THE JOY OF

EMBRACING GOD

Humanity's longing for the Eternal

JERRY DELL EHRLICH

Academic Christian Press
P.O. BOX 80247
San Diego, CA 92138-0247

(TELEPHONE) 619-422-8701
(FAX) 619-422-8749
E-MAIL acachrprsjdehr@msn.com

Published by Academic Christian Press
P.O. Box 80247
San Diego, CA 92138-0247

Library of Congress Cataloging-in-Publication Data

Ehrlich, Jerry Dell
      The Joy of Embracing God: Humanity's Longing for the Eternal.
      Includes bibliographical references, glossary, and index.
            ISBN 0-9710000-2-6 (ten digit)
        ISBN 978-0-9710000-2-5 (thirteen digit)
                  $17.50
1. Man: religious from the beginning. 2. Man's growing awareness of the idea of God. 3. Ways in which man believes God is perceived. 4. Mortal men crave immortality. 5. God seen as man's means to immortality. 6. Man's desire to embrace God and become eternal.

Library of Congress Control Number: 2005900947

10 9 8 7 6 5 4 3 2 1

TO

THOSE WHO DESIRE THE EMBRACE OF GOD

Also by Jerry Dell Ehrlich, M.Div., M.A., Ph.D.

From
Academic Christian Press
San Diego, CA   2001

PLATO'S GIFT TO CHRISTIANITY:
The Gentile Preparation for and the Making of the Christian Faith
ISBN 0-9710000-0-X $32

BUILDING A LIFE BY CARPENTER JESUS:
The Divine Teacher's Seven Steps to Wholeness
With
Supplementary Wisdom from both Western Classical and Eastern Sages
ISBN 0-9710000-1-8 $24

INTRODUCTION   9-10

CHAPTER ONE: PRIMITIVE MAN: SEEKING
      A HIGHER POWER TO LENGTHEN LIFE   11-37

I.   MAN: RELIGIOUS FROM THE BEGINNING
II   "BRILLIANT AND CREATIVE PEOPLE DO NOT
      BELIEVE IN GOD" IS CONTRARY TO THE FACTS
III. PRIMITIVE MAN'S RELIGIOUS EXPRESSIONS
      A. ANIMISM
      B. MAGIC AND OTHR METHODS FOR CONTROL-
         LING THE SUPERNATURAL POWERS
      C. FESTIVALS AND AGRICULTURAL FERTILITY
         RITUALS

CHAPTER TWO: MAN'S GROWING PERCEPTION OF
      THE ULTIMATE LIFE SOURCE: GOD   38-77

I.   GENERAL AND VAGUE IDEAS OF THE LIFE FORCE
II.   THE IDEA OF GOD
      A. DEFINITIONS OF GOD
      B. NAMES OF GOD
      C. THE NATURE OF GOD
          1. Nature/Cosmos as God
          2. Anthropomorphism -- God in Man's Image
          3. The Trend Towards Monotheism
          4. Monotheism And Its Complex Unities
          5. God Who is Beyond Being or Human Comprehension

III. WAYS IN WHICH MEN BELIEVE GOD PROCLAIMS
      HIMSELF
      A. GOD SPEAKS DIRECTLY TO HUMANS
      B. GOD PHYSICALLY APPEARS
      C. GOD APPEARS IN OTHER NON-HUMAN FORMS

D. GOD USES INTERMEDIARIES
    1. Visions
    2. Dreams
    3. God Sends Special Representatives
    4. God Used Heavenly Messengers, Angels to
       Communicate To Men
    5. Sons of God Are As God's Representatives
       On Earth
    6. Both Celestial And Human Hierarchies
E. NATURE DECLARES GOD AND HIS GLORY

CHAPTER THREE: GOD AS THE ETERNAL: MAN AS
    MORTAL   78-102

I. RELIGIONS OF MAN'S MORTALITY
   A. EARLY EGYPT
   B. THE HEBREWS
   C. THE EARLY GREEKS
   D. THE CHINESE
   E. BUDDHISM
   F. VARIOUS PHILOSOPHICAL VIEWS WITH RELIGIOUS
      ATTACHMENT
   G. BELIEF IN GODS WHO TOTALLY CONTROLED MAN-
      KIND AND BOTH PUNISHED MAN FOR REJECTING
      THEIR AUTHORITY AND IMPOSED LIFE LIMITATIONS
      ON MEN AS MORTALS
II. FORMS OF RELIGIOUS EXPRESSION
   A. THE CREATING AND ACTING OUT OF MYTHS
     1. Fertility Cults And Rituals
     2. Acts For Divine Protection
     3. Acts And Sacrifices That Sought Forgiveness And
       Redemption From The Wrath Of The Gods Or The God
   B. FORMULATED MORAL AND INSTRUCTIONAL
      LEGISLATIONS
     1. Law Codes From The Gods
     2. Sacred Writings

C. BELIEVERS' UNIFICATION BY CREEDS
D. ART

CHAPTER FOUR: GOD AS THE MEANS OF MAN'S
    IMMORTALITY   103-130

I.   GOD AS THE LIFE GIVING SPIRIT OF THE UNIVERSE
II. GOD AS THE UNIVERSE
III. GOD AS THE PERSONAL FATHER OF ALL
    A. SUMERIAN GODS
    B. EGYPTIAN GODS
    C. HINDUISM
    D. PLATONISM
    E. JUDAISM
    F. SOME STOICS
    G. THE ROMANS
    H. GNOSTICISM
    I. CHRISTIANITY
    J. ISLAM
    K. THE NORSEMEN

CHAPTER FIVE: MAN'S ASCENT TO THE ETERNAL 131-183

I.   THE LONGING FOR THE ETERNAL
II. PATHS TO THE ETERNAL
    A. PERSONAL COMMITMENT, SURRENDER,
       CONVERSION, AND FAITH
    B. MEDITATION, CONTEMPLATION, PRAYERS,
       AND DEVOTION
    C. MYSTICISM
    D. ASCETICISM, SELF-DENIAL, RENUNCIATION,
       AND NON-ATTACHMENT
    E. ETHICS, IMITATIO DEI, VIRTUES, AND SERVICE
       TO HUMANITY
    F. KNOWLEDGE
    G. LOVE

CHAPTER SIX: THE FINAL EMBRACE OF GOD:
    FRIENDSHIP AND UNION WITH THE ETERNAL   184-232
I.   ENLIGHTENMENT AND A DEEPER SPIRITUAL
       UNDERSTANDING
II.   PEAK SPIRITUAL EXPERIENCE
III.   PEACE AND JOY
IV.   THE FRIENDSHIP AND LOVE OF GOD
V.   THE EMBRACE'S ULTIMATE MYSTERY OF UNION
          WITH GOD
VI.   PASSING THROUGH DEATH
       A. A DIRECT AND INSTANT ARRIVAL IN HEAVEN
       B. SEMI-DIRECT PASSING INTO ETERNITY--THE
           NECESSITY OF JUDGMENT FIRST
       C. A JOURNEY
           1. Reincarnation
           2. Purgatory
       D. THE RESURRECTION OF THE BODY
       E. DEATH AND RESURRECTION OF THE COSMOS
VII.   THE ETERNAL EMBRACE OF GOD
       A. THE EMBRACE OF GOD
       B. VARIOUS IDEAS OF HEAVEN

CONCLUSION   233

GLOSSARY   234-235

NOTES   236-241

BIBLIOGRAPHY   242-250

INDEX   251-256

This book is based on the thesis that man was made by God, infused by God with a daimon of love that longed for Him and would not let man rest until he found, embraced, and beheld God, who is the Absolute and Eternal Beauty Itself, the Giver and Measure of all that is good and meaningful. It traces this longing for the Eternal back to the very earliest man, and there as primitive man fades from our knowledge of history, one can see evidence of his longing for the Eternal. When man first knows himself to be a different and unique person from all that surrounds him, including other people, then he already is showing his religious nature in reaching out to God. He may not have writings of doctrines and laws and the philosophy of God at his hands, but he does have the longing to live as long as possible and to rejoice in spiritual warmth and beauty. Different cultures show us that the greatest and the simplest concerns of men are universal in nature, despite men's having different cultures, weather, customs, and different times in which they experienced life in history. In fact as man grew up and his hopes of more joy and a quest for a more solid mental conception of the meaning of his life, his religious nature grew up with him becoming, not weaker in the presence of science, but stronger. His discovery of the infinite space and the beauty of it caused people like Pierre Teilhard de Chardin to write his *Hymn of the Universe* in which he sees the universe as the embodiment of God's beauty, depth, and infinity, and prompts the deepest feeling of Albert Einstein to declare: "I maintain that cosmic religious feeling is the strongest and noblest incitement to scientific research." In January of 2002 when the first pictures from the Chandra X-ray telescope showed us the absolute wonder and beauty of the center of the Milky Way in our very own galaxy, it was impossible not to be in a state of cosmic awe, feeling the universe to be the altar of God, and our own galaxy to be the Garden of Eden. It is easy to understand the proclamation of William Herschel (d. 1822) who upon discovering the planet Uranus stated: "The undevout astronomer must be mad." After 70 years of oppressive and atheistic communism, the people of Russia still retained the daimon of love within that reached out to God, and in a survey 71% proclaimed themselves in September of 2004 to be Russian Orthodox: this did not include the southern parts of Russia where Islam flourishes or the northwestern part of Russia where there are Lutheran and Catholics and various other believers. Despite two generations of Marxist education and culture 90% of the people outwardly proclaimed, not only to be religious, but to identify themselves with a particular religious group. Indeed there is a tremendous joy and thrill in reaching out beyond ourselves to feel ourselves part of the eternal and beautiful, and to partake of the great mystery of God. Abraham H. Maslow, after defending religious faith against the onslaught of some who thought of themselves as more advanced and scientific than the religious ones, and after also admitting that some of the organized religions have given totally inadequate answers to man's meaningful questions, still made this statement: "It is increasingly clear that the religious questions themselves --and religious quests, the religious yearnings, the religious needs themselves, that they are rooted deep in human nature, that they can be studied, described, examined in a scientific way." In this book, I have tried to show the progress men have made in both the questions they ask and the answers they give to those religious concerns. Man's religiosity is constantly growing into full adulthood as he learns more about himself and the wonder of the universe and the awe of the "deep deep eternity", to use a phrase of Nietzsche. From the early acts of "magic" and "ritual" to the period of the Scholastics to the modern Scientific Theologians the love and longing that God has planted into us to love and desire His Eternal Embrace is constantly becoming more apparent to our mental and psychological powers. We are simply dwarfed into cosmic awe, and yet uplifted by that same Beauty to higher religious joy than our forefathers could have ever experienced, for they simply could not have known the absolute grandeur of the creation. Yet, they too, from the very beginning felt the longing and the desire to embrace God and His eternity.

CHAPTER ONE

PRIMITIVE MAN: SEEKING A HIGHER POWER TO
LENGTHEN LIFE

I. MAN: RELIGIOUS FROM THE BEGINNING

Perhaps it is best at the beginning to try to understand the historical meaning of the word "religious", for, although I do not use the word in the title of the book, it is so common a word and so attached to any concept that refers to God or anything considered sacred, even one's conscience, that it is appropriate to try to define the term. *Religio* is a Latin word with the following usages: conscientiousness, respect for what is sacred, religious feeling or religious awe, observing the holy, and worship of the gods. Adolf Harnack defines it simply: "Not only is religion a life in and with God; but, just because it is that, it is also the revelation of the meaning and responsibility of life".1.1 This is probably the way it is most understood by the average American. However, in this book it will have a wider meaning, including all that the Latin word *religio* implies: any awe or fear of an unknown power of nature or that which is above nature is included. The honoring of cows or the worship of the Cat God, the rites given to a power that controls the rain and the fertility of the earth, any fear of fate or death, and any rituals or festivals that hopefully prolong life or give protection from an enemy, and other concepts are all included in the concept of being "religious".

It is also the contention of this book that as soon as man was conscious of himself as a being apart from others or nature he showed evidence of his being religious, probably in quest of self-preservation and a lengthened lifetime. Siegfried Morenz in his book *Egyptian Religion* states that in every aspect of early Egyptian culture, religion was not only present but was the basis of it. This is shown to be true in every aspect: art, literature and drama, science, philology and philosophy, historiography, government, and justice. He concludes his argument with these words: "Thus art and science, government and law are founded in religion, which in a nutshell is the womb of culture. Egypt provides particularly clear proof of this fact since in its early history it developed along autochthonous lines, i.e. without being greatly influenced from abroad".1.2 In a similar statement Joseph M. Kitagawa in his book *Religions of the East* stated: "Archaeologist, however, remind us that traces of religions go farther back, dimly to be sure, to the Old Stone Age."1.3 He then proceeds by referring to Maret that in studying the major institutions of mankind like family, tribe, state, government, law, morality, and art one always finds religion there also, until the very time that man himself fades out of history. E.O. James in his work *Seasonal Feasts and Festivals* makes this statement:

> From the beginning it would seem that man did not rely wholly
> upon his own initiative and ingenuity to ensure that all his needs
> were met. Therefore, when nature appeared to be in the balance
> at the crucial and critical seasons, he performed the rites pre-
> scribed for the control of the growth of the crops, or the increase
> of the flocks and herds, at regular intervals.1.4

Thus one can seen the why of so many agricultural and fertility gods and goddesses at the beginning of human history. Further, Bronislaw Malinowski in his *Magic, Science and Religion* opened his book with these words:

> There are no peoples however primitive without religion and magic.
> Nor are there, it must be added at once, any savage races lacking
> either in the scientific attitude or in science, though this lack has
> been frequently attributed to them. In every primitive community,
> studied by trustworthy and competent observers, there have been
> found two clearly distinguishable domains, the Sacred and the Pro-
> fane; in other words, the domain of Magic and Religion and that of
> science.1.5

These words are very similar to Alfred North Whitehead's when he said "The life of man is founded on Technology, Science, Art and Religion. All four are interconnected and issue from his total mentality...No social organisation can be understood without reference to these four under-lying factors".1.6

Since it seems that man from the very beginning was religious, one might ask himself why? The philosophers and theologians have given many reasons for this, and all the reasons seem to have a similarity: that is, that there is something innate in man himself that drives him towards that, which, in his mind, is the life-giving force of the universe. Plato taught that God made man for an eternal spiritual existence, for his soul was made as an eternal entity. However, God also delighted in giving man the experience of a temporary material existence in which he could experience life in a physical body. But, so that man would not forget his ultimate and real spiritual existence, he planted a daimon (sometimes transliterated daemon) in man's soul that longed for the eternal and through recollection of the mind man would remember that his real existence was in the eternal soul which, after the death of the body, would, if good, return directly to his eternal home and his Eternal Father. If he were less just on earth during his time here, he would have a prolonged journey back to the Father or even a possible reincarnation to "try it again" and be more presentable to the Father (Jesus said we are all invited to the Festival, but we will not be let in if we are not wearing the proper garment--virtue--when we arrive). This daimon is basically a longing love for God, the Absolute Good Beyond Being, the Absolute Beauty of all. Plato does refer to God as the Good Beyond Being as well as Beauty Itself. Plato stated in his creation story:

> ...and assigned each soul to a star...then in the first place it would be necessary that they should all have in them one and the same faculty of sensation, arising out of irresistible impressions; in the second place, they must have love...He who lived well during his appointed time was to return and dwell in his native star (his place in heaven), and there he would have a blessed and congenial existence (Timaeus 41d-e).

Plato discusses at length the longing of love for the Eternal in his work *The Symposium* (earlier called *The Banquet*). Below I have paraphrased and adapted 211 and 212 of the long dialogue.

> When the love which is implanted into our soul seeks to behold Absolute Beauty, it starts its ascent upwards by acknowledging the beauties bound into this world's order, but perceiving that

they are not the ultimate fulfillment, discards them, and resumes
its quest for Ultimate Goodness, and stepping upwards, one step
by one, seeks that which is the Eternal Good and Absolute Beauty,
knowing that what it has left behind will never satisfy it.
When it finally meets Beauty itself, face to face, that Beauty that
never decays or changes or fades, but gives its goodness to all reality, always and never wavering, then that soul knows he has become
a Friend of God, beloved and uplifted by the Same to his eternal
home.

In the *Gathas* of Zarathushtra (Zoroaster) are the following declarations.

O Mazda, from the beginning you fashioned for
physical bodies, an awakened conscience and a
directive intelligence through your own mind...
You granted us capacities to act and true teachings
to guide us so that we could choose to be with You. (Yasna 31.11)

When the full force of the Good Mind took
possession of me, O Mazda,
Then I realised You as Mighty and Bountiful. (Yasna 43.4)

Here we have the sending of the Good Mind into the mind and hearts of
men who then longed for the presence of Mazda.

In the *Srimad Bhagavatam* (The Wisdom of God) it is stated by the
worshipper "Thou art the innermost ruler of every heart...Thy lovers
meditate on thy blissful form, and become lost in the joy thereof" (Bk II,
Chapter III). The very existence of man seems impossible in Hinduism
without the union of the Soul (Atman) of God and the soul (atman) of
man.

The words of Gottfried Wilhelm Freiherr von Leibniz who greatly
influenced Alfred North Whitehead read as follows:

In the strictly metaphysical sense no external cause acts upon us
excepting God alone...We have in our souls ideas of everything,

only because of the continual action of God upon us, that is to say, because every effect expresses its cause and therefore the essences of our souls are certain expressions, imitations or images of the Divine Essence...God is the sun and light of our souls...during the scholastic period many believed God to be the light of the soul... and the fathers who were always more Platonic than Aristotelian in their mode of thinking.1.7

Is it no wonder that primitive man sought out help from a greater force than himself to survive dangers, receive a good crop to sustain him through the winter, and to prolong life. It was natural for him to do so, as we all seek to survive when in danger. But it was more than that. It was a longing to enjoy life and to have some relationship to the Power of Life that was outside of himself. While he may not have thought in terms of an eternal soul or a Heavenly Father, yet there was within him an emotional and rational hope that life could go on forever. Mircea Eliade has an article titled "The Yearning for Paradise in Primitive Tradition" in the Summer 1953 issue of Diogenes printed by U. of Chicago Press. He states in that article "We encounter the 'paradise myth' all over the world in more or less complex forms. Beside the paramount paradisial note, it always has a certain number of characteristic elements, chiefly the idea of immortality." Auguste Sabatier in his *Outlines of a Philosophy of Religion* stated:

> Why am I religious? Because I cannot help it: it is a moral neces-
> sity of my being. They tell me it is a matter of heredity, of educa-
> tion, of temperament. I have often said so to myself. But that ex-
> planation simply puts the problem further back; it does not solve it.
> The necessity which I experience in my individual life I find to be
> still more invincible in the collective life of humanity. Humanity
> is not less incurably religious than I am.1.8

Immanuel Kant believed that man was a moral person, but he could not possibly be a moral person without faith in God: "More than this, we cannot be moral without believing in God...The basis of religion must, therefore, be morality. Morality as such is ideal, but religion imbues it with vigour, beauty, and reality".1.9

As primitive man came to see himself as a separate unit from both society and the natural order, he then was acknowledging his own personality in which he found himself to be a "significant other". This too, claims Nikolai Berdyaev is from God.

> Personality is not born of the family and cosmic process, not born
> of a father and mother, it emanated from God, it makes is appear-
> ance from another world. It bears witness to the fact that man is the
> point of intersection of two worlds, that in him there takes place the
> conflict between spirit and nature, freedom and necessity, indepen-
> dence and dependence.1.10

Lastly, to close this section, I should like to refer to Gabriel Marcel's belief that all men have, feel, and experience the "need for transcendence". Man seeks to find his identity in the depth of reality. He feels homesick and in a state of exile without the inner presence of God in his heart and in his mind, and he wants his "place" within the depth of reality in the presence of God. He wants to be charmed by God's presence in which the depth of all being gives him identity and eternity. Marcel even refers to the philosophical longings of Nietzsche whose desires were revealed in his deeply thoughtful words of wonder and awe: "Die tiefe, tiefe Ewigkeit" (The deep, deep Eternity).1.11

II.   "BRILLIANT AND CREATIVE PEOPLE DO NOT BELIEVE IN GOD" IS CONTRARY TO THE FACTS

Nietzsche, Sir James Frazier, Bertrand Russell, the philosophical school of Logical Positivism, and Communism (religion is the opiate of the masses) certainly did not kill religion, faith in God, or the longing for eternity among the men and women of every class and intellectual level. Some think that modern man in the age of enlightenment and science, if well educated, does not believe in God. Therefore, I felt it important to put forth several men of the last 150 years that were extremely talented, free thinking, mentally brilliant, and also religious believers in both God and human immortality: Richard Wagner, Leo Tolstoy, J.P. Morgan, Albert Einstein, Otto Hahn, A.N. Whitehead, Jean Paul Sartre, Dag Hammarskjoeld, and Werner von Braun. Among them one finds a great musical composer, a literary giant, an extremely successful capitalist-financier-art collector, three of the 20th Century's premier scientists (the theory of relativity and E=MCsquared, the father of nuclear fission, and the father of modern rocketry and space travel), the most dramatic and charming of the Secretaries of the United Nations, the "high priest" of 20th Century existentialism and his last hour conversion to religion, a person who was creative in three fields--with a doctorate in science, music, and theology, and a very influential early 20th Century philosopher. While inserting this section at this point in my work, I felt it did, indeed, divert from the basic development of thought according to my fixed outline. However, upon second thought, I wanted to put forth, up front, a defense on behalf of those who believe in God against some common notions that rather arrogantly declare that God does not and can not exist according to proven knowledge, as if such "knowledge" could actually exist. There is no "knowledge" either of God's existence or His nonexistence. This is a book about the joy of faith in God as an Eternal Father who creates life and loves the beings of His creation, even to the point of extending their existence into eternity, that they might enjoy Him forever. This is my personal faith, the faith of those I shall refer to in this work, and the faith of more than two-thirds of the world's population. The preceding section has declared that this longing for the Eternal has been a common feature of men from the beginning of their awareness as individual beings, in every part of and society of the earth.

Richard Wagner, the brilliant composer of the greatest of German operas, was only too well aware of his achievements and led a rather pompous life and expressed his judgmental thoughts with a self-centeredness that few indeed could love. It has been said that he condescended towards journalist, Jesuits, Jews, and the French, and probably thought of himself, in Nietzsche's term, an uebermensch, the fulfillment of the ideal man far above the "masses". But something spiritual happened to him later in life: yes, he became religious. He experienced a **metanoia** (New Testament term for a total mind-set change: often translated "repentance" or "conversion"). He was baptized in the Evangelical Lutheran Church, and took on an almost missionary attitude towards others. Below are some of Cosima's, his wife, statements about Richard in her voluminous diaries.

In the evening started Meurer's life of Luther--great pleasure in the true German character, in which we recognize Goethe, Beethoven, and all that we venerate among the Germans; and here it is not a game, it concerns the very nerve center of life. "The absence of all ideality brings the soul blissful peace," says R., "and the way to this peace is through Jesus Christ." 25/10/1873

Yesterday (Friday) R. Earnestly reproached Malwida for not having her ward baptized. This was not right, he said, not everyone could fashion his religion for himself, and particularly in childhood one must have a feeling of cohesion. Nor should one be left to choose; rather, it should be possible to say, "You have been christened, you belong through baptism to Christ, now unite yourself once more with him through Holy Communion." Christening and Communion are indispensable, he said. No amount of knowledge can ever approach the effect of the latter. People who evade religion have a terrible shallowness, and are unable to feel anything at all in a religious spirit. 9-13/12/1873 [It is quite obvious here that the earlier association with F. Nietzsche had been broken].

R. (Richard) slept well, and we chat about all sorts of things at breakfast; of Christianity he says, "We lack even the rudiments of the education needed to understand such a phenomenon--we are in a state of complete barbarism."11/3/1879

R. Asks what priests are for; they are supposed to represent Christianity. Judas has triumphed, he says sorrowfully, and he speaks of Christianity, the relation of man to man--this will be his last work, he says. He reproaches Gob. For leaving out of account one thing which was given to mankind--a Saviour, who suffered for them and allowed himself to be crucified. 23/4/1882

R. Has finished the book on Buddha, and he reads to me the passage in it about deeds--that these, too, are finite and that the Atman is superior to them. This reminds us of the doctrine of grace in Saint Paul and Luther. 4/10/1882

R. Remarks how splendidly Luther's language suits the Gospels.

21/12/1882

In <u>Wagner's</u> *Parsifal* he puts in Parsifal's mouth his own feeling about his own earlier life of arrogance and unbelief and his now repentant mind.(trans.JDE)

> To him, whose deep complaints
> Which I foolishly with amazement received
> ...
> Pathless I erred, I hunted surrounded by a wild curse:
> Distresses without number, battles and conflicts
> Drove me from the path;
> I thought what was correct,
> Then as ordained despair controlled me..
> ...
> And I--I am he,
> Who has created this distress!
> Ha, what sin, what outrageous guilt
> Must this foolish head
> Be burdened with eternally!
> ...
> (Parsifal is baptized by Gurnemanz who then comforts Parsifal
> with these words)
> Now blessed be, you pure one, through that which is pure!
> So may you be separated from every guilt and sorrow.
> ...
> (Parsifal now feeling the joy of spiritual birth seeks then to baptize
> Kundry before she dies)
> ...
> My first duty I must perform
> Be baptized,
> And trust in the Redeemer.

Then Parsifal sees life and nature in all its beauty fully for the first time.

> How beautiful to me the meadows seem today!
> Such wonder blooming has greeted me,
> Seeking to embrace me even to my head;

Till now I have never seen such mild and tender
Blades of grass, flowers, and blossoms
Whose scent recalls my childhood's days
And speaks of loving trust to me.

The last four lines in German read:
    doch sah' ich nie so mild und zart
    die Halmen, Bluethen und Blumen,
    noch duftete All' so kindisch hold
    und sprach so lieblich traut zue mir.

The final words of the Parsifal are:

The Highest Holy Wonder:
Salvation to the Redeemer!
(Hoechsten Heiles Wunder:
  Erloesung dem Erloeser!)

Richard Wagner's transformation was truly a wonder, and it came by accepting the Gospel of Jesus.

    John Pierpont Morgan, successful capitalist, financier, and art collector, after identifying himself, proceeds to the First Article of his Last Will and Testament. It reads as follows:

I commit my soul into the hands of my Savior, in full confidence
that having received it and washed it in His most precious blood
He will present it faultless before the throne of my Heavenly
Father; and I entreat my children to maintain and defend, at all
hazard, and at any cost of personal sacrifice, the blessed doctrine
of the complete atonement for sin through the blood of Jesus
Christ, once offered, and through that alone.

He also asked in his will for a burial at St. George's Church in the city of New York, and bequeathed large sums of money to both the local Protestant Episcopal Diocese and to the same St. George's Church.

Albert Einstein, 1879-1955 the brilliant German-Swiss-American Jewish physicist, Noble Prize winner as physicist in 1921, known for his ideas about relativity and the relationship of mass to energy, was a devout Jewish believer in God. In fact, as few others do, he started his Last Will and Testament with these words: "In the Name of God. Amen." He continued his will with a large grant to his Hebrew University, obviously a testimony to his personal faith. Einstein certainly qualifies as a modern and brilliant scientist. Not only was this great scientist religious, he felt that it was the religious mind that aided science in its quest for knowledge, as he stated in his book The World As I See It: "I maintain that cosmic religious feeling is the strongest and noblest incitement to scientific research."

Leo Tolstoy, the great writer from Russia, whose personal faith was not settled until later in life, was extremely unhappy of what he considered the corruption of the Christian faith by the organized churches who controlled theology throughout the ages by oppressing those who were truly the followers of Jesus, whom he calls the Christ of God. After seeing the mass slaughter of Europeans by fellow Europeans, all of whom claimed to be followers of Christ, he wrote in angry protest his work *The Kingdom of God is Within You*. In a positive confession, he showed agreement with the words of William Lloyd Garrison which Garrison presented to and was adopted by the Peace Convention, held in Boston in 1838:

> Wherefore, we commit the keeping of our souls to God, in well-doing, as unto a faithful Creator. 'For every one that forsakes houses, or brethren, or sister, or father, or mother, or wife, or children, or lands, for Christ's sake, shall receive an hundred-fold, and shall inherit everlasting life.(Chapter One)

Tolstoy felt the Christ's teaching in The Sermon on the Mount was the only way in which mankind could become a harmonious and loving society, and to Tolstoy the only philosophy by which he could find meaning in life. Jesus had taught him to have a "divine life-conception" and he thus stated:

> The man with the divine life-conception no longer recognizes life to consist in his personality, or in the aggregate of personalities

(in the family, the race, the people, the country, or the state), but in
source of the everlasting, immortal life, in God; and to do God's
will he sacrifices his personal and domestic and social good. The
prime mover of his religion is love. And his religion is the worship
in deed and in truth of the beginning of everything, of God. (Ch. IV)

Tolstoy himself had made the journey to which he refers in the following
statement: "The whole historical life of humanity is nothing but a gradual
transition from the personal, the animal life-conception, to the social, and
from the social to the divine.(Ch.IV)

Albert Schweitzer, left Europe behind him and went to the Lambarene
district of the then "French Equatorial Africa" in order to use his talents,
not for money, but for an expression of the love which he felt the
historical Jesus tried to teach mankind. Now many others have done the
same type of thing in various countries throughout the world, but what
makes Schweitzer's action so admirable was what he left behind in order
to do what he did. He had Ph.Ds in philosophy/theology and music, and
also a Doctor's degree in medicine. Why would this brilliant and
multitalented person do such a thing? His motivation was "You shall
love your neighbor as yourself." He learned it as a commandment of
Jesus Christ. He stated: "The essential element in Christianity, as it was
preached by Jesus...is this, that it is only through love that we can attain
to communion with God."1.12 Brilliant people do not believe in God?
That certainly can not be maintained when one looks at Albert
Schweitzer and then acknowledge what he did to verify his faith.

Otto Hahn of Germany, 1879-1968, using Einstein's theory of mass
and energy, discovered nuclear fission of uranium in 1938, which was
during the high point of Adolph Hitler's influence and power in
Germany, as Hitler was riding high with a robust economy and appealing
to German pride, while only slowing revealing the uncontrollable hatred
he had for so many in the human race. But Otto Hahn was neither a
military man nor one to desire such power as his discovery would lead to.
After the Americans dropped the Atom Bombs upon Japan, Hahn needed
consoling. He earlier had contemplated suicide in 1939 when he first
realized that his discovery of fission might lead to such weapons, and he
then, again, on August 6, 1945 thought of suicide. Hahn's friends stayed
with him that night to make sure that it did not happen. Walter Gerlach,
chief of the German program that studied the fission discovery, was

upset because Germany had not built the bomb. But Hahn's response was completely different: "Are you upset because we did not make the unranium bombs? I thank God on my bended knees that we did not make a uranium bomb." Otto Hahn, a brilliant scientist, was deeply humbled before God, and knew how to thank Him for what did not take place. His fatherland, Germany, was not so important that it should have an additional weapon to harm humanity.

Alfred North Whitehead, influential philosopher, mathematician and educator was born in England in 1861 and died in Cambridge, MA in 1947. From 1924 he taught at Harvard University as a professor of philosophy, and was considered one of the most original and influential thinkers of his time. He was a believer in God, and the need to justify one's being by playing his part in God's creation. He begins his book The Aims of Education with these words:

> Culture is activity of thought, and receptiveness to beauty and
> humane feeling. Scraps of information have nothing to do with it.
> A merely well-informed man is the most useless bore on God's
> earth. What we should aim at producing is men who possess both
> culture and expert knowledge in some special direction. Their ex-
> pert knowledge will give them the ground to start from, and their
> culture will lead them as deep as philosophy and as high as art.1.13

He believed both in God and human immortality, and even jokes about what languages are worthy of heaven and concludes that only Chinese, Greek, French, German, Italian, and English will qualify. He further stated that "the blessed Saints will dwell with delight on these golden expressions of eternal life".1.14 Again he stated: "The life of man is founded on Technology, Science, Art, and Religion. All four are inter-connected and issue from his total mentality".1.15

Probably the most brilliant, and certainly the most charming, Secretary General of the United Nations, Dag Hammarskjoeld, was a deeply religious person of the Christian Faith. He was constantly comparing his life with that of Christ to motivate him to seek a higher and higher calling. His critics jestfully stated that they weren't sure if Dag wasn't thinking of himself as the Christ at certain times trying to solve all the world's problems. Hammarskjoeld kept some notes as a type of personal diary. After his death, they were found with an undated letter to his friend, Leif Belfrage, the Permanent Under Secretary of Foreign Affairs for Sweden, which ended this way: "If you find them worth publishing, you have my permission to do so--as a sort of white book concerning my negotiations with myself--and with God." In that published diary, published with the name *Markings* (in Swedish "Vaegmaerken") one finds such statements as:

On the bookshelf of life, God is a useful work of reference, always at hand but seldom consulted...He is a jubilation and a refreshing wind (p.16).

God does not die on the day when we cease to believe in a personal deity, but we die on the day when our lives cease to be illumined by the steady reliance, renewed daily, of a wonder, the source of which is beyond all reason (p.56).

Yet, through me there flashes this vision of a magnetic field in the soul, created in a timeless present by unknown multitudes, living in holy obedience, whose words and actions are a timeless prayer. "The Communion of Saints"--and--within it--an eternal life (p.84).

(He quotes St. John of the Cross) "Faith is the marriage of God and the soul" (p.97).

Thou who art over us,
Thou who art one of us,
Thou who art--
Also within us,
May all see Thee--in me also,
May I prepare the way for Thee,
May I thank Thee for all that shall fall to my lot,
May I also not forget the needs of others,
Keep me in Thy love
As Thou wouldest that all should be kept in mine.
May everything in this my being be directed to Thy glory
And may I never despair.
For I am under Thy hand,
And in Thee is all power and goodness.

Give me a pure heart--that I may see Thee,
A humble heart--that I may hear Thee,
A heart of love--that I may serve Thee,
A heart of faith--that I may abide in Thee (p.100).

Dag Hammarskjoeld was born in Joenkoeping, Sweden, in 1905, and died near Ndola, Northern Rhodesia, on September 18, 1961, when his plane crashed while seeking a negotiation in order to bring peace between the forces of the United Nations and the forces of Katanga: a man of faith who died trying to bring peace to others.

Jean-Paul Sartre, long an existential critic of religion, who proclaimed that man was "condemned to be free" because without God, man had no force outside himself to establish morality. Without God, man was free from powers without, but also then "condemned" to create a morality by which he could live. Man was called to be totally responsible for himself. However, late in life between 1974 and 1980 when Sartre died, as he aged and lost his eyesight, his relationship to his personal secretary Benny Levy, who was even more radical than Sartre in his own younger years, became one of deepest feelings and heart sharing. Either their thoughts merged or Sartre was under the influence of Levy, but whatever took place between them in thought-sharing, both of them turned to a form of mystical Judaism for spiritual hope and guidance. Yes, Sartre, once called the "High Priest of Existential Atheism" had become religious. When Levy announced that Sartre had taken on religious comfort, Sartre's followers and other skeptics refused to believe it. Therefore, Sartre, shortly before his own death, confirmed Levy's statement that he indeed had found religious comfort as he awaited eternity. Plato was right when he said that deep within each of us God planted a longing for Himself and the Eternal, and although some deny the longing, it is always there, pulling man's thoughts up to his eternal hopes.

Wernher von Braun received his confirmation at the age of 12 in Germany and his father gave to him, as a gift for his confirmation in the Christian Faith, a telescope. The rest was history. He went to the University of Berlin and eventually became the Father of Modern

Rocketry. In 1945 he came to the United States with more than a hundred of his fellow German scientists. They were put "on the back-burner" until, in 1961, Russia sent Yuri Gagarin into space. That was a wakeup call to the American political establishment. Von Braun was asked to be the Director of NASA and develop a rocket that could put, first of all, a man into space, and later to put a man on the moon (and bring him back). First he and his team invented the four-stage Jupiter rocket that launched Explorer I, the first satellite for the United States. Later he developed the mighty Saturn V rocket that put men on the moon. He was a man of absolute scientific brilliance and a man who had uncompromising faith in God, the Creator. During his years of scientific influence, he was a true evangelical spreading his faith to any who would listen, writing articles like "Why I believe in Immortality" in which he could say that when man was fully realized he "can stand straight and tall, assured in the face of apparent uncertainty, secure in his knowledge of the way home, at peace with himself because he is at peace with Almighty God."

Scientists, most all of the truly great scientists, have believed in the Creator of the universe, although often disagreeing how all was formed. From the beginning of the modern era of science they declared their belief in God: Nicolaus Copernicus, Galileo Galilei, Francis Bacon, Isaac Newton, Johann Kepler, Blaise Pascal, and many more, and, of course, Albert Einstein, Otto Hahn, and Werner von Braun. The 20th Century saw many great developments, but Einstein's theories, Hahn's nuclear fission, and von Braun's space travel are perhaps the three greatest steps forward for man in the 20th century, and in their discoverers they humbly loved and worshipped God. It is not just primitive man that believed in a power beyond himself. But now let us return, since I have shown that this study is also valid for the thinking man of the 21st Century.

III. PRIMITIVE MAN'S RELIGIOUS EXPRESSIONS

It is precisely because of early man's thinking powers that he realized the religious necessity of his being. Initially man saw the power that was external to himself in various forms and in various ways. He saw it in animals stronger than himself, he saw it in the wind and the thunder, he saw in the rebirth of the earth every spring and the power of rain, he saw it in any change or previously inexperienced action of nature and in anything unexplainable he knew was beyond himself. There was simply a power greater than himself whether it was called *mana* among the Egyptians or *moira* among the Greeks. He had yet to personalize it, but he knew it was there. Early personifications were actually not personal at all: Yahweh among the Hebrews simply meant "That which is" and Ptah of Memphis in Egypt meant "Powerful One". Nevertheless, with much usage such designations became personifications in the minds of the worshipers, and finally all virtues, attributes, and powers beyond human understanding became 'personal names'. Even in Christianity the name Jesus Christ means 'the anointed savior', but, obviously, since it was given to a visual and living man, it became his "personal name". Many languages do not exactly refer to a person's "name", but ask how they are known or how they are called. Wie heisst du? (German: how are you called?) Or in Spanish: Como se llama Usted? (How are you called?) Or people's "personal names" are just like the gods of old, according to function: Smith, Tanner, Butcher and so forth. Usage makes a name personal. So the student must learn that all names are really personal if designated to a particular being, god or man. "The Wind" or "The Rain" etc. can be designated as personal names of a god. Today it is common to say "The Wind God" or "The Rain God", but the primitive did not need to qualify the name that way. When Mind (or Intellect) is used by the Platonists it is a personal name. When Sun or Fire is used by Heraclitus or the Mithraic believers, that is a personal name. Before the movement towards monotheism, there were often many gods with many names according to their function or power. Therefore, in this section especially, it is to be remembered that if a man worshipped a "Cat" he was really worshipping the "Cat God", probably because a pride of lions was camped outside of his cave waiting for breakfast and the primitive man wanted to contact their master for help. Usage, then, made the name personal.

A. ANIMISM

Animism has been defined in various ways. The word itself comes from the Latin word *Anima* which also has several meanings: wind, air, breath, the vital principle or soul, and life. In its broadest meaning it can symbolize anything that has a type of life, even plants--for they are born, they grow, and they die. Among some ancients everything was filled with a soul or spirit, and thus had some power to affect its surroundings. On a narrower interpretation of *anima* the ability to move itself was necessitated, and that would eliminate plant life and leave only the "animal" kingdom. However, many non animals still could be perceived as be "animated" such as a tree when the wind hit it during a storm or the clouds themselves that seemed to move effortlessly across the sky and give rain. Likewise the planets, stars, sun and moon moved of their own accord (remember the earth was the center of the universe for primitive man). All such things that seemed to have movement and especially those things or beings that affected man's destiny came to be reverenced, feared, and prayed to. As a result, primitive man was much closer to nature than modern man is, and because of our distance from nature we do not reverence it nor even, sometimes, respect it. For us today, the command is to conquer it, which is not only understandable, but on many occasions, beneficial to mankind. But there is also a great danger when we diminish the sacredness of nature, both its plant life and its animal life. For they too are part of our greater existence and are also connected to the life principle, and in many ways help to purify that life principle (if it is air) that keeps us alive. Primitive man was overly fearful of nature, but we have scorned it, not realizing how "vital" it is to our own existence. Most modern religions still have some attachment to "animism", spirit, soul, or the "breath of life". Buddhism has, especially in the area between Eastern Pakistan and Thailand, countless spirits called "nats" and there are even places for their worship. Even today in this area people can be classified as "spirit possessed". In Java hosts of "yang" are believed to protect villages. Islamic lands still acknowledge the "jinns" that can be made to flee by reciting "In the name of Allah, the merciful and compassionate". Each person in many places has an individual spirit, which in reality is much like a modern person's idea of his personal soul; making the difference between us and the early animists much smaller than one tends to realize. Likewise, most people who are close to animals, are convinced that they have personal spirits or souls, and that these souls, like human souls, have an existence beyond the physical bodies they are presently occupying. In these areas of thought someone like Sir James Frazier would say than mankind has advanced beyond such primitive thinking and have entered the age of science, and, in fact, to him, it was time for many to give up religion completely--for he did see the close connecting between the most primitive people and some of our own sacred doctrines, even if now they are clothed in orderly and logical creeds. When one considers the "mystery" of the Christian Trinity, he sees a God beyond Being who is the Creator of all, but also a man Jesus Christ, and a Spirit of Holiness; and it is rather significant that Jesus said that the Holy Spirit could not come until he had left the earthly scene: the same scenario that the primitives had that after a man departed, his spirit was still there to inspire them and help them, and, unfortunately sometimes punish them. Jesus' own return after the resurrection was first supposed to be his "ghost" or "spirit" (Gk PNEUMA) by his disciples and they were scared (Gr PTONTHENTES) and terrified (Gr EMPHOBOI--like being wrapped up in a phobia), Lk 24:37: perhaps for good reason, they had denied and forsaken him, and even refused to come forward to bury him. My only point is that from the very beginning, mankind related to the sacred with hope and fear in the quest for protection of the life he had in his body and for his unknown future, and in that respect we can relate to him despite the different forms of religious thinking that were expressed between him and ourselves. Behind all modern religions there are vestiges of primitive animism, but, we have been released from the fear that the storm god sends floods because he is angry at us (most ancient religions had some type of myth that expressed an angry god who sent a flood to punish mankind), and we no longer have a pride of lions in our neighborhood looking for a meal when we open our door, and in these respects we have moved away from the negative elements of animism that gave so much fear to primitive man.

B. MAGIC AND OTHER METHODS FOR CONTROLLING THE SUPERNATURAL POWER

One of the devises that primitive man used to shelter himself from the evil spirits was that of magic. Sir James Frazer presents a very comprehensive study of magic and, religion in his well known book *The Golden Bough*, and for anyone who desires to study the subject this book must be read. He ties together magic with religion, and both are a way to either appease the supernatural powers or the nullify their dangerous acts against men. There is homeopathic magic that by imitating nature seeks to stimulate that same act in nature: a fertility cult would present man's act of procreation to the powers that they in turn would fertilize the earth. The concept of contagious magic is that contact with its power can be transferred, and if it is evil, transferred to an animal or an enemy. There is word magic, i.e. if you know how to call out to a particular power, by knowing its name, it will relate to your wishes and perhaps grant them. Names of these powers were usually well hidden from the masses by the priests who could make contact with such powers, lest everyone be able to call to them by name and get the desired response. The ancient Hebrews protected the uttering of the name of Yahweh, lest others might call out to him and receive the benefits of his power. This was true in many societies. The Norse people dedicated their children to the protection of their gods by giving the child the same name of a particular god. Thor was the most dramatic and powerful of the Norse gods and this can be seen easily by the names given to the people in the Icelandic sagas. In Njal's saga Thor is part of 25 different people's names and all the other names total only 88 people, none of them have a repetition of another god's name more than 4 times. In the King Harald's Saga Thor appears in names 15 times, and of the other ninety people the next highest number of a particular name is Sigurd who is the name of 4 women. In the Laxdaela Saga there are 179 people mentioned by name, and 57 have the name Thor within their name, Hall is second most with 11. From this, it not only implies that the Norse were very religious, but also incorporated the "magic" of the god's name to be a permanent feature of their named children. The fertility festivals will be mentioned in the next section, but the magic of the hunt, before man became an agriculturist, is traced back to the limits of our knowledge of primitive man. The Paleolithic caves served, not only for shelter, but for sanctuaries of magic as is shown by those paintings within them. The primitive image of a rhinoceros, the head of an antelope (probably) and a horse being shown falling into a pit (probably a trap). These imitative painting of the way to capture and what to capture for food, not only served as, perhaps, an educational devise, but also as a type of magic ritual in hopes of procuring food. The contagious element might simply a touching of the paintings and carvings to catch the power of the hunt. When I see a Notre Dame home football game I pay attention to the players touching the overhead sign as they run out of the tunnel and the declaration on campus of "Touchdown Jesus" one can see that we have not moved very far from the concept of primitive imitative and contagious magic.

Magic, of course, is very diversified. It can be expressed in offerings to the dead, in "power words" (the hocus pocus dominocus), ceremonies, taboos, charms and fetishes, symbolic designs, various rituals, divination, ordeals, witchcraft and sorcery, all of which still live on many T.V. shows and Big Screen movies. Here too we have not moved far from the primitive man. In all of these activities of the primitive man there is evidence that he desired as long a life as possible, perhaps even immortality, and he was reaching out to the powers that controlled what he could not. That is religion. We of a much more scientific and knowledgeable age, have discarded, for the most part, those methods, but we still long for friendship with the Ultimate Power of Life and seek and hope for its power, in some way, to be transferred to us that we might gain immortality. The essence of religion remains the same: to embrace God and attain immortality. Humanity can not do otherwise, for it is a deep part of what we are, and, I believe, it is the way God made us so that we do not feel comfortable without reaching out to Him.

C. FESTIVALS AND AGRICULTURAL FERTILITY RITUALS

Once man became an agriculturist, his life and religion radically changed. He created geometry in Egypt in order to separate individual's plots and water each from the Nile accordingly, In all places calendars had to be developed so that the sowing and reaping could be well planned--from the Druids (Stonehenge), to the Maya culture of central America, to the Greeks and Romans, and to the "fertile crescent"--a name that indicates the importance of fertile soil for an agricultural society. All had some type of calendar with usually 12 months (the word "month" comes from the word for "moon", and was based upon the moon's orbit around the earth-- a simple system, for the moon certainly was the easiest of the heavenly bodies that could both be visible and its stages of waxing and waning apparent). Others may have had an even easier system that was based on the rising and falling of the sun, but it was less detailed because it had only four "seasons": two solstices and two equinoxes. The New Year celebrations were often combined or derived from the Solar calendar and were probably originally celebrated during the Vernal Equinox (many ancient calendars started with our March--thus the beginning of the New Year: the Ancient Roman calendar was an example, and even today it has influenced our numbering of the months, for we call our ninth month (September--which means the Seventh month) and we call our tenth month (October--which means the Eighth month: and likewise for November (9) and December (10) which are our eleventh and twelfth). So the New Year's festival, even though now is at the beginning of January is really to be identified with the planting of the Spring sowing and the resurrection of nature in general, which starts to grow again after the long harsh winter. Mankind was reassured of another season of crops and the natural fruits because mother earth herself was resurrected from the dead. Every religion, at one time or another, was concerned about and had festivals to reenact the dying of nature and its rebirth in the Spring. For "Mother Earth" herself had to come alive again each Spring, for even before man himself was an agriculturist, he was a food gatherer, much the way vegetarian animals are today, and if Mother Earth did not produce food the Winter months would often be fatal as man would naturally lose his physical strength. During all of such festivals, man was reaching out to the power that bestowed life and fertility, both to the earth and to themselves. Often they would sacrifice cereal or animals to the gods both to show their gratitude and even maybe to nourish them and keep them alive that they might transfer their own powers to nature and women for the sake of reproduction. Very early in the religious art of mankind the female god is found to be the object of worship, for earth herself was female. It seems that for protection the Father God was called upon, but for food and sustenance, the Mother God was called upon. Both were obviously needed, and as man saw his gods anthropomorphically, both Father and Mother would be necessitated to create and sustain life. Fertility was of utmost importance.   O.E. James in his book *Seasonal Feasts and Festivals* presents evidence from the Paleolithic age of the worship of the Female God:

> They all resemble their Paleolithic prototypes generally known as 'Venuses' (e.g. the Willendorf, Lespugne, Brassempouy and Laussel female figurines) in having the maternal organs especially empha-sized, often with pendulous breasts, a protuberant navel, and some-

times highly developed buttocks. Most of them are in a squatting posture this being a normal attitude adopted in childbirth; others seem to indicate a state of pregnancy (pp.34-35).

While these are, by some, called "idols", one can see that the believers are reaching out to the "Mother of All Things" to provide children from the mother's fertility and food from the earth's fertility, at least by means of mimicking actual birth in their art. In most religions such fertility religions and beliefs developed into a Sky God (Father) and the Earth Mother, for it was what man did to reproduce his own children, and it was what the agricultural human did, plant the seed (male) into Mother Earth (female) and reproduction would take place. But without either the Sky God (often a rain god) or the Earth God, fertility could not take place. For example, in Indo-European worship the Sky-Weather God, Dyaus Pitar was united with (in Indian lore) Prithivi, the Earth-Mother, and they were then considered the Parents of Mankind. Similarly among the Greeks the earliest pair were Ouranus (the Heaven-God) and Ge or Gaia (the Earth-goddess) and by means of their union all was created. Zeus was the eventual Sky-God and Hera (his wife) was a Vegetation-God. It is also interesting to note the beginning of the Hebrew Torah where the gods (Elohim is a plural form of Eloah or El) decided to make mankind in their own image, so male and female made they them. If one would make a literal translation of Genesis I:26-28 it would read this way:

> Then the gods (Elohim, plural of Eloah or El) said, "Let us make mankind in our own image, according to our likeness; and let them have dominion over the fish of the sea...So the gods created mankind in their own image, in the image of the gods they created mankind; male and female they created them. And the gods blessed them, and the gods said to them, "Be fruitful and multiply".

This is certainly much like the creation stories of the other cultures. But as sexuality was gradually put aside from the creators, and monotheism was more developed in thought among the Hebrews, Elohim was unified into a single "person" and referred to as a male. Perhaps this was done to stress the difference of Hebrew theology with that of the Caananites whose land they had just invaded. For the Caananites had a religion that was strongly a fertility religion. Baal (Hadad) was a typical illustration of the Great Fertility God, but he himself suffered infertility (death) without the assistance of his "sister" Anat who brought his fertility powers back to life. Yahweh God certainly, then, at least according to the Yahwist, was the single God who was the cause of fertility (how often the phrase is in the Hebrew scriptures that Yahweh had or had not opened the womb for a woman hoping to have children). In Egypt Osiris and Isis were the God and Goddess of fertility, and Osiris rose to the top level of adoration of all the Egyptian gods and was, perhaps, worshipped longer than any other "named" god: From about 3,000 BC to and through the Christian era of Egypt until Egypt was conquered by Islam in the late Seventh Century AD. Each tribal group had a fertility goddess like Kybele of Anatolia, Inanna of Sumer, Ishtar of Akkadia, and the Greeks identified fertility wth many female goddesses: Hera, Dione, Semele, Kore (Persephone) etc. Festivals honoring such were celebrated with much enthusiasm throughout the world, and some such festivals grew into week-long celebrations in which even sporting events (Greek Games), litanies, songs, and even, sometimes, a sexual orgy (in the Spring festivals) to remind the fertility gods and their mates that they needed their services and blessings. All of these festivals tied together then, man's need for food to live and his religious nature: the desire to live for as long as possible in which he would need protection from animals and enemies (prayers and sacrifices to the Father God) and the food of Mother Earth (prayers and sacrifices to the Mother God). Among the Greeks such thinking was clearly evident as expressed by a Fragment (44) from Aeschylus:

Holy Sky desires to penetrate the Earth.
Love seizes Earth with longing for this marriage.
And rain, falling from her bedfellow the Sky,
impregnates Earth; and She brings forth for men
pasture for their flocks, and grain for them.1.16

In connection with the rise of the sun after the winter solstice and the rebirth of nature in the Spring that happened continually, the desire for man to live again and again, or at least pass through death to some type of renewal, confirmed in him a desire, not only to be a long-lived mortal, but to become himself renewable and immortal. Therefore the annual resurrection of nature was described in myths, such as those just referred to above, but within those myths were the proto-cults of the mysteries that developed into cults where people went through an initiation representing a rebirth that would last beyond death. Religion, the quest and longing to be eternal, was being institutionalized. The festivals were the public celebrations of such hopes, but the cults were the private celebrations whereby, usually in small groups, they encouraged each other with their hopes of eternal life, and the desire to embrace in a personal way the Ultimate Power of life. They sought to please the Spirit in such as way that It (used, not as an object, but as One that represents both sexes--therefore, not he or she) might transfer even the power of eternal life to them for, as a reward, their acts of piety and love. Mankind had always from the beginning sought to avoid death, but now he could have a program by which, according to his particular cult, he could be "assured by faith" that he would partake of eternal life. One could say that this was an expression of an awakened soul, although some still desired a type of physical resurrection like he had seen in nature in the Spring, while others desired to live among the departed "spirits" of their loved ones.

The idea of gratitude was used as a covering for prayers to the deities for continued blessings in the future. Among the Hebrews the "first fruits" of both the earth and the woman were presented to Yahweh. The first born son was "given" to Yahweh and then purchased back by the parents by means of an offering. The Norse religion had various customs such as leaving two to five of the fruits hanging on the tree as a gift to the god of fertility, and while banqueting, to set aside some food for the household gods. Likewise they placed a cup of broth "before" Berhta and Hulda before commencing a meal. Some, before drinking, would pour out some wine or beer into a vessel or spit some upon the ground for the Earth Goddess Zemynele.

In the Rig Veda, the oldest of all Indian religious literature, one can see that the prayers to Father Heaven and Mother Earth ask for, above all other things, protection from enemies, health-long life, children, and fruitful harvests.

Hymn 114: to Rudra "That it be well with all our cattle and our men,
that in this village all be healthy and well-fed....May his hand be
filled with sovran medicines, grant us protection, shelter, and a home
secure...Grant us, Immortal One, the food which mortals eat: be

gracious unto me, me seed, my progeny...harm us not, Rudra, in our seed and progeny, harm us not in the living, nor in cows or steeds."

Hymn 159: "I praise with sacrifices mighty Heaven and Earth at Festivals, the wise, the Strengtheners of Law. Who, having Gods for progeny, conjoined with Gods, through wonder-working wisdom bring forth choicest boons. With invocations, on the gracious Father's mind, and on the Mother's great inherent power I muse. Prolific Parents, they have made the world of life, and for their brood all round wide immortality...On us with loving-kindness Heaven and Earth bestow riches and various wealth and treasure hundredfold"

Hymn 185: "Heaven and Earth"." Endowed with understanding, I have uttered this truth, for all to hear, to Heaven and Earth. Be near us, keep us from reproach and trouble. Father and Mother, with your help preserve us. Be this my prayer fulfilled, O Heaven and Earth, wherewith, Father and Mother, I address you. Nearest of Gods be ye with your protection. May we find strengthening food in full abundance."

In these prayers one can find the full scope of the fertility festival: Two Gods, Heaven and Earth, have progeny in heaven, i.e. the other Gods, and on earth, the worshippers are asking for both the protection of the Father and the fertility of the Mother's "great inherent power" to bring forth livestock (wealth), agricultural fertility and children. Such thinking is continual in the Rig Veda and mankind, while desiring long life, as long as possible, abundance of food and children, still feels himself to be a mortal. But he desires immortality, but it is really in the later development of thought, especially in the Upanishads, that the doctrine of reincarnation is developed by which men, in prayer, are asking not to be mortal, but to become immortal.

This first chapter has sought to go back to man's earliest beginnings as far back as historically we are able to trace his thoughts to show that even from the very beginning of his perception of himself to be a separate unit from the rest of creation, even from then, he is seeking to live as long as possible. This can be shown by his paintings and his prayers. What can not be shown at this primitive state is that he sought to be eternal, but it can be expected that if he thought the Powers of Life were eternal, that he also desired such eternity for himself. Because he called himself a mortal before those who were immortal, it is inconceivable that he did not long for the eternal existence for himself also.

CHAPTER TWO

MAN'S GROWING PERCEPTION OF THE
ULTIMATE LIFE SOURCE: GOD

I. GENERAL AND VAGUE IDEAS OF THE LIFE FORCE

F.M. Cornford stated in his *From Religion to Philosophy: A Study of the Origins of Western Speculation* the following statement:

> We shall try to show how the ideas of Spirit or God and of Soul grew up out of 'Nature,' and passed into the inheritance of philosophic, as well as religious, thought...The point that now concerns us is simply this: that these three conceptions--Nature, God, and Soul--had all of them a long history which lay behind the first utterance of philosophy (p.6).

The Ultimate Power and Life Source had not yet attained the name of God, but, as seen in Chapter One, was acknowledged in nature and its many variations. But the implication seems to have been that something was there that could be touched and moved to action by cultic acts, prayers, mimicking magic, and sacrifices. This "Force" concept among many peoples was similar to the Greek *Moira* which even controlled the gods who, although, they were immortals, seemed to be subjected to the power of *Moira. Moira* is often translated Fate or Destiny; It was moral, It was just, and It administered order even among the gods. Originally, according to Hesiod the cosmos was divided into three realms of control by Moira: Earth, Sky and Sea. But later the accepted worldly order was: Zeus in control of sky and earth, Poseidon the oceans and large bodies of water, and Hades controlled the underworld. Each God in His own appointed area was supreme, but to step into another's appointed area was *hubris* (arrogance), for he tried to usurp the order imposed by Fate or Destiny (*Moira*), and for that the god could be punished. Each god in his area could appoint lower gods within his realm to certain appointed tasks: Diana for the hunt, Hera as companion to Zeus in the act of creative acts like fertility (although these often were not exclusively given to one god alone--certainly Dionysus was the most popular god of fertility), and Apollo and his son Aesclepius were appointed the art of healing. (As a diversion: I often wondered why Zeus would give the art of medicine and healing to Apollo and Aesclepius, for he himself was always eager for prayer and praise and sick people pray much. After much pondering of the question, without any aid from any other, I found my answer: He simply did not want to be known as Doctor Zeus!).

Confucius, used the term "Heaven" for that ultimate source that the contemporary Greeks used for *Moira*. One does not offend "Heaven" for there is no sacrifice left to him, no expiation, i.e. he will be punished. "He who offends against Heaven has none to whom he can pray" (BK III. 13). "The superior man thinks of Moral Force, the small man thinks of comfort. The superior man of "Heaven", the small man thinks of things of the earth" (Bk IV.11)."Heaven" is very much in control. When a man is sick it is so appointed by "Heaven" (Bk VI.8). The solution, Confucius taught, was to be moral, for "Heaven" establishes justice, and to offend Heaven is to be of a small mind.

These basic concepts of justice, personal limits, respect for the territory of others, an awe of the eternal and unknown, a fear of death and hope of life all were, and are experienced by all humans, not just the believers in God. Abraham H. Maslow stated:

> There is, then, a road which all profoundly "serious," "ultimately concerned" people of good will can travel together for a very long distance. Only when they come almost to its end does the road fork so that they must part in disagreement.2.1

Maslow continues by referring to Rudolf Otto's work *The Idea of the Holy* and picks the following religious concerns from that work in which both the theist and the atheist can walk side by side, until the end's necessary departure. Such religious concerns imbedded in all people and discussed in Otto's work are: feelings of sacredness, of being a creature--a sense of smallness in the universe, a sense of thanksgiving for the blessings one has received, an awe in confrontation of the great mystery of the depth and grandeur of the universe, personal awareness of limitations and sometimes a sense of powerlessness. Inquiries and discussions of concern about such can be shared by all, for all have them. Maslow then concluded: "This road can be traveled together by all who are not afraid of truth, not only by theists and non-theists, but also by individuals of every political and economic persuasion".2.2

II. THE IDEA OF GOD

The Idea of God is a very diversified concept, sometimes not more than the thoughts presented above, i.e. a Moral Force that directs the universe and those within it in such a way that the good prosper and the evil are eventually punished or at least less blessed. And while the statement of Plato that God is "past being found out" and by the Sufi Sanai (Hadiqa) 2.3 "No human mind can attain an understanding of the form of being which is called God" are correct, yet man seeks to believe and even to "know" more. It is indeed a noble quest, but not a scientific one, and is filled with dangers. That is why some present the "via negativa" that predicates that one ought to say what God is not, before they present the via positiva, of what He is. Sarvepalli Radhakrishnan believes that religious experiences by individuals affirm the reality of God, but that trying to symbolize either the experience itself or God is no more than a personal interpretation of that experience. He cautiously explains his faith with these words:

> So also we may not know the ultimate meaning of God, though we may know something about God or what answers to God in reality through religious experience. The creeds of religion correspond to theories of science...However, we are realizing that it is simply im- possible to form any picture at all of the ultimate nature of the physical world...Similarly, we have certain experiences which we try to account for by the assumption of God. The God of our imagi- nation may be as real as the electron but is not necessarily the reality which we immediately apprehend. The idea of God is an interpreta- tion of experience.2.4

G.W.F. Hegel taught that there were four elements to the "knowledge of God": faith, feeling, representation, and thought. He argues that faith (Glaube) is not in opposition to certainty (Gewissheit), but is a form of knowledge. The second element is feeling (Gefuehl), which, although very subjective is touching on the very core of the person:"What one has in one's heart belongs to the being of one's personality, to one's inmost being." Yet, "there are severe limitations to feeling" and therefore one must pursue the form of knowledge known as representation (Vorstellung). "Hence when it comes to the matter of truth, representation is prior (to feeling)." This is a statement which is critical of Schleiermacher, who, Hegel felt, put too much emphasis on feeling. This representation usually took form in images (Bilder), but also in stories of representation about Zeus or like the story of Jesus as the image of God. For such representations say much more, at least in a communicative way, than personal feelings. Finally thought (Denken) whereby a person can draw mental images, concepts (Begriff) which more closely hold together the religious experience in a logical form. Plato and Epicurus, as well as their followers after them, taught that, in the words that <u>Cicero</u> put into Velleius' mouth in the dialogue *The Nature of the Gods*, "...that gods must exist because nature herself has imprinted an idea of them in the minds of all mankind."2.5 Yet, one must be aware that each person's experiences and ideas of God are different, are molded by our own age and culture, and therefore there is no room for arrogance when speaking of one's concept of God when relating to another's concept of God. For as the pre-Socratic Greek philosopher <u>Xenophanes</u> warned:

Mortals believe that the gods are begotten,
and that they wear clothing like our own,
and have a voice and body.

The Ethiopians make their gods snub-nosed and black;
the Thacians make theirs gray-eyed and red-haired.

And if oxen and horses and lions had hands,
and could draw with their hands and do what man can do,
horses would draw the gods in the shape of horses,
and oxen in the shape of oxen,
each giving the gods bodies similar to their own.2.6

A. DEFINITIONS OF GOD

Because all mankind felt within the existence of an Eternal Force beyond himself, it came to a point where he tried to go through the four stages referred to by Hegel. Also, he wanted to define It, then name It, try to understand Its nature, and how It related to the universe, and finally how It related to man himself. These then will be the following sections of this second chapter.

Defining the Ultimate Life Source and Moral Force of the universe was perhaps just a small step away from what was already said, nevertheless, thinkers of all ages came up with various definitions. From Lao Tzu's the "Mother of all things" to Tertullian's "Ground of Being", from the "Infinite" of Anaximander to the "Good beyond Essence" of Plato, from the "Water" of Thales to the "Air" of Anaximenes, from the "That which is" of the Yahwist to the "One" of Neoplatonism, from the pantheistic "Soul of the Universe" to the "Absolute Other" from the "Fire" and "LOGOS" of Heraclitus to the "Intellect" or "Mind" (Greek NOUS) of Anaxagoras, and from the "Unchangeable That Is" the "Ultimate Reality" of Parmenides to the active Fate as a Force of Morality of the Stoics, from the "Supreme Good" of Anselm to the Swedenborgian Trinity "Divine Love, Divine Wisdom, and Divine Use," from Empedocles' "Love" or "Harmony" that is a "Sacred Mind" (Phren hiere), all have tried, in their own ways, to define "God" in such a way that others would seek their God and be comforted by It. Plato described God as the Unity of All Virtues, and often called him by those virtues: NOUS (Intellect of Mind), the First Cause of creation, Absolute Goodness, the Good beyond Being, Absolute Beauty, and the Creator and Father of the universe. All men, during polytheism, simply called them the Immortals. Abraham H. Maslow was irritated by some of the modern theologians and philosophers who did not use the name God and reverted to other definitions somewhat like the preceding.

> "Even the word 'god' is being defined by many theologians today
> in such a way as to exclude the conception of a person with a form,
> a voice, a beard, etc. If God gets to be defined as "Being Itself," or
> as "the integrating principle in the universe," or as "the whole of
> everything," or as "the meaningfulness of the cosmos," or in some
> other non-personal way, then what will atheists be fighting against?

They may very well agree with "integrating principles" or "the principle of harmony."2.7

The person or personhood of God will be further developed in the next few chapters, but one can see Maslow's discomfort with impersonal names or definitions. But from God's point of view, I doubt that it would keep God from caring about someone reaching out to Him/Her in love and hope simply because the worshipper used the definition by which he came to by the influence of his culture.

B. NAMES OF GOD

As I mentioned earlier in Chapter One, there is very little difference between a definition of God and a name for God, for I believe that usage of a definition for God for a period of time eventually became the name of the God. But they are separated here and called names because of a lengthy period of use. Theologians who have accepted the fact that God is beyond all anthropomorphisms and beyond gender, even beyond being itself--as Plato, are not disturbed by "non-personal" names, such as "definitions", for in their minds it does not take away from the "personhood" of God to do so. It reminds me of a question a child asked her father. "Has anyone ever been to the planets?" "No", said the father. "Then how do we know their names?" asked the child. Same with God: we have named Him/Her!

Before going to the numerous ways in which man has named God, I would like to use a story that Jalaludin Rumi, a Sufi, told.

"Four people were given a piece of money.
     The first was a Persian. He said: 'I will buy with this some angur.'
     The second was an Arab. He said: 'No, because I want inab.'
     The third was a Turk. He said: 'I do not want inab, I want uzum.'
     The fourth was a Greek. He said: 'I want stafil.'"

Because they did not know what lay behind the names of things, these four started to fight over how they would spend their one coin. They each had a name and a concept, but no knowledge of the names of the others. One man of wisdom present could have reconciled them all saying: 'I can fulfill the needs of all of you, with the one coin. If you honestly give me your trust, your one coin will become as four; and you, four at odds with each other, will become united in agreement.'

Such a man would know that each in his own language wanted the same thing, grapes."2.8

If that is kept in mind, the spirit of this chapter and the rest of the book may be better understood.

The *Corpus Hermeticum*, Libellus I, starts with Hermes Trismegistus declaring that he had a vision of Light that spoke, and the way that God, within the Light, described himself was: "That Light is I, Intellect (NOUS: also Mind), the First God." Later NOUS is called the Father of all. In Libellus XII it reads: "NOUS, my son Tat, is the very substance of God, if indeed there is a substance of God; and of what nature that substance is, God alone knows precisely". So what we have for personal names given by a vision and a doctrine are actually no more than definitions that have been accepted as personal names within the Hermetic literature.

Sri Chinmoy in his Commentary on the *Bhagavad Gita* stated: "AUM is the mystical symbol supreme. AUM is the real name of God. In the cosmic manifestation is AUM. Beyond the manifestation, farthest beyond is AUM."2.9 Swami Nikhilananda confirms that to the Hindu, AUM is indeed the name of God.

One of the most significant symbols of Brahman, both personal and impersonal, is Aum, often written Om...This syllable Om is indeed Brahman. This syllable is the Highest.2.10

However, Swami Prabhavananda takes more tolerant view, as Hinduism in general is more tolerant than most religions, and he quotes from Sri Chaitanya the words which he encouraged his followers to remember:

Various are thy names, Oh Lord,
In each and every name thy power resides.
No times are set, no rites are needful,
    for chanting thy name.
So vast is thy mercy.2.11

One can see the simple sincerity of one reaching out to God: no rites or times or rituals are needed to accompany the prayer of the believer, for God is vastly merciful and can see into the heart, and does not demand such formalities.

In the *Gathas* of <u>Zarathushtra</u> Ahura Mazda is proclaimed God, but He is also defined as "First and Last of all Eternity, as the Father of Good Mind, the True Creator of Truth, and the Lord over the actions of life."2.12 Again, it is near impossible to separate definitions from personal names. Ahu, in Avestan, signifies "the indestructible life essence of Ahura, therefore, the "Living One" and Mazda seems to have connotations of wisdom: therefore, Ahura Mazda, personal names, means the Living One who is Wise. Again, a "personal" name, becomes personal by the continual usage of the definition of His nature.

As mentioned earlier, the Hebrew name, the Tetragrammaton, transliterated "Yahweh" is likewise a name by usage of the definition, for the definition is something like "That Which Is", which implies Absolute and Eternal Existence. People who follow the Torah, both Jews and Christians, see it today as a personal name, given by Yahweh himself, so that the calling upon the name of Yahweh gives the same intimate comfort that a Hindu has by calling upon AUM. It is likewise with Islam, for Allah actually means, "The God", and theologically for the Muslim, it means the One and Only God. Yet Allah also is used as and considered a personal name. For a Christian to refuse to use the name Allah, he is, in actuality, simply rejecting the Arabic word for God, and in a sense is saying that he refuses to use the name God, which, in English, comes from the German word for God, Gott. As far as Islam goes, there are, of official usage, 99 names for God, Allah, being only one of them. Some of the other names for God are: Ar-Rahim (The Merciful), As-Salaam (The Source of Peace), Al-Khaliq (The Creator), Al-Ghaffar (The Forgiver), Al-Hakam (The Judge), and Al-Wadud (The All loving). Again one can see that a quality or a function by usage can become a personal name for God.

In the <u>*Prose Edda*</u> by <u>Snorri Sturluson</u> (1179-1241 AD) there is the tale of "The Deluding of Gylfi", in which there is a conversation about the highest God and his name. One name, of course, can not totally define him, and even his actions must be mentioned before Gylfi would know the foremost of the gods. The question is answered this way:

> Gylfi began his questioning: 'Who is the foremost or oldest of all the gods?'
> High One replied: 'He is called All-Father in our tongue, but in ancient Asgard he had twelve names: one is All-Father; the second, Herran or Herjan (Lord or Raider); the third, Nikar or Hnikar (Spear-thruster); the fourth, Nikuz or Hnikud (Spear-thruster); the fifth, Fjoelnir (Much-knowing); the sixth Oski (Fulfiller-of-desire); the seventh, Omi (Booming Voice); the eighth, Biflidi or Blindi (Spear-shaker), the ninth, Svidar; the tenth, Svidrir; the eleventh, Vidrir (Ruler-of weather); the twelfth, Jalg or Jalk (Gelding).2.13

These names are yet not enough to "know" the foremost God. Gylfi asks, "What kind of power does He have and what does He do?" The answers are that He lives forever and ever, He has created heaven and earth, and he has made man with an eternal soul so that man can also live forever and ever.

Many gods with many names are mentioned in the Rig-Veda, the almost endless volume of hymns to the gods. In hymn Bk X, 121 it is asked: "What God shall we adore with our oblation?". The answer is "Prajapati! For You only comprehend all these created things, and there is none besides You." One may ask how such monotheistic views can be held in a religion which constantly praises many different gods by many different names. Because, from its very outset, Hinduism was a religion of great tolerance and was open to all the views expressed by those longing for God. No heresy trials, no burning at the state, no set formulas that all had to agree to. Much later reformers, like Shankara (686-718 AD) tried to bring some consistency to Hinduism, but the task was really impossible to accomplish by its very nature of openness for the religious mind. Generally many hold that The Great Atman (Brahman) was the ultimate unifying principle of reality.

The Egyptians likewise were normally very open and tolerant to the many concepts and names of God. Herodotus, himself from the polytheistic Greeks was amazed that the "Egyptians worshipped everything" as he felt everything was made a god by them. But Egypt did have a graded hierarchy. The names of the most established gods there were: Amon (the Hidden One), Khons (the One Who Travels across the Sky, i.e. the Moon), The Sun-god was Re, Horus was "the Lofty One",

Sekhmet was the "Mighty One, and Isis meant "the Throne". The meaning of the name of Ptah and Osiris are unknown. Thomas Aquinas thought the best name for God was "He Who Is", which is not far from many other such designations, especially "Yahweh". The female Christian mystic, Julian of Norwich said:

> As verily as God is our Father, so verily God is our Mother; and that
> showed He in all, and especially in these sweet words where he says:
> I it am. That is to say, I it am, the Might and the Goodness of the
> Fatherhood; I it am, the Wisdom of the Motherhood; I it am, the
> Light and the Grace that is all blessed Love: I it am, the Trinity; I
> it am, the Unity.2.14

The common Judeo-Christian Bible (canonized Hebrew and Greek scriptures) presents many names by which it refers to God: "That Which Is - or - I Am Being" (Ex. 3:14; Rv 1:4,8); "Life" (Jn 11:25, 14:6); "Light (I Jn1:5); "God" (Gn 28:13, Ex 3:6, Is 40:28); and many other names such as Good, Beautiful, Wise, Beloved, God of gods, Lord of lords, Holy of holies, Eternal, Existent, Cause of the ages, King of kings, and Ancient of days. A profitable reading would be a Christian work that discusses the Names of God (Divine Names) by Pseudo-Dionysius.

C. THE NATURE OF GOD

From definition to name to nature is really a short and overlapping journey, because they are so very interrelated, yet there is room for mental separation of the three categories. As previously stated, sometimes the names are simply well used definitions, and sometimes those definitions also are relative to the God's function or nature. I have decided to make five divisions, which I believe follow a logical development of man's thought about the Power beyond themselves: Nature itself or the Cosmos as God; the gods in man's image--anthropomorphism; the difference between polytheism and monotheism; complex unities and "trinities"; and finally God beyond being and human apprehension and symbolism.

1. Nature/Cosmos as God

   Shinto, the true indigenous religion of Japan, is a religion that is totally tied to nature, as there is nothing supernatural in their belief. Although they pray to many gods, those gods are all linked to the natural order, and therefore, all things in nature have a type of divinity to them. Life, all life, is a participation in divinity, and therefore their is no negativity about human life as experienced in the now. Rather it is to be groomed and beatified, and as the Japanese Shintoists beautify their gardens, they also try to beautify their lives and enjoy the beauty of nature, for all things participate in the divine. They have no concern about the "soul" or the afterlife, or theology that goes into the supernatural. The gods who are worshipped are all elements to nature: the Sun Goddess, Amaerasu, is the most significant God, but also highly praise are the Sky God and the Food God. Their nature poetry is for them an expression of praise and love for the Divinity.

   Even in a single leaf of a tree
   Or a tender blade of grass,
   The Majestic Deity reveals Himself.

   Heraclitus, who is rather obscure to begin with, wanders, sometimes inconsistently from subject to subject--this is probably due to our judging him on the bases of the existing fragments of his work--but Fire often seems to be God Himself. But other times, God seems to be everything:

   God is day and night, winter and summer, war and peace, surfeit
   and hunger; but he takes various shapes, just as fire, when it is
   mingled with spices, is named according to the savour of each.

   All things are an exchange for Fire, and Fire for all things.2.15.

   In the Srimad Bhagavatam it is stated:

   You attained knowledge and gained power through your devotion
   to God; yet some ignorance remains in you, for you still see difference, and not the unity that pervades all things. Now must you

therefore seek the highest truth, so that you may find one God, the divine Self, in all beings and in all things, and thus be forever free from delusion.2.16.

In Cicero's Nature of the Gods, he puts into the mouth of Velleius a criticism of Balbus, and his Stoic beliefs, stating:

But Zeno--and I come now, Balbus, to the men of your school-- Zeno thought that God was to be found in the law of nature, which is powerful to enforce what is right and to forbid transgressions. But how one can attribute life to a law, nobody can understand. And God must surely be a living God! Then in another place he identifies the aether with God...In other works, he takes the view that the divine power is to be found in a principle of reason which pervades the whole of nature. He attributes such power to the stars, and even to the months and years and changing seasons...Zeno ignores all our natural or acquired beliefs about the gods, and banishes Jupiter, Juno and Vesta, and all these persons...He says in fact that the universe itself is God.2.17

Balbus does not disagree: "...and so by this argument too we may infer that the universe is God."2.18

Pierre Teilhard de Chardin in his *Hymn of the Universe* certainly disturbed many more traditional theologians by a few "pantheistic" statements, yet one must not close one's mind to the beauty of the work, for even the traditionalist who insists that there be a separation of God and his person from the creation (as I myself do) can, nevertheless, derive a deep appreciation of God's nearness to us from the Hymn. Like many great works, it is not necessary to agree with all that is said to be spiritually edified by such works. De Chardin's Hymn is one of those works. Nevertheless, a couple of statements are definitely espousing pantheism:

For me, my God, all joy and all achievement, the very purpose of my being and all my love of life, all depend on this one basic vision of the union between yourself and the universe. Let others, fulfilling a function more august than mine, proclaim your splendors as pure Spirit; as for me, dominated as I am by a vocation which springs

from the inmost fibers of my being, I have no desire, I have no ability, to proclaim anything except the innumerable prolongations of
your incarnate Being in the world of matter; I can preach only the
mystery of your flesh (the material universe).2.19.

Later in the work, de Chardin presents God as saying about the universe,
"hoc est Corpus meum" (this is my body). For those who are pantheistic
in their theology, this is an absolute must read. Even for others, there is
so much beauty to the work that it will deepen a persons faith in a God
that gives to humanity such a beautiful and filled with life universe.

2. Anthropomorphism -- God in Man's Image

How to think of God, and then to make such thoughts communicable
to others has always been a difficult task for theologians and philosophers. For that which is "Wholly Other" than humankind to be expressed
in human words with human concepts makes the task totally impossible
(in Plato's mind), yet necessary. Therefore, mental and symbolic
concessions must be made. Early man made conceptions and symbols of
God based on similar characteristics and functions, as has seen to a
limited degree in Chapter One. If it were strength and frightening power,
then perhaps God was made or spoken of in the form of a lion, or if high
above all and yet able to see all, in the form of an eagle. As man
developed his own thinking power and with his reason was able to
conquer the greatest of the wild beasts he raised his image of God to his
own level only stronger, wiser, faster, and above all invulnerable.
Nevertheless, man saw his own image as that closest to God, therefore, it
seemed logical that God created man in his own image, and to speak of
God in the highest image he had, his own, man then anthropomorphised
his mental concepts and artistic forms of God in his own image. This
even implied that the gods formed families, since they too had sexual
relations and took pride in their children. Hesiod's entire Theogony is a
work that puts order into the hierarchy of the Greek gods, so that the
Greeks would know, in King James' language, who begat whom. He
even refers to the family of the gods as a holy race. True, most of the
early Greek gods were symbols of virtues or charactistics, and their status
in the holy family probably was a way of teaching what values are to be
preferred to others. Nevertheless, they were, at least in the popular

mind-set, gods. Likewise, man's nature was not quite so pure, and to make God in man's image often represented God or the gods doing some of the self-centered things that man often did. One of the first, at least among the Greeks who rejected such ugliness ascribed to the gods was Xenophanes of Kolophon (6th Century BC). He wrote the following rejections of the crude anthropomorphisms used by his Greek predecessors about God or the gods and the "insults" to their nature.

> Homer and Hesiod have ascribed to the gods all things that are a shame and a disgrace among mortals, stealings and adulteries and deceivings of one another.

> But mortals deem that the gods are begotten as they are, and have clothes like theirs, and voice and form.

Xenophanes then declared his own position: "One God, the greatest among gods and men, neither in form unto mortals nor in thought."2.20 Heraclitus had much the same criticism of trying to draw concepts of God based on man's image of himself: "Man is called a baby by God, even as a child by a man...The wisest man is an ape compared to God, just as the most beautiful ape is ugly compared to man."2.21 But Cicero explained it this way, speaking by the mouth of Cotta in his The Nature of the Gods, he has Cotta say:

> Do you imagine that an eagle, or a lion, or a dolphin prefers any other shape to his own? So is it any wonder if in the same way nature prescribes that mankind should consider no shape to be more beautiful than theirs? This I think is the reason why we think the gods similar to men. (Bk I.76-77)

About the Egyptians' tendency to anthropomorphise the gods, E.A. Wallis Budge stated:

> To the great and supreme power which made the earth, the heavens, the sea, the sky, man and women, animals, birds, and creeping things, all that is and all that shall be, the Egyptians gave the name *neter*... But side by side with *neter*, whatever it may mean, we have mentioned in texts of all ages a number of beings or existences called *neteru*,

which Egyptologists universally translate by the word "gods." Among these must be included the great cosmic powers and the beings who, although held to be supernatural, were yet finite and mortal, and were endowed by the Egyptians with love, hatred, and passions of every sort and kind.2.22

The bickerings between Horus and Seth, and their having to have the other gods come in and make judgments between them is further evidence of the passions of the Egyptian gods--just like men.

The Romans likewise had very anthropomorphic gods, and are so described in Ovid's *Metamorphoses*: Apollo lusted after Daphne; Jove, the Almighty Father, lusted in passion for the Arcadian girl, a nymph, "and fire ran through his marrow-bones," and he impregnated innocent Semele, who then was punished by the jealous wrath of Juno. Many other stories of the jealousies, pride, and disgrace among the popular deities. But, to be fair all the good traits of men also were magnified among the Roman gods. But either way, the gods were made in man's image, for better and for worse.

In the Srimad Bhagavatam, God, Brahma, brooded over Naga, rested, and even closed his eyes during rest (Beginning of Chapter Two). The Teutonic gods are often seen in a state of complacency and joy, but also can fall into a fit of wrath and vengeance, and Loki a spoiled and precocious child grew more self-centered and violent as the years passed so that all the other gods condemned him. Idun's apples were stolen, and Thor had a duel with Hrungnir.

Jahweh, in the *Hebrew Scriptures*, often became angry, sometimes insecure, always jealous, and vengeful. From taking away life and inflicting death because man disobeyed his rules in the fruit garden, his violent anger to send a devastating flood upon his created children, his attempt at destroying man's unity by confusing their language because of his insecurity that if the tower was built high enough nothing would be out of man's reach, his creating millions of people but loving only a small portion of them and giving them special relationship to himself.

There were, in fact, no early religions that personified God or the gods that did not transfer, not only the images of justice, truth, protection, and even love to their gods, but also the bad human traits as well.

3. The Trend Towards Monotheism

Among the early polytheistic religions, after such religions received a reforming of thought and a desire to give some organization to the celestial realm, usually an established hierarchy among the gods was developed, such as was presented by Hesiod for the Greeks. Even though all gods still were prayed to and accepted of being worthy of man's worship, there eventually emerged one God who became the Supreme Master of the heavenly realm. In Hinduism this transition can be seen in the change of theological perspective that took place from the time of the Vedas to the time of the later Upanishads. For example, in the Vedas there were 33 gods. First Brahman becomes superior to the other gods, and from the myth of Kena 14-28 declares the dependence of the other gods, nature gods, upon Brahman; for Agni (the god of fire) can not even burn a blade of grass without the support of the will of Brahman, and Vayu is not able to blow hard enough to move a small piece of straw without the will and consent of Brahman. All gods are now subjected to Brahman to such a degree that they can not even perform their activities in their own realm of authority without having a sense of fear of Brahman that, perhaps, they have exceeded their authority (Greek Hubris). At this point, depending on how one defines "God", there is already monotheism, for the other gods have become lower gods and are actually helpers of the Supreme God, Brahman.

Among the Norse, as presented earlier, there were many gods, but usually with one who was a Supreme God, the High One, who was called the "All-Father" of the other Norse gods. In the Deluding of Gylfi, Snorri Sturluson proclaimed:

'Odin is the highest and the oldest of the gods. He rules all things and, no matter how mighty the other gods may be, they all serve him as children do their father. His wife is Frigg and she knows the fates of all men, although she does not prophesy...Odin is called All-Father because he is the father of all the gods. He is also called Valfather because all who fall in battle are his adopted sons. He allots to them Valhalla and Vingolf, and then they are called Einherjar. 2.23

The Norse hierarchy became limited to 14 gods, and 'Odin (sometimes: Wodin) was their Father and Leader. This says something of Norse values, for 'Odin was also the god of wisdom, having given one eye for the sake of wisdom. While Thor was a mighty warrior, and no one emphasized war heroes more than the Norsemen, yet the highest respect was to the God of Wisdom, 'Odin, which sounds of Platonic values.

Dr. Mueller-Kriesel compiled a list of 89 Egyptian gods, and while some were much higher than others, a strict monotheism never developed among the ancient Egyptians, which speaks well of their tolerance, not to force people in any particular way in their religious thinking. However, Osiris and family (Wife Isis and Son Horus) were the most prayed to and beloved of the Egyptian gods. The image of Osiris was indeed so very powerful that his image became that of a "Universal Hero", and therefore his appeal was great and his influence upon other later developing religions was probably quite enormous. He was already popular in Ancient Egypt as early a the 26th Century BC, and may have been worshipped as early as 3000 BC. He continued to be worshipped by some until Islam conquered Egypt in the late 7th Century AD. But no other god in human history was worship by name for so long a time. The Osirian myth presented him as a god who united and loved his people, the Egyptians. His image penetrated the lives of both pharaohs and peasants. He was the Lord of Fertility, the human king who shared work, life, and death with his fellow humans; and the righteous one who, in bringing good to others, was betrayed and brutally killed, even by those closest to him. Yet this Hero overcame evil and death and thus broke through the barriers that most hold mortals in bondage and fear, and even this victory he did not hold selfishly. Graciously he offered this same victory over evil and death to those who loved him and kept his commandments for living justly and kindly to others. The dying took on His name at death (the deceased was known as "Osiris John Doe") in the hopes that he would give them eternal life, and his own eternal presence. The *Breaking Forth of Day* (the Egyptian name for the book called by Westerners *The Book of the Dead*) will usher in the new eternal era and those who followed him will celebrate their being his children forever. That was about as powerful a message and a promise that the ancient world could give by means of a religious teaching. One can certainly see the parallels between the Osirian religious thought and that of Christianity. While Ancient Egypt never went to monotheism, yet in practice, Osiris was certainly beloved above all. In addition to the preceding, he also presented the ideal family pattern to the Egyptians: a more than loving wife in Isis and a loyal and honorable son Horus. It might be interesting to Christians that the greatest Christian mind of the Third Century of the Christian era, Origen, used for his name, in the Greek language, the expression "Of Horus born" -- "Hori-gene".

In like fashion Zeus rose to the top of the Greek pantheon, as did Jupiter among the Romans. Israel started out as a polytheistic religion, and then proceeded to, what one often calls, a henotheistic theology: i.e. there are many gods, but only One is to be worshipped by the people of Israel by covenantal contract, Yahweh. Later, perhaps during or after the period of Isaiah's message, Israel became a monotheistic religion. The traces of early polytheism among the Israelites are not only the plural form of Genesis One (Elohim = the gods), but also in Genesis 6:1-4 where a hierarchy of gods were born from the lead God, and from the story of Rachel who stole and hid her family's gods under her garments in flight from her father, Laban (Gen.31). Laban certainly spent enough time and energy to recover them to give evidence that he was of the faith that such gods existed.

4. Monotheism And Its Complex Unities

Today most people, if they believe in a heavenly realm, believe in a rather strict monotheism, at least to One who stands so far above any other heavenly creatures and that all are totally dependent upon that One. Probably the closest to absolute monotheism is Islam, for it has few other eternal beings in the heavenly realm, Gabriel certainly being one of them. Gabriel is prominent as the first from heaven to contact him about his call from God, he accompanied Muhammad on his night journey to Jerusalem, and it was Gabriel who accompanied him to the door of heaven that was guarded by another angel. In the Second Sura, Satans, the angels of God, and His Messengers (Gabriel and Michael) are mentioned. In fact twenty times in the Koran angels are mentioned., and they play a long prominent part of the creation story in Sura XV, where Iblis will not bow down before Adam, for Adam was a mere mortal. For such action, Iblis (Satan) received the curse of God. But, by and large, Allah is the only One, and he has no son, for he himself was unbegotten and he himself begat none.

Comparable to Islam in declaring itself monotheistic is present day Judaism, although, after the Hellenistic influence they believed in many other heavenly creatures known as his messengers (Greek--AGGELOI). And evidently, even though only a few are known by name, there is a great number of them. Of those known by name at the time of Jesus and taken from the book of Enoch there are seven: Uriel, Raphael, Raguel (Reuel), Michael, Saraqael, Gabriel, and Remiel. Early Israel's journey from polytheism to monotheism was addressed earlier and shall not be reviewed here. But since about the time of Isaiah, with the exception of the angels, there is only One in the heavens.

Platonism also focused upon the One, The Good beyond Being, the Absolute Beauty, and known also as the Intellect or Mind (NOUS) of the universe, and more in concession to man's limited way of anthropomorphically thinking, God was the Shepherd of Mankind, the Pilot of the Universe, and the Father and Creator of all that is. Plato called the other heavenly hosts created by the Father and Creator "lower gods" for to Plato and most Greeks those creatures made unchangeable and eternal by the Creator were called gods. When Judaism filled its heaven with those creatures, and their functions equal to Plato's lower gods, it called them angels, instead of gods. More of the Absolute One will be discussed in the next section.

The challenge to stay "monotheistic" and yet have teachings that relate to other eternal beings, was not so simple for several religions who have long academic and logical battles within, came to a complex of beings within the One. The Egyptians tried to solve their desire for unity within plurality with a series of Trinities: Ptah and Sokaris and Osiris for one; Amon and Re and Ptah for another; and yet, Osiris, Isis, and Horus for a third (sometimes known as the Triad of Abydos), and even the Egyptian view of the Syrian gods were seen by the Egyptians as a Trinity: Kades-Astarte-Anath. All within each group could be prayed to without any seeming conflict to the very open and tolerant of thought Egyptians.

The Hindus also had variations of the Trinity of Gods. In each, however, the greatest God was always Brahman, and the different Hindu trinities were either slightly lower than He or else were modes of Himself. The Fourth Khanda of the Talavakara Upanishad states: "Therefore these Devas, viz. Agni, Vayu, and Indra, are, as it were, above the other gods, for they touched It (Brahman) nearest." The most common of the Hindu trinities in sacred literature is a Trinity in which Brahman, the non-personal and beyond anthropomorphisms God, is expressed in three ways: as a Creator (Brahma), as a Preserver (Vishnu), and as a Destroyer ((usually Shiva (Siva) or Rudra)). But the One God above all is Brahman who is known as the Imperishable Infinite, and often is called by the name AUM.

Zarathushtra, likewise believed in One God, yet the One God, Mazda Ahura, or simply Mazda, was always accompanied by Armaiti (his daughter) and Good Mind. It seems that Good Mind and "Love and Compassion", his daughter Armaiti, are only expressions of his attributes and qualities. In the 45th Yasna it is stated:

I declare this to you,
Mazda, who knows all things,
has established the best life in harmony with Truth,
He is the Father of the empowering Good Mind,
and his daughter is Armaiti (Devotion) and
nourisher of good deeds.

Sometimes there seems to be a Trinity with Mazda Ahura, His Benevolent Spirit, and the Good Mind. A self-blessing, that somewhat reminds me of the blessing given at the end of many Christian worship services (The Love of God, the Grace of Our Lord, Jesus Christ, and the fellowship of the Holy Spirit be with you), is prayed with these word (Yasna 45):

May Mazda Ahura be gracious to me
through His Benevolent Spirit in whose adoration
the Good Mind has guided me.
May He, in His Wisdom, teach me the highest.

So, even though, Zoroastrianism is a monotheism, yet one can see that there is a three fold complex involved.

In Christianity there is no doubt that the One God is a complex of three identities (names or persons) that form a Superessential Unity of Being, generally referred to as the "Holy Trinity" or "The Father, Son, and Holy Spirit". Yet that very Godhead is always seen as One. Because of criticism from others that Christianity really has three gods, especially after its rejection of modalism, the teaching is often referred to as "The Mystery of the Holy Trinity". Modalism was a teaching of some early Christians that God was One, but he appeared in three modes corresponding to his three activities on behalf of man: as Creator, as Redeemer, and as Comforter. However, such a teaching was rejected by the majority of bishops who voted it out, and in general the teachings ascribed to the theology of Athanasius and developed about a century later and linked to him was designated as the Athanasian Creed. In it the personhood of all three "persons" of the Trinity was defended and each in its own behalf was God, yet there was only One Godhead. The logical variations from this teaching were numerous and many still exist that are usually influenced by Arius, Nestorius, or Eutyches, and certainly do not need further discussion here.

5. God Who Is Beyond Being Or Human Comprehension

While some religions do not feel that naming the Ultimate Being is improper, they also feel that to try to capture the fulness of God in a particular anthropomorphic word, however well intentioned, does not do full justice to the dignity of God. For He is so far above and beyond our thinking capacity. The Hindus came to the conclusion that one may properly refer to Brahma, Vishnu, or Sive as God and use such personal names without the need to feel guilty of any type of hubris, yet they prefer to teach that there is a total incomprehensibility to the Ultimate Being of God, which they designate with the word Brahman, but to whom they attach no human concepts or passions. Shankara taught: "Supreme, beyond the power of speech to express, Brahman may yet be apprehended by the eye of pure illumination. Pure, absolute and eternal Reality--such is Brahman, and 'Thou art That'".2.24   In the *Srimad Bhagavatam* it is stated (Chapter II):

"Words cannot express Thee,
Intellect cannot know Thee,
Senses cannot find Thee,
Mind cannot conceive Thee:
Thou art beyond all.

....
There is nothing beyond or above Thee.
From thee all religions spring forth,
Thou art the source of all Scriptures,
Thou art the fountain of all knowledge.
Yet none of these can fully reveal thy infinite nature,
For verily thou are supreme;
Infinite, absolute, impersonal, beyond all name and form art Thou.
(trans. Swami Prabhavananda)

Master Lao (Lao Tzu) is known for the work *The Tao Teh King* (*Ching*) and in it he immediately speaks of the Infinite Tao as something that is far beyond a name or the possibility of such naming. It is the everlasting and unchanging Tao, but having no name a person can say that it was the Originator of heaven and earth, but if one wants to give It a name he may refer to It as "The Mother of All Things". Man has a natural desire to know It and try to be familiar with it, but he will always be on the outside of this Reality in substance and thought.

"Always without desire we must be found,
If its deep mystery we would sound;
But if desire always within us be,
Its outer fringe is all that we shall see" (trans.J. Legge)

For Ultimate Reality is a mystery, and sages do not use words or any power of speech to make it known.

Platonists follow the concepts of Plato, often using terms like The Intellect or Mind (NOUS), Father (PATER), Creator (POIETES), and Maker (DEMIOURGOS), but likewise refer to the Good Beyond Being (Republic 509b). Plotinus is emphatic that only the Good Beyond Being is in reality the One from Whom all else emanates. He called NOUS the "image" of the One. For all things are derived from the One: "The One, however, is the power productive of all things"; and "The totality of beings must come after the One because The One itself has no determinate form" (Enneads V.1). The Pseudo-Dionysius, authored by an unknown Platonic Christian around the year 500 AD, likewise declared: "The Good transcends everything, as indeed it does, therefore its nature, unconfined by form, is the Creator of all form"(Divine Names 697A).

Kabir was a 15th Century AD mystic who was a mixture of Hindu and Islamic (Sufi) beliefs. The Sufi mystics, unlike most of Islam, were very open to spiritual knowledge from other religions, Kabir is a prime example of a willingness to unify the truths, as he saw them, from both sides. Based on a translation by Rabindranath Tagore, his 49th Song declared that

"Some contemplate the Formless,
And others meditate on form:
but the wise man knows
that Brahman is beyond both.
That beauty of His is not see by the eye:
that rhythm of his voice is not heard by the ear."

For God was truly the Infinite, beyond man's mental capacity to apprehend, and, therefore, beyond his capacity to form words to express him.

The Christian mystics, who rebelled against some of the strict doctrines of the Church, by which the Church sought to confine God to certain names, creeds, and essences, themselves were very careful always to point out that what they say and the object of their meditation and the One who receives their love, devotion, and praise is far above their abilities to understand Him, name Him, or restrict him to most anthropomorphic representations of Him. The words of a few of them are presented.

God is not communicable in the uncommunicability of His essence (Maximus the Confessor).2.25

It is by his energies that we say we know our God: we do not say that we can come near to the Essence Itself, for His energies descend to us, but His Essence remains unapproachable (Basil). 2.26

The divine and deifying illumination and grace is not the essence but the energy of God (Gregory Palamas)2.27

From a work called The *Cloud of Unknowing* written by an unknown Christian mystic, the following is taken:

> You have brought me ..into that same cloud of unknowing, ..For of all other creatures and their works, yes, and of the works of God Himself, may a man through grace have a fullhead of knowing, and well he can think of them: but of God Himself cannot man think. ...He may well be loved, but not thought. By love may He be brought near and held; but by thought never.2.28

This line of thinking, which will be softened later, but for now, is the ultimate basis of being honest about our perception of God. We can love, adore, and worship That That Is and The Infinite One, but for the sake of human longing and grasping and teaching, we can use anthropomorphisms such as Father of Humanity, Shepherd of our souls, Creator and Pilot of the Universe, and Mother of All Things. They are indeed necessary if we are to communicate or represent Him at all. However, while putting our anthropomorphic views into creeds in order to try to communicate our faith, if we then use such inferior vessels to house "truth", we are very close to the sin of hubris if we then take those symbolic creeds and judge others by them, treat them as less "godly" and even persecute them (as has been done in the past by many religions). Such arrogance must ultimately be religiously self-destructive, for one has abandoned the Mystery of Being Himself and diminished Him to human mental capacities.

III. WAYS IN WHICH MEN BELIEVE GOD PROCLAIMS HIMSELF

A. GOD SPEAKS DIRECTLY TO HUMANS

In the Judeo-Christian culture it is very evident that believers hold strongly that God, at certain time and in certain places, has spoken directly to an individual, especially if God wanted to give him or her an assignment to carry out. But even from the beginning God is presented as speaking to his first born human creatures: Adam and Eve. Personal conflict resulted when Adam and Eve disobeyed God's instructions, and God then announced face to face the future punishments that would result and be applied, not only to Adam and Eve, but also all life that would proceed from them. God also is said to have spoken to the serpent and put him under an everlasting curse as he did with man. God carried out many further conversations: with Cain, Noah, Abraham, Jacob, Moses, and the prophets. In the Christian Scriptures God no longer speaks directly to man, but by angels and by means of visions, dreams, a dove, and a cloud: which will be discussed later.

In the popular Greek myths, the gods are quite active within human society and are often found talking to men and women, but even in these cases the gods are usually in disguise. Occasionally a god or goddess would speak directly to a human: Themis spoke to Deucalion and Pyrrha; Apollo speaks to and tries to seduce Daphne, but since she does not seem to recognize him, he must have been somewhat disguised; and The All-Seeing Sun spoke to Phaethon But the general appearance of a god was in disguise.

In the Gatha Ahunavaiti (Yasna 29) it is said that Ahura Mazda spoke directly to Zarathushtra. In the Egyptian faith there is the belief that God "speaks" directly, but not in words, but put a type of inspiration directly into the hearts of men: 'God puts it into his (Amenophis II's) heart to do it"; and about King Petubastis it is said that he proclaimed: "God put all this into my heart so as to make my lifetime on earth long". It is in the heart where God communicates with men.2.29

B. GOD PHYSICALLY APPEARS

In Exodus 24:9-11 it is claimed that at Sinai-Horeb that Moses, Aaron, Nadab, Abihu along with 70 of the elders of Israel ascended the Mountain and there they saw God...they saw God and they ate and drank However, in most religious literature people do not see God face to face, as did Moses and the 70 elders of Israel. For He usually appears in another form, and when that form is human, it is considered an incarnation usually for some type of intervention within human society or even for the benefit of all men of all ages. The Hindus believe that the second person of their Trinity, Vishnu, has become incarnate at least 10 times during the course of human history for the purpose of helping mankind when he seemed to become spiritually lost. The most popular of these incarnations of Vishnu is Krishna. The *Srimad Bhagavatam* declares it this way.

> "But Sri Krishna, the embodiment of love and divinity, is in his
> special manifestation. Whenever the Truth is forgotten in the world,
> and wickedness prevails, the Lord of Love becomes flesh to show
> the way, the Truth and the life to humanity. Such an incarnation is
> an avatara, an embodiment of God on earth."(Bk I, Ch.1)

Christians believe that the Logos of God became incarnate in the person
of <u>Jesus</u> of <u>Nazareth,</u> for the same reason, the salvation of mankind, who
then became the second person in the Christian Trinity, similar to
Krishna's position in the Hindu Trinity: the Second Person of the Trinity
who became incarnate for the redemption of mankind. <u>Walter</u> <u>Hilton</u>, a
Christian Mystic who died in 1395 AD, try to comfort those who had not
ascended to God in a mystical experience in which He could be
perceived at the high point of man's spiritual perception. He reminded
them that going to God is very difficult and they should take comfort that
He came to humanity in the person of Jesus, and to contemplate the life
and love of Jesus was also a peak experience of the soul. He stated:

> "Nevertheless, in order that the devotion of those souls that are
> incapable of such elevated contemplation of the Godhead should
> not be misdirected, but be comforted and strengthened by some
> form of interior contemplation of Jesus to forsake sin and the love
> of the world. For God tempers the ineffable light of His divinity
> and cloaks it in the bodily form of Jesus' humanity. He reveals it
> in this way to the inward vision of the soul, and sustains it spiritually
> through the love of His precious manhood."2.30

The Author of the <u>Gospel</u> of <u>John</u> stated at the end of his work about the
accounts he has given of Jesus presence among them "are written that
you may believe that Jesus is the Christ, the Son of God, and that
believing you may have life in his name."
Among the Romans Jupiter (Jove) also came down in to earth and took
the form of a man to see if mankind was as evil and spiritually lost as he
had heard (Jupiter speaking):

> "Cancel your pious cares; already he (Lycaon)
> Has paid his debt to justice and to me;

Yet what his crimes, and what my judgments were,
Remains for me thus briefly to declare.
The clamors of this vile degenerate age,
The cries of orphans, and the oppressor's rage,
Had reached the stars: 'I will descend,' said I,
'In hope to prove this loud complaint a lie.'
Disguised in human shape I travell'd round
The world, and more than what I heard I found.
....
I enter'd his inhospitable door.
Just at my entrance, I display'd the sign
That someone was approaching who was divine:
The prostrate people pray, the tyrant grins,
And adding profanation to his sins.(trans. Dryden)

Lycaon then proclaimed he will prove Jupiter a fraud and planned to kill him during the night as he slept. But killing The Great Immortal God was not possible, and Jupiter in his anger turned the critical and evil king into a wolf (certainly a little different attitude than Jesus' "Father forgiven them for they know not what they do"). But Jupiter was the Father of the Gods, and because he cared for mankind, he could not tolerate the sufferings brought upon the people by this cruel tyrant. This part of the Creation Story then declares that heaven does care for men in their misery: "Yet still with pity they remember man, and mourn as much as heavenly spirits can." But Jupiter did more, he intervened in human history and relieved the sufferings of men under this cruel tyrant.

C. GOD APPEARS IN OTHER NONHUMAN FORMS

Of the ten incarnations (*avatara*) of Vishnu five are human: the Dwarf (*Vamana*), the Human (*Parasurama*), the Warrior-Hero (*Ramachandra*), the Shepherd (*Krishna*) and the *Buddha*. The other five are: the Fish (*Matsuya*), the Tortoise (*Kurma*), the Boar (*Varaha*), the Man-Lion (*Narasimha*), and a future incarnation designated as *Kalkin*. In contrast to the Hindu idea of incarnation, i.e. for Vishnu to come to earth was always for mankind's benefit, the Roman myths expressed some rather devious motives for the incarnations of the Gods. While Jupiter's incarnation, aforementioned, to help mankind by punishing a tyrant, was noble, many other incarnations, including those of Jove (another name for Jupiter) himself were not for the sake of mortals but for some negative and destructive emotion of an upset god or goddess. Jove himself saw the beautiful Aracadian girl and lusted after her, but not to alarm her immediately, appeared as a gentle Diana (a female goddess). In the Hebrew scriptures, although Yahweh did not himself take on an earthly form, yet his presence was represented in the cloud that came down upon Israel. The polytheistic Greek legends and myths proclaim that non-human gods exist and the planets themselves are such, and their adorations of the planets were practiced among the Romans also. The planet Venus shows up in many different legends: Ishtar, Aphrodite, and the male Lucifer (i.e. the Bearer of Light). Likewise the Sun disk was worshipped by many as a god also: Amun-hotpe IV-Akhenaten of Egypt declared to Aten (The Sun): "(you are) sole god, without another beside you; as the appearance of Ahura Mazda; and by those who believed in Mithra, who was very popular in Roman thought during the early Christian Era.

D. GOD USES INTERMEDIARIES

1. Visions

The ancients, when they had a vision of some sort, believed, by in large, that it was a communication of some sort from above. Visions abound throughout the ancient religions. In the Hebrew Scriptures Yahweh came to Abraham in a vision (Gn 15:01), "And God spoke to Jacob (Israel) in visions of the night (Gn 46:2), Isaiah received a vision (Is. 1:1), Jeremiah had a vision (24.1), Daniel received a vision at night (Dn 2:19), Obadiah saw a vision (1:1), and most of the other prophets also received a vision from Yahweh. In the Christian Scriptures the author of the Gospel according to Matthew called the incident of the "transfiguration" a vision: "Jesus commanded them, 'Tell no one the vision, until...'. The Greek words for vision (horama or horasis) are few in the Canonical New Testament. Other than in Paul and Luke there is only one other use of the word in Rev. 9:17. Luke likes the word and uses it continually throughout both his Gospel and the book of Acts: only twice in his Gospel, but eleven times in Acts--when no one else in the New testament uses it more than once, and only is it mentioned one in Matthew and Revelation. But, according to Luke, God was directing the early church by means of visions that gave them instructions as to how to proceed in its missionary work: Ananias, Peter and Paul were involved.

2. Dreams

While it is difficult for me to distinguish between a dream and a vision that happened during the night, I have chosen to have a separated section for each. God spoke directly through dreams and angels of God spoke through dreams in the Hebrew Scriptures. Some dreams were explicit and others to be interpreted by professionals. Joseph was both a dreamer and an interpreter of dreams, and saved Pharaoh's economy by his expert interpretation and thus won Pharaoh's favor. Nebuchadnezzar had a dream (Dn 4:18). Dreams are predominate in both Genesis and Daniel, but used rather sparingly in the rest of the Hebrew Scriptures. But they are present throughout the entire canonical Hebrew Scriptures, and without a doubt the writer of those scriptures and the people in general believed that God did indeed speak to them by means of dreams. In the Christian Scriptures the word for dream (ONAR) is used only by Matthew: five times in the first two chapters of his Gospel and once in Chapter 27. The Greek word (ENUPNION) for "things seen in sleep" could be used for either dream of night vision, is used, but only once in Acts 2:17. Since Matthew has a strong Hebrew oriented flavor, probably written for Jewish people, and sense visions and dreams were very common in the Hebrew Scriptures, he seems to be using their concepts to present his own. Since no one else in the Christian Canonical Scriptures uses the word ONAR. Yet every ancient culture had to consider dreams and well into the Christian period dream interpretation continued to this very century. Macrobius, a Neo-Platonic of the 4th and 5th centuries AD, wrote a commentary *The Dream of Scipio (Somnium Scipionis)* written by Cicero, and in Macrobius' work he also used as reference the work of Artemidorus (first century AD) by the name of *Oneirocritica* from the Greek word (ONEIROKRITES). In it Macrobius has five classifications of dreams including nightmares (EPHIALTES--however he used the aeolian variant EPIALTES). Among the Sufis there are three classifications of dreams: 1) God send the dream directly and its meaning is clear; 2) an angel brings the dream and interpretationis often needed for them; and 3) the dreams comes from one's nafs or Satan himself, and such a dream is to be discounted and run off with along with Satan.

3. God Sends Special Reprentatives

Ahura Mazda, the Omniscient, declared that "One man alone has listened to our Decrees. He is Spitama Zarthushtra. He is eager to proclaim the glory of Ahura Mazda and His Truth, so let him be blest with sweetness of speech." (Yasna 29) And Zarathushtra accepts the call with this prayer: "I pray for the abiding support of Your ever-expanding Spirit of Benediction. All my actions I dedicate to Truth. May the Wisdom of the Good Mind guide me." (Yasna 28). Zoroastrians believed that this one man alone was sent to bring truth to humanity that men may know the truth and live it fully and thereby gain eternal life. Prophets that foretold the future also were seen as the gifts of the gods for the sake of mankind. Balbus, the spokesman for Stoicism in Cicero's *The Nature of the Gods*, defends his belief in prophets who foretold the future against the criticism of the Skeptical school of Carneades and the humorous and witty criticism of the Epicureans, stating: "The gift of prophecy above all seems to me the strongest proof that the divine Providence concerns itself with the welfare of men, although I know both of you are likely to be quick to attack me on this point." (Bk II.162). Some Stoics did believe in such a form of prophecy. But, other than some very vague oracles of Delphi, stated in such a way that regardless of what happens in the future, they can be "proved to be correct", the Greeks generally did not believe in such prophecy. If one did know the future, he would probably go crazy, as did Cassandra--if we can believe Pindar and Aeschylus. The Hebrew prophets, who predicted likely events in the very near future, based on the political situation of the day, were the most likely to be believed that they were true representatives of Yahweh. Basically the Hebrew prophet would see a bad situation caused by the leaders of Israel and he would declare in the name of Yahweh that if changes were not made and repentance from the leaders of the country, then Israel would either be conquered by a foreigner or Yahweh himself would punish them in some way. Sometimes, however, the prophet was sent to comfort a confused and fearful people that things, although they may now look threatening, Yahweh would protect them. "Comfort ye, comfort ye, my people" was Yahweh command to Isaiah (40:1), and throughout Isaish this encouragement was given many times. Isaiah was the prophet of comfort. One of the most well known passages of prophetic comfort given by Isaiah came when Judah, while Ahaz was their king, was threatened by a coalition of the Northern Ten Tribes (called Israel) and Syria to destroy Judah. Isaiah comforted Israel that a child would be born by a young damsel, and by the time he was two years old, the threat of the northern coalition would be gone. For they were just two fire brands that were now burning themselves out. Isaiah stated it this way:

> Therefore the Lord himself will give you a sign, a young woman
> shall conceive and bear a son, and shall call his name Immanuel
> (i.e. God is with us). He shall eat curds and honey when he knows
> how to refuse the evil and choose the good (that is, when he is two
> or three years old). For before the child knows how to refuse the
> evil and choose the good, the land before whose two kings you are
> in dread will be deserted. Yahweh will bring upon you and upon
> your people and upon your father's house such days as have not
> come since the day that Ephraim departed from Judah. (Is 7:14-17)

Yes, Judah will soon be liberated from the coalition, and within three years the people of Judah will be eating curds and honey (a land of milk and honey was symbolic of the blessings of the promised land) and things will be as glorious for Judah as during the time of David (before Ephraim, that is the Northern Ten Tribes, succeeded from the united Kingdom of David). This verse, unfortuanately, was allegorized and distorted by the early Christians (The author of Matthew's Gospel) to try to prove to the Romans that Christianity was not a new, and therefore illegal religion, but was the continuation, even the fulfilment of, the long established Jewish faith which was legal under Roman law. The author of Matthew was well aware of Roman law and wrote his gospel after the persecutions of Christians began with Nero. When Nero realized that Christianity was a distictly different religion than Judaism he declared that they were no longer COLLEGIA LICITA (permitted religions and associations granted by the Romans to the people that they had conquered because they were part of the pre-Roman heritage; but new associations or religions were forbidden as Romans saw them as coverings or fronts for anti-Roman political activity). Therefore, the

Author of the Gospel According to Matthew, written about 75-80 AD, after more than two decades of Roman persecution, tried to allegorize this passage and many others in order to legitimize Christianity in the eyes of the Romans. Isaiah was not a fortune teller for the distant future, but was called by Yahweh to comfort his people at the time of Ahaz the King of Judah. Let Christians not misuse this passage for the sake of Christian comfort by using a type of "prophesy" to prove God's existence the way that Balbus, the Stoic, was using it as Stoics used it to provide "proof" of the existence of God.

4. God Used Heavenly Messengers, Angels To Communicate To Men.

As ancient kings liked to stay close to the throne, they used messengers to bring their concerns and edicts to various parts of their realm. So too the gods. In the Hebrew Scriptures they appear early as two angels came to Lot (Gn 19) and continued as God needed them until the Hellenistic period, when, influenced by the Platonic "Lower Gods" who had names and particular functions the angels took on the form of the Platonic lower gods. By the time of the book of Enoch (c. 50BC), an entire array of angels were present for certain events, and book of Enoch itself named them, as also the Greek "Lower Gods" had personal names, and gave to them particular functions as the Greek Lower Gods had. The "Enoch Seven" were: Uriel, Raphael, Raguel (Reuel), Michael, Saraqael, Gabriel, and Remiel. It is worth noting that none of them were named after Yahweh, but the universal term for God, El. As Israel was more and more influenced by other nations, the name tended to supplant Yahweh in many cases. The earlier prophets were mixed like "My God is Yahweh" or in Hebrew El (God) i (my) Jah (Yahweh)--Elijah. But among the minor prophets are Obadiah, Zephaniah, and Zechariah all relate to Yahweh, and as prophets are Yahweh's messengers. Only Joel has the El in it, but it is only Elijah in reverse Jo (Jahweh--the J and Y are interchangable in pronouncing Yahweh or Jahweh) is El, i.e. Joel means Yahweh is my God. Likewise prophets such a Abijah (my father is Yahweh), Isaiah (Yahweh is my salvation), and Jeremiah (Yahweh ...unknown). But the word El seems to gain in popularity as Israel becomes more aware of the greater world, as it is a more generic or general term for God. Ezekiel (later than both Isaiah and Jeremiah) has the meaning "El Strengthens", and Daniel, "El has judged". While this trend is not conclusive or consistent, yet it is note worthy that all the above named angels of Israel are attached to El and not Yahweh. Uriel means "El is light"; Raphael "El is the Healer"; Raguel "Friend of El"; Michael "Who is like El?"; Saraqael "El explains or shines forth"; Gabriel "Man of (or Strength of) El"; and Remiel "El is exalted". At any rate, by the time of Enoch the Hebrew faith had a heaven full of messengers that served Yahweh or El, the God of the Hebrews.

Among the Greeks and the Romans there were many gods and they all seemed to have the same messenger: Hermes for the Greeks and Mercury of the Romans. Hermes then was the Messenger for the other eleven Greek Olympians, and Mercury for the Roman pantheon. Plato, in his teaching of monotheism, arranged the popular gods under his One God, and classified them as lower gods, who then became The Good Beyond Essence's messengers or helpers.

In the Greek Christian Scriptures there are many angels indeed. However, it is evident that Gabriel had emerged as God's main messenger who made the announcements of John the Baptist's and Jesus' births, described only as the angel of the Lord in Matthew, but identified as Gabriel in Luke. Angels appear often during the ministry of Jesus and their presence is seen throughout the entire Canon, beginning with his birth as a host of heavenly angels announced his birth and sang joyously about what it would mean for humanity. At his resurrection angels appeared at the tomb, and before he departed he declared his return with the angels of heaven accompanying him (Mt 25:31).

As mentioned earlier, Islam also had many angels, and 20 times in the Koran they are mentioned. Gabriel appears early in the life of Muhammed but Michael also is mentioned by name. In the 49th Yasna of Zoroastrianism, Zarathushtra is praying that he and his friend Frashaoshtra: "May we be at all times Your angelic messengers". The concept of an angel or a messenger from God is more important to those religions in which God is far beyond all else, and He alone rules. With many gods, one can play the role of contacting men, but when the One God becomes so Majestic so that man can no longer look upon Him, then God has mercy upon man and sends a messenger or two to comfort him or give him directions in answer to his prayers.

5. Sons Of God Are As God's Representatives On Earth

Among Christians Jesus is proclaimed the Son of God, and indeed that is probably the main thesis in both Gospels: Mark and Matthew. When Jesus asked his disciples who they thought he was, Peter answered that he was the Christ, the Son of the Living God, and with that answer Jesus was well pleased. The Son of God was seen, not only as a representative sent from God, but one who was "begotten" of God and therefore had similarities to the Father just as human sons have features of their fathers. They also could rule in the Father's stead. But, as in the case of Jesus, the Father's Kingdom was an eternal one, not of this world, and that was the kingdom that Jesus proclaimed. Different from the Christian concept of Jesus as the Son of God, was the Egyptian in which the Pharoah was ruling the earth on behalf of God. Akhenaten, in his hymn to Aten, declared: "Since you are Re (Sun God), you reach as far as they do, and you curb them for your beloved son (Akhenaten); and "You are my desire, and there is no other who knows you except for your son, for you have apprised him of your designs and your power." Even the kings of the Hebrews were ordained to represent God--the concept was at first rejected by the Jewish prophets, for they felt God could rule on his own behalf and did not need an annointed (messianic--messiah means the annointed one) one to handle God's works. But after the rule of the first two kings it was quite well accepted and subsequent Judaism took great pride in the Star of David and the glory of his reign. Because the concept of the Son of God made the son alittle too close to the Majesty of God himself, Islam completely rejected that anyone was the Son of God, and it may be for that reason that Islam does not in its 99 names for God have the word Father, for he has no consort and therefore does not produce a son. Allah has no son, and Muhammed is his prophet!

6. Both Celestial and Human Hierarchies.

With all the beings of heaven, the hosts, the spirits, the saints, and the angels, Christianity has what some would say "a rather cluttered heaven with so many eternal beings doing their things". It was recognized early in the church and the authror of the work known as The *Pseudo-Dionysius* ordered the Christian heaven much the way that Hesiod ordered the realm of the Olympian Gods. He defines a hierarchy as a sacred order, and each level is "uplifted to the imitation of God in proportion to the enlightenments divinely given to it", for the entire purpose of the heavenly creatures is to be "uplifted to imitate God as far as possible" (this, of course, had been taught by Plato and for the 800 years between Plato and the Author of the Pseudo-Dionysius). He answers the question as to why all heavenly beings are generally classified simply as angels. He stated that there are many subdivisions of the angels such as "archangels, principalities, authorities and powers". He likewise speaks of the differences between the seraphim, the cherubim, and those sitting on thrones. He does settle for three ranks. The first comprises the seraphim, cherubim, and thrones; the middle rank, authorities, dominions and powers; and the third and lowest rank, comprised of principalities, archangels, and angels. It is an interesting work, and, as a whole, is quite devotional and spiritual. It is basically Platonism in Christian form. He also discusses the earthly or Ecclesiastical Hierarchy, for "Thy will be done on earth as it is in heaven". An orderly church is to imitate the celestial order, and like the celestial order it is all for the purpose of each rank or station seeking to imitate God's nature as much as possible. The focus is always God and sometimes in the Ecclesiastical Hierarchy the focus is Christ: thus the imitation of Christ is the church's highest calling. Other religions also have types of earthly hierarchies. In general we may think of three or possibly more gates to heaven among men according to their earthly station. The lowest gate is one of ethical living and basic goodness, the middle gate are those whose lives are filled with spiritual concepts and motives, mystics and monks of every religion. The highest gate or station in life is that of the philosophers and theologians whose entire existence is one of thinking and trying to perceive the ultimate being of God, and to lead all others to a higher level. The Hindus actually have four main castes that imply the same spiritual level. The caste system according to the Laws of Manu are; the Brahmans who are from the mouth of God (priests and philosophers), the Kshatriyas from the arm of God (the warriors and knights), the Vaishyas from the thigh (traders and agriculturists), and the Shudras from the foot of God (the servants of the other three castes). A fifth caste, though not an "official caste" is that of the untouchables, perhaps not even worthy of being a servant.

These then are the ways in which God is seen as using intermediaries in order to reach mankind and help him ascent to Him, that they might be like him as much as possible and enjoy him as much as possible. Humanity felt that there is help for it in seeking out God, for God has supplied these intermediaries to succor mankind in his spiritual quest.

E. Nature Declares God And His Glory

Sometimes there is a thin line between one who sees God in his creation and one who believes that creation itself is God, or at least, part of God. I am presenting this section as one that declares that nature and creation have been created or at least molded by God and in essence are separate from his being, which is beyond being or essence. Reverting back to Plato for my definition of God is that He is The Good Beyond Essence. Therefore creation can declare itself to have a Maker or show the beauty, to a degree, of the Maker, but in itself does not participate in that Ultimate Self that controls, molds, and beautifies it. And while I am certainly aware that many people throughout human history have found God to be in nature, pantheism, I feel that the great majority of people who have a metaphysical (beyond the physical) perspective naturally feel that God is Someone beyond the physical. The Hebrew Psalmist (19:1) stated "The heavens speak of God's glory and the firmament proclaims his craftsmanship". I, myself, have been spiritually stirred at times when I have looked to the heavens, both during the dawn and dusk periods of grays, yellows, reds, white, and blue and various other mixtures brightly shining in the sky. Likewise in middle of the night, when all is clear from the clouds which bring earth such beauty during the day, the sometimes arrangements of the planets and the moon, whether full or crescent, display such sparkling lights in the midst of darkness that it is difficult not to give thanks to God for this method of making us look upward and notice the breadth and majesty of all, even the background of galaxies that add such depth to our perception of all reality. Throughout the history of mankind, men have seen what they believed to be evidence of God's existence by such beauty, brilliance, and depth. Xenophanes looked to the sky and said that "The One is, namely God".

However, it was Plato in his *Timaeus*, a work written in his maturity, that one finds the sparkling Beauty of God Himself in His own creation that He then called His "son". Plato taught that the Maker and Father of the universe was good, and not envious in any way, and decided to share existence by creating a beautiful universe in the empty space and fill it with movement and life of all kinds. He wanted it to be as perfect as the material He used would allow, and therefore worked from a pattern of eternal perfection. God used this thought-out model of eternal perfection by which to construct His material universe, that Plato called the Cosmos (KOSMOS), a word which means in Greek "the beautifully ordered one" (hence our word "cosmetics"). God gave this beautifully ordered universe movement and life (soul), and directed its movements in harmony that all might see His own beauty in the beauty of the cosmos (the Son as the Image of the Father). He made the parts of the cosmos alive with soul, and thus was the creation of the lower gods, the stars and the planets, whom God called his children, who were to imitate His goodness and love in all that they did. He was not jealous and gave to them the most perfect material beings that were possible, and when it moved in its beautiful and harmonious way, He was delighted and rejoiced. The creation, then, to Plato, was a loving and generous gift of a good and non-envious God, who delighted in sharing life with all His creation. Man was implanted with a soul that sought to enjoy the beauties of the creation and with a longing, then, for the Eternal Beauty, God Himself, the Father and Maker of all, who rejoiced in man's longing for Him.

Cicero in his *Nature of the Gods* puts into the mouth of Balbus, who represents the Stoic philosophy,

> For what could be more clear and obvious, when we look up to the sky and contemplate the heavens, than that there is some divinity of superior intelligence, by which they are controlled? if it were not so, how could Ennius have been universally applauded when he wrote: "Lift up your eyes to that bright firmament, Which men call Jupiter", and not only Jupiter but the Lord of the universe, who sways all nature by his nod and is, as Ennius says, "the father both of gods and men", a present and a mighty God...And so, both in our own country and in others, the worship of the gods and the sanctity of religion grow firmer and fairer day by day. And this does not happen blindly or by chance but because the gods time and again declare their presence."2.31

Likewise, in the *Corpus Hermeticum*, the Platonic argument is restated:

And do you say 'God is invisible'? Say it not! Who of Himself
is more revealed than God? For this He has made all things, that
through all things you may see Him. This is God's Goodness,
this is God's excellence (ARETE), that He manifests Himself
through all things. Nothing is invisible, nothing is without body.
Intellect (NOUS) is seen in its thinking (NOEIN), and God in his
doing. (Libellus XI.2 -22a).

Paul, in his letter to the *Romans*, follows the same reasoning and
claiming that no one can say he is without knowledge of God:

...because the knowledge of God is manifest among them, for God
has manifested it to them. For the invisible aspects of God from
the very creation of the cosmos are known and clearly seen, both
his everlasting power and divinity, therefore they are without excuse (Rm 1:19-20).

In a poem, Boethius declared that men could find the ways of peace
among themselves if they would just look to the peaceful and
harmonious heavens where the Lord, by his counsel, has established
peaceful co-existence among the heavenly bodies.

Look to the highest heavens where never does the fiery sun impede
the axis of Phoebe (the goddess of the moon), nor the vortex of
the world the rapid path of the Bear...Vesper sustains the opening
door of darkness, and a fostering Lucifer brings back the day. So
love brings back, one after the other, those that run the eternal
course, so that discordant war is exiled from among the stars.2.32
(trans. JDE)

It should be noted that Lucifer did not have either a negative or a satanic
meaning, for the word means "bearer of light" and was used as a personal
name by leaders of the church and could even be applied to Jesus who
was the "light of the world" in the Gospel of John. In this poem Boethius
refers to the Morning Star (Venus) who preceeds the coming of the sun,
and thus is seen as the bearer of the coming light (the sun).

Maximos the Confessor in his *Four Hundred Texts on Love*, stated,
(number 96), "We do not know God from His essence. We know Him

rather from the grandeur of His creation and from His providential care for all creatures. For through these, as though they were mirrors, we may attain insight into His infinite goodness, wisdom, and power. 2.33

Leibniz put the declaration of God by the heavens this way:

> Furthermore every substance is like an entire world and like a mirror of God, or indeed of the whole world which it betrays, each one in its own fashion; almost as the same city is variously represented according to the various viewpoints from which it is regarded. Thus the universe is multiplied in some sort as many times as there are substances, and the Glory of God is multiplied in the same way by as many wholly different representations of his works. It can indeed be said that every substance bears in some sort the character of God's infinite wisdom and omnipotence, and imitates him as much as it is able to. 2.34

Many others from Rumi to Kabir to Emerson have repeated such elements of faith that God does indeed reveal at least his existence in the universe itself. The natural awe a person feels when he looks at the depth and beauty of the universe does give a deep sense of humility, and to most, a sense of sanctity and the feeling of standing before the Divine Essence of Being. Therefore, in man's quest to embrace God, he sees God also reaching out to him, sometimes directly and sometimes indirectly through intermediaries, and sometimes in the beauty of the universe.

If one were to read the words inscribed on the two stelae of Nabonidus found in the ruins of the Great Mosque in Harran, one would find, almost a summary of this second chapter. Nabonidus talks of the heavens and his God, Sin, in many of the terms expressed here in this chapter. He sees many gods, but Sin is the Head of the celestial hierarchy. He believes that he as king is the appointed son of Sin, as the King of all gods, Lord of all lords, and the Divine Crescent, has also appointed, as his representatives, Shamash, Ishtar, Adad and Nergal to watch over him and take care of him. He comes about this conviction by means of a dream. Even the rotation of the celestial beings, sun and moon and stars, are appointed to bless Nabonidus. Shamash, the lord of oracular decisions, has seen to it. Nabonidus also had his faith confirmed by visits to the diviner who was an expert in dreams and interpreter of signs. And he was absolutely convinced that when he went to war the Divine Crescent, Sin, would treat him with favor because Narbonidus was his son.2.35

Man's perception of the Ultimate Life Source has therefore moved from a rather impersonal, yet real, awe of the Otherness of Power that controls all things and to which he is greatly inferior and in fear of, to one of, not only openness by which men can talk to God and praise him, but also Divine tenderness by which God himself takes an initiative to comfort man that He is indeed present. He can be called by many names by the different tribes of the earth because he has shown himself in various ways to all of them: by the beauty and depth of nature and the universe; by using numerous forms of intermediaries, and at certain times by a personal incarnation when humanity had lost its spiritual way; and even on special occasions He has appeared in person, although in various forms and even disguises. Man has always been religious, but as he grew spritually he has been conviced that the Wholly Other wills to be known and honored, and has made himself, in various way, available. Humanity, in response, has desired the joy of embracing Him, and even longs for a personal and eternal existence that he might enjoy Him forever.

CHAPTER THREE

GOD AS THE ETERNAL: MAN AS MORTAL

I. RELIGIONS OF MAN'S MORTALITY

Even though man naturally had a longing to live after death and envied the gods as immortals, in some religions there was no faith, belief, or opinion that they, as mortals, would in any way become immortal themselves, and expressed no creedal statements to that effect. The following religions, or the early period of such religions, fall into such a category.

A. EARLY EGYPT

An Ancient text from the one called Papyrus Berlin 3024 describes a man discussing with himself whether to try to go on living or to simply die. The "to be or not to be" dilemma expressed in ancient Egypt. He says his soul is drawing him towards death, and tries to convince him that this is the way to go, especially in times of difficulties and problems. But he is confused as his soul is too stupid to comfort him in his miseries, yet it holds him back from death. Then again, life is a transitory state, like the trees that, even though they live long, also are temporary and fall into death. His "soul" asks him that although he is alive, what profit is there to simply being alive? Yet he yearns for life, but there is, however, rest from his problems and pains in death. This struggle over the benefits of life or death goes on for some time as he weighs both his desire for life and his personal miseries and the violence and brutallity inflicted upon him by the unrighteous. For there are no just persons and no possibility of an intimate friendship. But if he chooses death he will never again see the sun. Finally his soul decides to hang on to life until the body takes its natural course and returns to the dust of the earth.3.1 In general, in early ancient Egypt, life was held in high esteem and death was a depressing thought, for it was seen as a state of darkness and deprivation of all that had been experienced in life. The lone exception for this general belief was the teaching of the godliness of the Pharaoh, either as a god himself, or as God's (Re's) son, and such a position for him was thought great enough to merit eternal life. And to live in heaven as he lived on earth, he would need all of his servants and nobles who were important to him with him in heaven also. But other than this attachment to the pharaoh, at least in primitive Egypt, there was no hope for others to attain eternal life.

B. THE HEBREWS

As one can see from the prayers of the Psalmist, it is protection from enemies and the extension of earthly life that are constantly pursued in the prayers. For Yahweh loves those who hate evil deeds and protects the lives of the holy ones; He rescues them from the hands of the wicked (Ps 97:10). Yahweh came to Jeremiah when he was arrested and comforted him that he would not be given over to them that he feared, for Yahweh will rescue him and he does not need to fear the sword (Jer 39:17). Judah is counseled not to fear, for Yahweh their God will deliver them out of the hand of all their enemies (II Kg 17:39). Salvation of the righteous means that Yahweh will rescue those who trust him from the hands of the wicked who desire to harm and kill them (Ps 37:40). The fact that man was confined to brief existence weighed heavily upon the author of Ecclesiastics, and he declared life itself to be empty of any value, for all was vanity. Better to have never been born: for the dead already were more fortunate than the living (Ecc 4:1-3). Yet, paradoxically, a living dog is better than a dead lion (Ecc 9:4). Death makes everything vain. Rudolf Bultmann stated it plainly in his *Primitive Christianity*: "Life like the flesh itself is mortal and ceases to be upon death...the Old Testament invariably confines human life to this earth.3.2

C. THE EARLY GREEKS

Pindar accepted that men were mortal and tried to immortalize them in his odes of praise, usually to the victors of wars and the games of the athletes, but also in joyous songs and friendships and love. Even though God alone never tastes the woe of death, yet men are happy and poets sing of him when he wins a foot race (Pythian X.2). Happy is Phylakidas of Aigina, who won the boy's contest of strength, and even the Gods honor him (Isthmian VI.1). Pindar tells man to know his place as a mortal, and when good things come in this life, enjoy them and rejoice, but he is always to remember his mortality.

> If a man fares well and hears his good name spoken.
> Seek not to become Zeus!
> You have everything, if a share of these beautiful things come to you.
> Mortal ends befit mortal men. (Isthmian V.1)

Achilles was praised even by the Goddesses: for the Immortal ones thought it was proper to give a brave man, even though he was dead, his praise from the Goddesses (Isthmian V.6). Aristotle represented these early views of most Greeks by stating in his Nicomachean Ethics: "The most fearful thing of all is death; for it is the end, and once a man is dead it seems that there is no longer anything good or evil for him"(1115a, 25). God, for Aristotle, is in just the opposite state, that of Immortality. "And God is in a better state. And life also belongs to God; for the actuality of thought is life, and God is that actuality; and God's essential actuality is life most good and eternal. We say therefore that God is a living being, eternal, most good, so that life and duration continuous and eternal belong to God; for this is God" (Metaphysics 1072:25-30). Other Greeks thought different from the general consensus, at least beginning with Pythagoras and those who followed him and those of the Orphic cult: these will be presented in another section.

D. THE CHINESE

The doctrine of a metaphysical immortality is never spelled out in ancient Chinese philosophy. There may be spirits of ancestors, a life force in "heaven", and idealized kings of the past, but for individual immortality, there simply is no clear statement of such a belief. For Lao Tzu one must be content, virtuous, and trusting that a good life will be rewarded with long life, maybe, and possibly fame. But even if life is shortened, it is not to be worried about: contendedness within the natural order of the creation is man's only legitimate concern. For all else is beyond his knowledge. Sometimes he must choose between fame, i.e. dying for something virtuous or a just cause to help others, and life itself. Master Lao is never easy to translate or understand; one can meditate upon the following (Chapter 44).

Or fame or life, which do you hold more dear?
Or life or wealth, to which would you adhere?
Keep life and lose those other things;
Keep them and lose life: -- which brings
Sorrow and pain more near?
Thus we may see, Who cleaves to fame rejects what is more great;
Who loves large stores gives up the richer state.
Who is content needs fear no shame.
Who know to stop incurs no blame.
From danger free, living long shall be.

Lao claims that caring for others is a defense against death; the thinking seems to be that if one is full of care for the welfare of others, he will have no natural enemies that will bring a sudden death upon him and when he himself is ill, others will reciprocate and nurse him back to health the way he himself helped them with his caring. This reciprocity of nature and the "way of heaven" is common thought for most Chinese philosophers. Lao's 67th Chapter in his *Tao Te Ching* preaches just this kind of gentle caring for others and the merits of heaven it gains. My adaptation of James Legge's translation is the following:

The rest of the world declares that my teaching (Tao) is good, but
when compared to the systems of others, it is simple and inferior.
But it is great because it is a simple system of thought. If it were
an attempt to mimic other systems, it would have been forgotten
long ago. I hold only three things to be precious: the first is a gentle-
ens towards others; the second is a basic and fair economy; and the
third is withdrawing the desire to have precedence over others...
Gentle caring is a sure way to victory when battling the problems of
life, and heaven will save and protect its possessor, for his very way
of being gentle to others is natural protection.

There is presented here no reward in heaven, but a reward from heaven for this temporary mortal life. In Lao's 74th Chapter there seems to be a caution issued to the powerful in society not to threaten others with death for some purpose, for the wise man has already accepted the reality of death and therefore its threat does not mean anything. Lao also warns that it is nature that rules over death, and if man usurps such power himself from nature to inflict it upon another, for in his acting on behalf of nature, he acts clumsily and will do harm to himself as well as others. An unschooled novice acting like a proficient carpenter will likely cut off his own hand trying to do the work of the expert. All rewards and punishments for man are relegated to this life, and nothing is ever implied that there is another or eternal realm whereby justice will be served to man in another life. This trend is also in Confucianism, Monism, and 'Neo-Confucianism". Indigenous Chinese thought in antiquity was never focused on a metaphysical life.

E. BUDDHISM

When Siddhartha Gotema rebelled against Hinduism, he was driven by a desire to solve the problems of life that man experienced, especially the problems of pain, suffering, and death. Salvation was basically a release from such. When man had finally merited release he experienced Nirvana, which was a void of existence. For where there is life, there is suffering. Non-attachment to life is vital to Buddhist thought. In this sense initial and basic Buddhism is very negative towards life, but because one can not be released from the cycle of endless lives of suffering, whereby man is continually reincarnated, until he merits release from life, Buddhism is a very moral religion. Its ethics are comparable to Plato's and Kant's, and, perhaps, even "too much" for man to bear. For the pleasures of life are scorned, and the joy of sex is tabooed more than in any other religion (although parts of Christianity has at times equaled Buddhism in its repression and scorn of earthly pleasures, especially the sexual ones). A couple of quotations from the Sermon at Benares attributed to *Siddhartha* himself state:

> "Whatever is created will be dissolved again, and to worry of one's self is vain...This pure state of mind is one that realizes that there is no self, and that the cause of all man's troubles, cares, and vanities is a mirage, a shadow, a dream...Self is a transient vision, a dream; but truth is wholesome, truth is sublime, and it alone is everlasting. There is no immortality except in truth, for truth alone is forever."

F. VARIOUS PHILOSOPHICAL VIEWS WITH RELIGIOUS ATTACHMENT

Above, Aristotle's views were presented, and, although he belongs in this section, his views will not be repeated here. However, among the Greeks both the Epicureans and some Stoics had no interest in talking about individual immortality. The Epicureans, somewhat similar to Master Lao, did not go into speculation as to man's future, believing the gods, even though they exist, have absolutely no interest in mankind, for men were simply mortals who did not concern their own functions or lives in heaven and certainly, after their deaths, not in the future either. Cicero putting Stoic concepts into the mouth of Balbus stated:

(Referring to man's ability to use nature and interpret the heavens--the eclipses of sun and moon for example)-- Balbus continues, "When the mind contemplates these phenomena, it learns also knowledge of the gods. So religion is born, and with it goodness and all the virtues which make up the good life, a life which reflects the divine life. We need to be inferior to the gods in nothing except our mortality, which need in no way hinder us from living well.3.3

For one interested in the First Century BC views of Greek philosophy concerning the Gods, I would recommend the reading of Cicero's Nature of the Gods as translated by Horace C.P. McGregor, as it is a splendid and interesting dialogue between "representatives" of the Skeptical Academy, the Stoics, and the Epicureans. Stoics themselves were in many ways simply eclectics who, in general believed that Fate ruled, but was given life itself by the World Soul, and therefore, it was expressed by the rules of nature which itself was brought to life by the World Soul. Many Stoics felt that individual souls after the death of the body merged into the World Soul, without any personal immortality. But the Stoics were not unified on this, and Epictetus, who will be discussed in the next chapter definitely felt very close to the Creator God and entertained the hope of life beyond death for his own person.

G. BELIEF IN GODS WHO TOTALLY CONTROLLED MANKIND AND BOTH PUNISHED THEM FOR REJECTING THEIR AUTHORITY AND IMPOSED LIFE LIMITATIONS ON MEN AS MORTALS

From ancient Mesopotamia and into the popular myths of both Greeks and Romans, there was the presentation of the gods that saw them as rather self-centered and vindictive. They made man, it seems, for the one purpose of men serving them for a brief period of their existences and then dying. This was the good-news, and the bad was that if they did not serve properly the gods (represented by their priests, of course), then they were inflicted with continual punishments such as ill health, victims of evil crimes, betrayal by loved ones, blindness, starvation, war and many other "god inflicted punishments" before they could die, and if they sought to avoid such by suicide, the priests would dishonor them in burial and possibly put some ban on the family survivors. These are the gods that send fire and brimstone, floods, destroy human unity by raising one nation against another, confusing their language, and bring draught and plagues upon the peoples. These myths are often quite personal, turning a particular person into a spider (Arachne) or a pillar of salt (Lot's wife), or even a tree or some other non human being. The flood story is one of the most common, with generally one person and either his wife, family, or artisans being saved in order to recreate a new subservient race of humans to satisfy the needs of the gods or a particular God. The Sumerian flood story, the first flood story, features Ziusudra as the favorite to build the ark; the Babylonian version gives the role to Utnapishtim who saved animals, family, and craftsmen: "All my family and kin I made go aboard the ship. The beasts of the field, the wild creatures of the field, all the craftsmen I made go aboard". These two stories were the stories popular at the time of the writing of the Biblical account of Noah, who saved the animals and only his immediate family, indicating that Yahweh restricted even more severely than the "great gods" of the Babylonians (Anu, Enlil, Ninurta, Ennuge, and Ninigiku-Ea) who would be spared death in the flood. In the Roman version, Jove (Jupiter) was even more limited in his charity for he saw only two people worthy of surviving his wrath by flood: Deucalion for "there was no better man", and his wife, Pyrrha for "there was no other woman more scrupulously reverent".

Needless to say, man felt very insecure before such personalized powers (gods) that controlled the weather, the plagues, wars, and sudden deaths of individuals. These negative concepts were thought to be overcome by many things: magic, by means of sacrifices, priestly intercessions, and other acts which usually cost money and benefited the priests of that particular god or religion in general. Only later did a true quest for morality take place and man could stand alone before his God and offer his love and his just and ethical life. Of course, today, most religions, and this will be extended much more in subsequent chapters, try to reflect a God of love and beauty, one who is tender to all people of the earth, and requires simply a kind and righteous life, treating all others as one would like to be treated himself.

II. FORMS OF RELIGIOUS EXPRESSION

Despite the often negative feelings between men and the gods, man still struggled to make better the relationship because he was by nature religious and he also needed, in his own mind, the blessings of the gods for his own welfare and survival. I have divided such forms of religious expression into four areas: creating and acting out myths; moral legislations; creeds for community unifications; and artistic expressions.

A. THE CREATING AND ACTING OUT OF MYTHS

When man tried to explain something he was ignorant of, but believed in some way that it took place, he created a story that tried to manifest the truth as he saw it. Lacking direct knowledge, and unable to clarify to himself, an obvious truth, man turned to myth making. This was not done to purposely lead astray others, but to give a mental vessel by which man could carry in his mind a concept that brought forth an unknowable truth that was beyond man's capacity to rationalize it. Having stored the concept in his mind he was able to teach and explain the unexplainable to others who constantly sought answers about those very things. In this way the myths became 'aetiological', i.e. an explanation of something beyond our normal thought processes. There are many good books on the making of myths, but I would recommend three of many books: one edited by Henry A Murray in which 21 articles are presented by 21 different authors, *Myth and Mythmaking*; Robert Graves' *The Greek Myths*; and the various works of Joseph Campbell.

Aristotle, who tried to bring rational thought into the quest of knowledge of first things and first causes was quite critical of Hesiod: "The school of Hesiod and all the mythologists thought only of what was plausible to themselves, and had no regard to us. For asserting the first principles to be gods and born of gods....(then he questions why those who did not taste nectar and ambrosia became mortal...and why if the gods needed food how could they be eternal by nature and of themselves produce the very nectar they themselves needed to remain immortal?)", and concluded..."But into the subtleties of the mythologists it is not worth our while to inquire seriously"(Metaphysics 1000a, 9-18). But it was with the first of the Greek philosophers, beginning with Thales, that the quest was for LOGOS (Gr. rational thought expressed logically in words) to replace MUTHOS (Gr. initially word, then used as a tale, story or fable). Heraclitus even declared that it was LOGOS that was the driving force of creation and the harmony of the universe. Plato later classified LOGOS, theologically, as the action of NOUS (Gr. Intellect or Mind), the word that Plato used for God 22 times in his later dialogues, and eventually such Platonic thinking found its way into the Gospel of John: "In the beginning (of creation) was the LOGOS)", and in that sense the Gospel of John was following Heraclitus by means of the Platonists. A very good book for this progression of thought from myth to logic is F.M. Cornford's *From Religion to Philosophy: A Study in the Origins of Western Speculation.*

While it may be natural to condescend to our ancestors in this field of thought, we are warned by Karl Jaspers not to be too arrogant with our own creeds to which we today subscribe, and in some churches it is necessary that we subscribe to them. He declared:

> All metaphorical representations of God without exception are
> myths, meaningful as such when understood to be mere hints
> and parallels, but they become superstitions when mistaken for
> the reality of God Himself.3.4

It is well that when we today speak of the abstract and immaterial it is necessary to speak in what Walter Lippmann referred to as a "method of accommodation" to the actual reality we are trying to express. Myth may be used as a form of allegory but that is like translating a thought of the mind of one person (his "language") into the thought of the mind of another (another "language"), and therefore the element of interpretation becomes important. John Smith, the Christian Platonist, in his writing *A Christian's Conflicts and Conquests*, stated: "Truth is content, when it comes into the world, to wear our mantles, to learn our language, to conform itself as it were to our dress and fashions."3.5 This is most certainly true of God also. He is contented to be expressed, praised, loved, and honored by symbolic and abstract, even mythical and allegorical, concepts and ways of thinking, especially if that is the best we can do when expressing the Eternal and Absolute Good--but, with this caution, that we never impose our views upon others declaring them to be Truth Itself. God is always pleased when we reach out to Him within the capacity of our thinking process, but to think that our thinking process is to be demanded of others is very displeasing to Him, for He has his relationship with the others just as He has his relationship with us. How dare we infringe upon God's relationship to others! What HUBRIS! How can we declare our allegorical symbolization of God as truth but classify another's as childish "myth"! Humility is always our first priority before God, for that is always the natural expression of one who is in love before his Beloved. It is the symbolic content of the myth as well as the symbolic content of a creed that is to be set before us logically and sacredly that we can value for ourselves. For logical words, simply because they are human words, must also be treated as symbolic and not the ultimate truth they try to represent.

1. Fertility Cults And Rituals

Such cults and their rituals were briefly mentioned before, but now is the time to expand and show the depth and breadth and longevity of such even into the present day, where, if they are not still in an earlier form, still influence some to the more sacrificial and sacramental aspects of some modern religions. When there was a draught and the Spring did not blossom, then the ancient worshippers would first complain to the gods about their difficulties:

Ishtar has gone down to the underworld, and has not returned.
And since Ishtar has gone down and not returned,
The bull does not embrace the cow,
 and the donkey does impregnate his mate,
In the city the men are not impregnating the young women.
The man stays to himself, and the women turn aside.3.6

In another complaint of Hittite origin, *The Telepinus Myth*, describes the results of God's anger, i.e. withdrawing fertility from both animals and vegetation. Telepinus, the God of Fertility, is presented as one who left his work undone and left humanity stranded. The grains of the field did not grow, and cattle, sheep, and men not longer reproduce. Even the younger men are infertile, and all vegetation dried up, for the pastures had no moisture and the springs no water. Even the other gods were upset because men could no longer offer them cereal and animal sacrifices. It is understandable that all ancient cultures had some god to pray to for the sake of fertilization. The Norse prayed to both Wuotan and Donar (who needed help from his mother), and such led to having harvest-ceremonies to honor those gods. Osiris and Isis were the main fertility gods of Ancient Egypt, and indeed became the most favored and loved of all Egyptian gods, perhaps because of the regularity of the flow of the Nile that gave people a justified confidence in the fertility of their land. The Greeks had Demeter and Persephone; the Syrians, Astarte and Adonis; the Phrygians, Cybele and Attis. Because the Hebrews depended upon only one God, Yahweh, he then also became a god of fertility: opening the wombs of the women and sending the rain to nourish the earth.

2. Acts For Divine Protection

   This was discussed earlier and only a brief mention of it is necessary here, for magic, songs and chants to the powers that be, various sacrifices, and some religious taboos are were indeed ancient man's way of trying to control those forces which he feared.

3. Acts And Sacrifices That Sought Forgiveness And Redemption From The Wrath Of The Gods or The One God

When the above actions and forms of religious expression did not work, then someone would declare that the people had offended the Divine Order, and a form of repentance was called for. There were many forms of contrition to be shown, some for the entire tribe or nation, some for the priests, and some for the individual who felt he was suffering because of a bad relationship with God. Oracles could be consulted, priests could offer sacrifices, and prophets could call for moral reform as they implicated the people for breaking faith with their Metaphysical Provider. The people believed they were at the mercy of some angry gods and goddesses and that some kind of reconciliation with them was necessary to once again receive from them social and agricultural blessings and protection from enemies.

B. FORMULATED MORAL AND INSTRUCTIONAL LEGISLATIONS

1. Law Codes From The Gods

Every religion has some type of code of ethics, whether it is stated in established laws (Hammurabi), a certain amount of commandments (Torah's Ten Commandments), in confessions (The Egyptian Negative Confession), or sermons (Buddha's Sermon at Benares or Jesus' Sermon on the Mount), or, perhaps a list of guiding principles. Some of them are stated so that the anger of a god can be soothed, some more for practical social unity, and some to develop the personal holiness of the individuals of a particular group. They also all claim to be from the inspirations of a particular god or at least from a holy man. *The Code of Hammurabi* is almost totally secular in the nature of its laws, with the few exceptions where a man must go through an ordeal before his god or city-god and when he must affirm what he says by a god, i.e. takes an oath in the name of God. Yet the claim for its sacredness is made, for the stela upon which it was written has a bas-relief that presents Hammurabi receiving the law code from Shamash, the god of the sun and of justice. In the Egyptian *Book of the Dead* (ought to be translated *The Breaking Forth of Dawn*, pointing to the dawning of a new day in eternal life), several times in the Negative Confession that must be declared to the judge in the afterlife, the confessor claims he has not been sacrilegious, and the entire ethical code of 40 innocent pleas are social laws that hold the key as to whether or not the individual is worthy of life after death in the heavenly abode, and in the presence of Osiris. The Jewish Law, in its briefest form, the Ten Commandments, presents two "tables", a series of four laws that govern man's acts towards Yahweh, and six laws that are social in nature; and they claim to have come to Moses directly from God on Mount Sinai. Confucius made the claims in his *Analects* that his teachings were in keeping with the will of "heaven", even though the teachings were secular in nature in the sense that if the power of "heaven" were to reward or punish one, it would be in this present world order. Buddha was considered the Enlightened One and therefore his *Sermon at Benares* in which he presented the 'Setting in Motion of the Wheel of Righteousness' was given by the power that enlightens. Even though Buddhism did not have a "god", one must remember that for a Buddhist, Buddha, being the Enlightened One was the person through whom one reached the knowledge of the ultimate good and absolute reality. For the simple formula recited by Buddhists, even today, is:

> I take my refuge in the Buddha (The Enlightened One),
> I take my refuge in the Dhamma (The Righteous Teaching)
> I take my refuge in the Sangha (The Order).

These are often declared as the Three Treasures. The strength of these "given by God" or "from above" laws is that they help to control those in society who need curbs to their self-centered acts that are harmful to others. However, the theological aspects of the laws can divide one group of believers from another group that has a theological flavor that is different. If such theological aspects are enforced strictly, then they become divisive elements in human society, and have even caused wars between people who consider killing other believers more important than their own reaching out to God and trying to imitate his love and righteousness. This is perhaps both a strength and a weakness in Buddhism, for it has no theology and no God, and therefore they avoid theologically motivated hatred and conflict with others, for the Buddhists are certainly the most peaceful of all religions towards others.

2. Sacred Writings

The Holy Scriptures of all religions seek to give enlightenment to their followers by means of history, sermons, devotional discourses, prayers, stories, and fables, all for the purpose of explaining the elements of life that befall them so that they will have living examples and mental concepts to help them to live a more satisfying life. Those writings that proved themselves to be useful or educational enough through the generations then became canonized and declared holy. For since they have proved so inspirational to others, they themselves undoubtedly were considered inspired in the first place, by either God or His Spirit. Moral teachings (doctrines) are then derived from such writings for the purpose of spiritual guidance. They represent the Way or the Truth or the Life, that Christians believe are all present in the Person of Jesus, His works, His teachings, and His life. Even Hegel, mainly against Schleiermacher, taught that a religion must have "representations" of truth that are more formidable than feelings alone. But Schleiermacher was also correct when he declared that religion is much more than scriptures and representation, one must feel with one's heart the joy and the presence of God. Kabir, declared the same thing: "Put your cleverness away: mere words shall never unite you to Him. Do not deceive yourself with the witness of the Scriptures: Love is something other than this."(LIX) The Hindus believe one may think of Brahman, the Ultimate Being, in two ways: one as the Supreme Brahman, who is beyond representation; and the Lesser Brahman, who can be represented with attributes and personality. When reading the sacred writings of the Hindus it is best for one to keep this in mind. In a similar way of expressing God, some religions use both the via positiva and the via negativa (i.e. the things which one can say about God in terms of attributing to Him characteristics, and this in concession to human communication, and the other "negativa" is a declaration of things that God is not: unjust, incorruptible, incomprehensible). Such writings, prayers, and stories are necessary for human communication, but the danger with this form of religious expression is that one forgets that words are themselves only symbolic, to say nothing of the difficulty they have in translation to another language, which is also symbolic and from a different cultural viewpoint.

C. BELIEVER'S UNIFICATION BY CREEDS

This step towards unification of the believing community by creedal expression can be a most dangerous step, in many ways. Above it was mentioned that representation, even in stories and prayers, can be difficult in terms of expressing God, and at very best can only be symbolic on a rather low level. And, of course, they can be, not only poor representations of the Deity, but they can be misleading also. Any teaching about God must be clothed in deepest humility, and then with the Hindu's view of the Supreme Brahman and Plato's view of the Good Beyond Being in mind, one must constantly be aware that he is dealing, not so much with God's Ultimate Nature, but with man's desperate attempt to declare it. The danger of Creeds is that they usually take on an absolute and unbending character, claiming ultimate spiritual truth, and forsaking their original intent of being only symbols. How many "heretics" have been burned at the stake for such arrogance of shallow religious fanatics? How many wars have been fought to kill the infidels, the pagans, and the heathen? While it is understandable that a community of believers wants to represent what it believes in simple words, it must certainly know that they are, at very best, an inferior and human view of the Divine, and if taken to be Truth Itself, that that is absolute hubris before God and the appearance of utter foolishness before men. Justification for an act of violence or discrimination ought not to be "It is in our Scriptures." or "It is in our Creeds." Maybe that is fine to designate who should be or not be in that particular group of believers, but to use such statements seriously as representations of Truth Itself is spiritual arrogance, which is a far greater evil than any "misunderstanding" of an "attribute" of God. As religious expressions, "yes!" to creeds and scriptures, they are necessary for our communicating our faith and its implications for living a good and holy life, but for unbending declarations about the very nature of God Himself, then "no!" to them.

D. ART

Art can be expressed visually, literally, and musically. But each area must consider the cautions mentioned above. But again, for the sake of human communication of the most precious hopes that man has in reaching out to God, such expressions are necessary, and in art they meet their most beautiful form. In fact, subconsciously, when one hears the word "art" he is already anticipating something beautiful. From the very beginning, as expressed in Chapter One, art was present in the lives of men and women, and religion was in its content. Art, as nothing else, can express the Joy of Embracing God and Humanity's Longing for the Eternal.

Plato spoke much of the purpose of art and the desire of the Beautiful in many of his dialogues and all of these discussions pointed man to the good moral life, the good function of the material, the educational value of such art, and the initial steps of man's ascent to the form of Beauty, Beauty Itself, that is beyond created existence, but that gives love for itself, The Beautiful, as the first element of creation. He also spoke much of the levels of art, i.e. the degrees to which they are removed from Beauty itself, or the eternal Form of the object of art. Likewise, an object that is for a basic function, a utilitarian vessel, was also to be expressed as a form of art by the excellence (ARETE) of its function. Yet, the prime purpose of art for Plato was to create good humans who, lifted up by art, would be enhanced in their efforts to be as much like God as possible. For the entire natural order of the cosmos (KOSMOS), was an ordered beauty that pointed men, not only to a creator, but to Beauty Itself, for Plato taught that God Himself was Absolute Beauty and Goodness, and created his cosmos in his own image as much as possible, for He had to work with the innate inferiority of the material realm. This He did in order to show mankind His own beauty, goodness, and love that He had for his created realm, and all that dwelt therein. Plato taught that indeed a man who viewed the heavens, knew the power of mathematics, and had a sense of wonder would come to see God in his creation, as well as his loving attributes. For the creation was God's son and was made in the image of God Himself. Some have erroneously taught that Plato had a negative attitude towards the creation, and that is simply not true, for he saw it as the first born child of God, in the very image of God's great beauty. In the Phaedrus Dialogue, Phaedrus takes

Socrates out of the city to a tree and a scene that he wanted Socrates to see. Upon seeing it, Socrates spoke such:

> ...a beautiful resting place, full of summer sounds and scents. Here is this lofty and spreading plane-tree, and the agnus castus high and clustering, in the fullest blossom and the greatest fragrance; and the stream which flows beneath the plane-tree is deliciously cold to the feet. Judging from the ornaments and images, this must be a spot sacred to Achelous and the Nymphs. How delightful is the breeze: --so very sweet; and there is a sound in the air shrill and summer-like which makes answer to the chorus of the cicadae. But the great-est charm of all is the grass, like a pillow gently sloping to the head. My dear Phaedrus, you have been an admirable guide(Phaedrus:230).

If a person was not aware that Plato was a poet before he took up philosophy, he certainly can see such in the above passage. Plato, not only loved beauty but wrote in some of the most beautiful prose ever written. But, again in the walk of the Athenian, the Cretan, and the Spartan, from Cnosus to the cave and temple of Zeus, the pleasantness of the journey itself was, not only in the dialogue, but from the loveliness and practicality of nature itself.

> The distance...is considerable; and doubtless there are shady places under the lofty trees, which will protect us from this scorching sun. Being no longer young, we may often stop to rest beneath them, and get over the whole journey without difficulty, beguiling the time by conversation. (Cleinias responses) Yes, Stranger, and if we proceed onward we shall come to groves of cypresses, which are of rare height and beauty, and there are green meadows, in which we may repose and converse (Laws 625:a-b).

Plato criticized those poets whose poetry presented the gods in an ugly fashion with characteristics that Plato said one would not say about a decent man, let alone attribute the gods with such passions and self-centeredness. For that very reason he spoke critically especially of Homer's works, and declared that in a good city set upon the goal of developing human goodness Homer would automatically be banned. Literature and poetry were to present the Beauty of God and the loveliness of the creation in hopes that man himself would be moved to extend himself towards nobility and virtue, and in that way fit into the creation of beauty and reflect in some way the Beauty of God Himself. All art was seen as an imitation of the real thing, i.e. foremost God Himself, but also the absolute virtues which existed as ideals or forms. The better the imitation, the more moral value the piece of art would be. Therefore, art could also play, for good or for bad, a role in the education of children, And for this reason, all play and study of children were to reflect the goodness of nature and God. A secondary but important role of art for children was that it was to create an imagination that in turn would develop, as artisans, elements of the material realm that would serve other men by the quality of their function. To Plato there was really no such thing as pure play or simple work, for in every element of man's activities the goal was to educate for goodness, and for things like knives and bows and arrows, goodness was in the excellence of their function. In summary, then, for Plato, all art whether written, plastic, athletic, or dialogue was moral, religious, and an enhancement in the soul's quest to be like God. Even the acknowledgment of a beautiful woman or man was the first step up in the quest of the soul to embrace Beauty Itself. My summary of Diotima's dialogue with Socrates in the *Symposium* (in the past the dialogue was called *The Banquet*) follows.

> When the love which is implanted into our soul seeks to behold
> Absolute Beauty, it starts its ascent upwards by acknowledging
> the beauties bound into this world's order, but perceiving that they
> are not the ultimate fulfillment for which it longs, it puts them
> aside and resumes its quest for Ultimate Beauty and Goodness,
> and stepping upwards, one step by one, seeks that which is the
> Eternal Good and Absolute Beauty, knowing that what it has put
> aside will never fully satisfy it. When the soul finally meets
> Beauty Itself, face to face, that Beauty that never decays or changes
> or fades, but gives its goodness to all reality, always and never
> wavering, then that soul knows it has become a Friend of God,
> beloved and uplifted by the Same to its eternal home (Adapted
> from Plato's Symposium 211-212).

All art in Plato is to aid that journey of the love-inspired soul of him who seeks the Joy of Embracing God and fulfill his longing for the Eternal.

All subsequent religions has been influenced by these Platonic teachings, and if not, they have probably died out. In Plato, all images, icons, and, indeed, all forms of art can be beautiful inasmuch as they themselves serve their function. Greek art in itself was always spiritually utilitarian with its statues, icons, paintings and all other forms of art as being helpful in man's reaching out to God. During the iconoclastic conflict of the Christian Church, the Hellenistic, and especially, the Platonistic, influence saved the Church's quest of expressing their love and longing for God by means of the beauty of the arts. Maximus of Tyre, a Second Century AD Platonist, and contemporary of the other great Platonists (Iamblichus, Apuleius, and Celsus) realized the problem of God's being so wholly other than man, and therefore, did not disapprove of images and earthly things being used to awaken and strengthen faith in God whose majesty and being was far beyond what we can express in the material world. He stated:

> God himself, the Father and Fashioner of all this is, older than the sun or the sky, greater than time and eternity and all the flow of being, is unnamable by any lawgiver, unutterable by any voice, not to be seen by any eye. But we, being unable to apprehend his essence, use the help of sounds and names and pictures, of beaten gold and ivory and silver, of plants and rivers, mountain peaks and torrents, yearning for the knowledge of Him, and in our weakness naming all that is beautiful in this world after His nature--just as happens to earthly lovers...Why should I further examine and pass judgment about images? Let them know what is Divine, let them know: that is all. If a Greek is stirred to the remembrance of God by the art of Pheidias...I have no anger...only let them know, let them love, let them remember.3.7

It was also the Platonic Christians who gave impetus to the Renaissance that brought forth such beautiful Christian works of art. The Church, in this, as well as in many other ways, followed Plato and not Moses where such works and images were strictly forbidden.

In the *Srimad Bhagavatam* written by Vyasa in the 6th century AD, Krishna declares nature and the works of artists are indeed capable of directing people to the knowledge of Him. "Those who, knowing my true nature, worship me steadfastly are the first among my devotees. Worship me in the symbols and images which remind thee of me, and also in the hearts of my devotees, where I am most manifest."3.8

The Sufi, Rumi, told a delightful story in which he presented the Chinese and the Greeks at competition before a king in which each tries to show forth in art the greatest of all beautiful things. The Chinese suggested that a curtain should divide a large room, on one side the Chinese would work and on the other side the Greeks. When both were finished the king could draw away the curtain and compare the two works. The Chinese asked for dyes of a hundred different colors and their variations with which they would create their work. The Greeks then asked for no colors at all, as they were not necessary for the work they had in mind. The Greeks instead spent all their time cleaning and polishing the hard surface of the walls of the room until they were as pure and clear as they could be. The Chinese meanwhile applied all their colors and assured themselves of victory by the beautiful arrangement of all the colors, and when the king entered their side of the room he was, indeed, astonished by the gorgeous color and detail. Then the Greeks pulled aside the curtain and there against the pure colorlessness of their walls was the reflection of the Chinese paintings, but they seemed to have come to life, for with each change in the light from the sun that shone in, the colors moved and blended into new and even more beautiful scenes, much like a turning kaleidoscope (a Greek word meaning: the viewing of the beautiful forms). Rumi then concluded that a true Sufi find the living beauty of life in the purity of his reflection of God, from whom all beauty comes. This is a wonderful thought for all art: the art of painting, writing, sculpturing, and, above all, the art of living.

Martin Luther added the old *Book of Passions* to his 1529 edition of his *Personal Prayer Book*, and used pictures (later editions used woodcuts of Duerer's *Short Passion History*). The iconoclasts of his era who followed Moses' directive of no images had criticized him earlier for such images of the Holy. But, in anticipation, of their criticism, he stated, "I do not care if the iconoclasts condemn and reject this. They do not need our advice and we do not want theirs, so it is easy for us to part company." He further stated that for children and simple people (only four percent of the Germans of Luther's day were literate), divine stores were more aptly taught by pictures, painting on walls, and all forms of art, for Satan was working against faith and therefore all arts were needed to teach the gospel which was to be preached, taught, written, read, illustrated, and pictured. The woodcuts that were added included images of God, Adam and Eve, Noah, the rain of manna, Mary and Elizabeth, the Nativity of Jesus, and many of Jesus in his ministry. Against the Calvinists, Lutherans represented Protestantism with an openness to and the use of art to exemplify the Beauty of the Holy Things as well as God Himself. This was in the tradition of the Western Catholic and Eastern Orthodox Church. In fact, if one has never seen the beauty of the Orthodox Church's icons and worship areas, he is depriving himself of a truly beautiful religious experience. For Lutherans I would recommend a work in German called *Luther und die Folgen fuer die Kunst* that I was able to purchase at the Kunsthalle in Hamburg.

Johann Sebastian Bach was a deeply devotional Christian and a follower of Martin Luther in every sense of doctrine and feeling of the great reformer that he had towards his God. Bach's medium was music, and his music was truly a spiritual poetry of the soul, both at play and at worship. He lived in a deep rapture of feeling towards God, an honest enthusiasm (being in God: EN THEOS) of his entire being. In his music he lived in the presence of God, and hoped that it would bring the same sacred moments to those who participated in it or even those who only listened to it. In life and in death his hands were outstretched to God. The final words of his Easter Cantata are:

"Letzte Stunde, brich herein,
Mir die Augen zu zudruecken!
Lass mich Jesu Freudenshein
Und sein helles Licht erblicken,
Lass mich Engelen aehnlich sein.

So farh' ich hin zu Jesus Christ,
Mein' Arm' tu ich ausstrecken;
So schlaf' ich ein and ruhe fein,
Kein Mensch kann mich aufwecken:
Denn Jesus Christus, Gottes Sohn,
Der wird die Himmelstuer auftun,

Mich fuehr'n zum ew'gen Leben."

"Come in, last hour,
To close my eyes!
Let me behold both the joyous shining of Jesus
And the brightness of his light,
Let me become like the angels.

So I go forth to Jesus Christ,
I stretch out my arms to him:
So I fall asleep in graceful rest,
No human can awaken me:
For Jesus Christ, God's Son,
He will open heaven's door,
And lead me to life eternal."

Many people hear both the music and the words to Beethoven's Ninth Symphony, The Choral, but seldom, probably because it is sung in German, are the words understood and theme recognized. The theme is that joy and both God's beauty and presence are not to be separated, and therefore, if all men are to live in joyous harmony, they must do so under the wings of God. The words and theme were written by Schiller who had written much on the purpose and power of the arts. Those words that are used from his "Ode to Joy" by Beethoven for his Choral are shown below, first in German and then in my English translation.

Freude, schoener Goetterfunken, Tochter aus Elysium
Wir betreten feuertrunken, Himmlische, dein Heiligtum!
Deine Zauber binden wieder, Was die Mode streng geteilt;
Alle Menschen werden Brueder, Wo dein sanfter Fluegel weilt.

Wem der grosse Wurf gelungen, Eines Freundes Freund zu sein,
Wer ein holdes Weib errungen, Mische seinen Jubel ein!
Ja, wer auch nur eine Seele Sein nennt auf dem Erdenrund!
Und ser's nie gekonnt, der stehle Weinend sich aus diesem Bund.

Freude trinken alle Wesen An den Bruesten der Natur;
Alle Guten, alle Boesen Folgen ihrer Rosenspur.

Kusse gab sie uns und Reben, Einen Fruend, geprueft in Tod;
Wollust ward dem Wurm gegeben, Und der Cherub steht vor Gott!

Froh, wie seine Sonnen fliegen Durch des Himmels praechtgen Plan,
Laufet, Brueder, eure Bahn, Freudig, wie ein Held zum Siegen.
Seid umschlungen, Millionen, Diesen Kuss der ganzen Welt!
Brueder! Ueberm Sternenzeit Muss ein lieber Vater wohnen.
Ihr stuerzt nieder, Millionen? Ahnest du den Schoepher, Welt?
Such' ihn ueber'm Sternenzeit! Ueber Sternen muss er wohnen.

Joy, The sparkling beauty of God, Daughter of Elysium,
Fire-inspired, we enter, into the heavens, your sanctuary.
Your magic binds again, all that custom has harshly divided;
All men become brothers, where your tender wings linger.

Whoever has received the abundant gift of friendship,
Whoever has obtained a charming wife, unite in jubilation,
Yes, who also calls only one soul his own upon the round earth!
And he who cannot rejoice, removes himself tearfully from our circle.

All creatures drink of joy on the breasts of nature.
All who are good, all who are bad, follow her sweet smell of roses.
She gave us kisses and the grapevine, a friend proven even in death;
Even the worm was given full joy, and the cherub stands before God.
Cheerfully, as the sun flies its splendid course through the heavens,
So also brothers, run you race happily, as a hero to victory.

You millions, you are embraced, this kiss is for the entire world!
Brothers! Above the canopy over the stars, there must dwell a
   loving Father.
Do you kneel before Him, you millions?
World, do you acknowledge your Creator?
Seek Him above the covering of the stars.
It is above the stars He is obligated to reside.

This most beautiful *Ode to Joy* by Schiller touches upon almost every
aspect of this very book: *The Joy of Embracing God: Humanity's longing
for the Eternal.* The Joy of a Loving Father, human harmony for those

under God's wings, the desire to seek Him, acknowledge Him, and come to Him because our hearts are fire-inspired, a burning zeal, to approach the "sparkling beauty of God". And Beethoven's music put to this Ode immortalized it in the history of music. Beethoven himself, even though he talked of his run-ins with God, still was deeply religious and had a strong interest in how his predecessors developed the Christian themes in their music. In a letter to Breitkopf he asked about such: "...I should be grateful if from time to time you would send me most of the scores that you have, as, for example, Mozart's Requiem, etc., Haydn, Mozart, Bach, Johann Sebastian Bach, Emanuel, etc.."3.9 According to Bettina Brentano Beethoven said to her: "I know well that God is nearer to me in my art than to others. I consort with Him without fear, have always recognized and understood Him, nor am I at all anxious about the fate of my music"...and again "So always art represents the divine, and the relationship of men towards art is religion: what we obtain through art comes from God, is divine inspiration which appoints an aim for human faculties, which aim we can attain...Music is the electric soil in which the spirit lives, thinks, and invents."3.10 It is in Beethoven's Ninth Symphony that the spiritual thoughts and artistic excellence of Beethoven and Schiller come together and blossom. This is to say nothing of Beethoven's other church music.

Jaroslav Pelikan in his *Jesus Through the Centuries* notes well that Christianity did not follow Moses' prohibition of religious images, but rather followed the Greeks, and possibly over the course of centuries did even more with the arts than the Greeks themselves. He stated:

The victory of Jesus Christ over the gods of Greece and Rome in the fourth century did not, as both friend and foe might have expected, bring about the demise of religious art; on the contrary, it was responsible over the next fifteen centuries for a massive and magnificent outpouring of creativity that is probably without parallel in the entire history of art.3.11

Alfred North Whitehead in his *The Aims of Education* stated:

"You cannot, without loss, ignore in the life of the spirit so great a factor as art. Our aesthetic emotions provide us with vivid appre-hensions of value...when your population widely appreciates what art can give--its joys and its terrors--do you not think that your prophets and your clergy and your statesmen will be in s stronger position when they speak to the population of the love of God?" 3.12

In this chapter I have tried to present adequately a stage in many religions that considered man to be mortal and the gods to be immortal, yet that did not keep them from expressing their faiths in many ways, in fact they are the same ways, for the most part, of those who believe in a heavenly Father who also offers his children eternal life. From the representations of the myths to the wonder and logic of the philosophical mind, man sought and still does to express himself by cults and rituals, by sacred writings and laws, by creeds, and above all, at least to me, by the arts of beauty. Perhaps the arts, often using words, but also often liberated from them, seem to soar above all other expressions in the deepest form of both mental and emotional desires to reach out to God. The great stage of worship in which the plastic arts present the setting, the literary arts the words, and the music and acting out of a religious drama often including ritual is the climax of man's artistic talents in reaching out to God, to embrace Him, and declare their hopes of immortality. Richard Wagner used all such elements of art in his opera the *Parsifal*. The next chapter will focus upon man's reaching out to God as a child to his father, with the additional hope that the Heavenly Father will bring him "home" through the passage of death to the eternal realm in which the Father lives. Man's religion will be moved beyond the state of that of a mortal man to the man who sees himself as an immortal being, and thus has experienced a tremendous difference in his outlook, hopes, and his ultimate longings.

CHAPTER FOUR

GOD AS THE MEANS OF MAN'S IMMORTALITY

I. GOD AS THE LIFE GIVING SPIRIT OF THE UNIVERSE

There were in the history of mankind many religions that believed that God was the Life Giving Spirit of the universe, but did not believe that the immortal life was given to men. These have been discussed before, and the subject of this chapter is the concept that God, as The Life Giving Spirit of the universe, gave or shared that Life Giving Spirit to men as an eternal possession, or, at least, the possibility of immortality. Some religions, initially were faiths with no belief in man's immortality, but were heavily influenced by others throughout the ages, and became split into parts as some of its adherents adopted the idea that they were indeed blessed with the gift from the Creator that they would be able to become immortal with His blessings. This is true of some groups within such religions as Buddhism and Judaism. By the time of the Pharisees it is evident that there were some in Israel that believed in some type of resurrection, usually a physical one, and some of the Buddhists, at least by the time of Asoka likewise believed to have some type of other life or life beyond the present cycle of lives. The early Greeks were split, but the masses who believed in the Olympian Gods did not hold much hope for man's immortality. The others, i.e. those of Orphism and followers of Pythagoras indeed had hopes of eternal life, and they appeared before what one would generally classify the Classical Period of Greek history. After Plato, with the exception of the Epicureans and Aristotelians, belief in the existence of a Father-God who implanted each person with an immortal soul that it might rise through death to its most real and eternal home was adopted by the vast majority of Greeks, and thereafter Platonic Theology was the soul of Hellenism. It is not the purpose of this work to be overly scholastic concerning these developments, but rather present them within the flow of humanity's thought that pointed to and arrived at the belief that each person, in some way, partakes of the eternal life that God gave from Himself to be part of the living universe.

Even some of the animists believe that life after the death of the flesh is something to believe and look forward to, and that the particular fate of the individual is dependent upon either the degree of virtue that one had in this present life or the very thought that one had at the moment of death. Others (e.g. Bakauna of Melanesia) did not speculate on whether or not there existed punishment after death. Some did not see the afterlife as very desirable, like the Aztecs who saw the afterlife as a rather dreary and cold place. The Confucians, although by no means metaphysical, did honor their ancestors as if they were alive, for they believed that there was a life principle passed from one generation to the next, much like the genius of the ancient Roman families, and thus both Confucians and Romans honored extensively their ancestors. But it was only in such cases when the belief took hold that that life giving principle was shared by each person, instead of the corporate tribe, that each person was brought to the faith that he himself had an eternal divinity, spirit, or daemon within him that would partake of another life after the death of his body. Zarathushtra could call Ahura Mazda "the Spirit of Eternal Life"(Yasna 28). And that eternalness would eventually be shared by all humans:

> So understand, O mortal men, the Decrees which Mazda has
> established regarding happiness and misery.
> There will be a long period of suffering for the wicked,
> and salvation for the just, but thereafter
> eternal bliss shall prevail everywhere (Yasna 30)

The Hindus also believe that the one firmly grounded in Brahman (i.e. the "Brahamsamstha"), obtains immortality. As will be discussed later, all will eventually obtain immortality, but there is a system of spiritual justice that will need several lifetimes to be satisfied that the individual has reached the spiritual level by which he deserves eternal life. In the last chapter of this book it will be discussed in more detail. For the Upanishads taught that the Life Giving Spirit was Purusha, the Lord of immortality, and it embodied itself in each man, and in due time, all would reach the Eternal Abode of blissfulness. All Platonists follow Plato in believing that the Creator put a good daemon within each man that recalled the soul's former existence (former to its being incarnated), and in that "recall" was a longing to return to the eternal realms which was his real home, the origin of his soul. The Christian Creed refers to the Holy Spirit as the Lord and Giver of Life. Man had been moved to the mindset that he was an eternal being, so designed by the will and love of the Creator, and that for which humanity had always longed, eternal life, was a reality, and that knowledge deepened and enlivened man's character and thought process so that even with that faith, before his final journey to his eternal hope, he could now in the flesh live a life "more abundant".

Some of the more mystical thinkers, who will be discussed in the next chapter, saw an almost symbiotic linkage between themselves and the universe, some inclining towards a pantheism, and others who saw the entire universe as the Garden of Eden and earth as the very sanctuary of life, that here and now God and our relationship to him can be as fully enjoyed as in the future world. Such thinking is present in the teachings of men like Kabir and Pierre Teilhard de Chardin. From the writings of Kabir are the following quotations.

Within this earthen vessel (material universe) are shade trees
    and groves, and within it is the Creator:
Within this vessel are the seven oceans and the unnumbered stars.
The touchstone and the jewel-appraiser are within;
And within this vessel the Eternal shouts out and the spring wells up.
Kabir says: "Listen to me, my Friend! My beloved Lord is within."

The light of the sun, the moon, and the stars shines bright:
The melody of love swells forth, and the rhythm of love's
    detachment beats the time.
Day and night, the chorus of music fills the heavens; and Kabir says
"My Beloved One gleams like the lightning flash in the sky."
Do you know how the moments perform their adoration?
Waving its row of lamps, the universe sings in worship day and night,
 There are the hidden banner and the secret canopy:
 There the sound of the unseen bells is heard.

Kabir says: "There adoration never ceases; there the Lord of the Universe sits on His throne." (From songs VIII and XVII)

You will know that He transcends this universe. (Song LXXVI)

Pierre Teilhard de Chardin in his Hymn Of The Universe in which he declared that the Presence of God or of Christ can not be confined to space or any one material symbol begins his Hymn with these words.

Since once again, Lord--though this time not in the forests of the Aisne but in the steppes of Asia--I have neither bread, nor wine, nor altar, I will raise myself beyond these symbols, up to the pure majesty of the Real Itself; I, your priest, will make the whole earth my altar and on it will offer you all the labors and sufferings of the world...
My paten and my chalice are the depths of a soul laid widely open to all the forces which in a moment will rise up from every corner of the earth and converge upon the Spirit. Grant me the remembrance and the mystic presence of all those whom the Light is now awakening to the new day.

...those yearnings you implanted in me as a child...

...like the monist I plunge into the all-inclusive One; but the One is so perfect that as it receives me and I lose myself in it I can find in it the ultimate perfection of my own individuality.

One simple story that I remember from somewhere also speaks of the unity of the Universe and God, not that they are one, but that to see one is to see the other. It goes this way: God looked into a mirror to see Himself and was happy at the sight of Ultimate Beauty, but He tired of looking into a mirror and decided to make the universe as an image of himself, so that he could see Himself in His creation, and could do away with the mirror. He decorated the night with different kinds of flowers that we call stars and planets, in order that we see the universe as a growing and beautiful Garden and therefore the universe itself is the Garden of Eden or Paradise in which God is still with us. We are not cast out of this paradise, but held within its beauty by God's love. In this mass infinity we are able to see His majesty, power, and beauty. He is very close to us and we hear His voice of comfort in the sounds of nature. It is in the universe that He holds us near to Himself and within it we can look upon His gentle and loving presence.

II. GOD AS THE UNIVERSE

There is in many authors a line that separates God as Being within the universe that was made by Him to declare Himself as Creator and those who believe that God is the Universe Itself, and sometimes that line of distinction is very thin. Indeed both Kabir and Pierre Teilhard de Chardin have made other statements that seem very much like a form of pantheism. The argument of the Pantheist is basically something like this: God because He had nothing else by which to make and form the universe (i.e. creatio ex nihilo), He had to make everything from His own being, and inasmuch as everything that exists came directly out of God's Being, then everything in a way is part of God Himself. The ancients in the Western World usually avoided the problem by stating that there was a void or a chaos out of which God created the universe, and then avoided defining those vague terms. In order to "put the best construction on everything" it is morally better not to judge how the pantheists come to their conclusion, but to listen to the spiritual concepts they offer in order that one might just be lifted up to a new and closer appreciation of close association with our Creator. Some Stoics believed that one can judge the justice of God by the acts of fate and the rules of nature, and that when we die, our souls merge into the World Soul, from which we have received life in the first place by our participation in that very World Soul, and to return to it does not nullify our existence but lifts it up within the eternal world of incorruption and union.

In the Hindu work The *Srimad Bhagavatam* one finds this prayer:

"O Lord, your infinite power dwells in all.
You are in the fire, You are in the sun,
You are in the moon, You are in the stars,
You are in the water, You are in the earth,
You are in the ether, You are in the wind,
You are in the smallest elements of the universe:

You are in everything.
Save and protect Durbasa with your power that loves all.
In You may we all find peace."4.1

The Hindu, <u>Shankara</u>, tries to separate them, that is, the universe and Brahman, by saying that since all came from Brahman, the universe is Brahman: "The universe is Brahman". However, he continues, Brahman is real and the universe is not, i.e. while the universe is Brahman, Brahman is not the universe, but rather the source of it. "The universe, therefore, is nothing but Brahman. It is superimposed upon Him. It has no separate existence, apart from its ground (Brahman)."4.2 Suffice it to say that Hinduism, while expressing many concepts that seem to imply "pantheism", it expressly states that only Brahman is real in the ultimate sense and all that is is dependent upon Brahman for its existence. One might say that Brahman has put on clothing, and that clothing is the universe, but it is not the Ultimate Reality that is Brahman.

The <u>Shinto</u> faith projects "kami" as the vital life force in all of nature. There is no god apart from nature and that very Life Force, called "kami". It is Kami that brings forth growth in nature, fertilizing all nature, including man, with the power of its life force. Joseph M. Kitagawa, in his *Religions of the East*, put it this way:

> More important, perhaps, is the fact that the notion of *kami* provides the foundation for the Japanese attitude toward life and the universe. To put it another way, the cosmological orientation of the early Japanese took it for granted that they were an integral part of the cosmos, which to them was a gigantic organism permeated by the *kami* (sacred) nature.4.3

The Life Force was part of and intertwined with nature itself, and therefore all nature was sacred. This attitude can be seen in the Japanese closeness to nature and its respect for it. From flowers in a window to luxurious gardens, from nature paintings to native animals one finds an hallowed closeness of the Japanese to his natural surroundings. This sacredness of feeling towards the native land also is reflected in Shinto's deep patriotism and honor of their leaders, and in the past the sanctity of their emperor. Even though in Shinto there are stories of gods and goddesses (male and female *kami*: Uzanagi and Izanami respectively), all of those, even in the Plain of High Heaven, were dependent upon *kami* for their life force. But because they represented the Plain of High Heaven, mountains took on a special sacredness. Indigenous and uninfluenced Shintoism was a pantheistic "all things are united in their need of the sacred life force, kami, that was intertwined with nature itself."

In the Hymn of the Universe by de Chardin, there are passages that have indeed been interpreted as his giving homage to pantheism, for he clearly stated that God had been incarnated in the universe and the universe was his body.

> "For me, my God, all joy and all achievement, the very purpose of my being and all my love of life, all depend on this one basic vision of the union between yourself and the universe...I have no desire, I no ability, to proclaim anything except the innumerable prolongations of your incarnate Being in the world of matter; I can preach only the mystery of your flesh, You the Soul shine forth through all that surrounds us."4.4

It is from such passages as the above that de Chardin's theology has been attacked as pantheistic, and, as a matter of fact, it does lean in that direction, but only sometimes. It is a beautiful work and can help to lift up the soul and find a sacredness to all reality that sometimes the more "orthodox" person does not see, and, in not seeing, loses some of the great mystery and majestic awe of the Christian faith. The most important point of this section is merely to show that humanity in longing for and reaching out to God, believed all was from Him and all showed forth His majesty, power, and beauty. Many simply could not separate in concept the awesome greatness of the universe from the very being of God Himself. This is in no way to be taken negatively so that great judgment is to be cast because they approach God in that way, but rather thanks ought to be given to God who has so decorated the universe with beauty that men would naturally think of Him. For humanity has nearly always reached out for God because of both the inner longing for Eternal Goodness and Life as well as what he has seen with his eyes, i.e. the beauty of the Infinite, within which is an almost infinite universe:

Plato certainly used both as causes of man's reaching out to God to embrace Him.

III. GOD AS THE PERSONAL FATHER OF ALL

In my own mind, I believe that this is the most sacred and intimate concept in all theology, for it predicates that I am a child of God, and a very well beloved child, similar to the way an honorable father looks upon his children. Yes, it is an anthropomorphism, and will have its limitations, but for an expression that gives room for the necessary concessions that are important to communicate those concepts beyond words, I personally feel it is the best one. This also, of course, applies to those who use the "Mother of all", and this, perhaps even more so, represents the tenderness of God towards her, in many ways, infant children. The concept, The Father of all, is found in almost all religions, and I believe, all the religions that seek to stress the most intimate relationship of God and his love with his creatures. Malinowski speaks of the views of Andrew Lang that declared that some the natives of Australia referred to an All-Father who was the caretaker of their particular tribes, and the Rev. Pater Wilhelm Schmidt in his studies felt that "there was much evidence proving that this belief is universal among all the peoples of the simplest cultures and that it cannot be discarded as an irrelevant fragment of mythology, still less as an echo of missionary teaching."4.5 Even in infancy, men, in their longing to embrace God, looked to Him as a Father figure. This gives religion life and intimacy, for religion, as defined by most, is a relationship between man and God, and if that relationship is defined as Father and son, then indeed, it becomes intimate and creates a warmth of spirit.

A. SUMERIAN GODS

Even though there are references to the gods that show some feeling between the creature, man, and the makers, the gods, there is no indication of a joyous future after death. The "life" portrayed in the nether world, was far inferior in every way than life on earth, which in turn was far inferior to life in heaven, that is, the domain of the gods. The nether world was dark, impersonal, and devoid of all the possible pleasures of life on earth. As described it can remind one of the movies made about "the living dead" that roam around the earth, but in <u>Sumerian</u> lore, they roam around in the ugliness of the nether world. <u>Samuel</u> <u>Noah</u> <u>Kramer</u> put it bluntly: "The Sumerians held out no comforting hopes for man and his future." Yet, the relationship between man and god, even if it offered no hope of a future life, could, at least a few times, be seen as one of some type of affection. I found two instances in which a human addressed a god as "father": Gilgamesh, in his desire to see Enkidu again, even if it were only his "shade", pleaded to "Father Enlil" that it could happen. Father Enlil granted his wish. Enlil was also referred to as a "worthy shepherd". On another occasion a sufferer prayed to an unnamed god, and addressed him: "My God, You who are my father who begot me, lift up my face." It seems that the female gods were more accessible and understanding. There are two instances of female gods who have some linkage with humanity: Ninhursag and Nanshe. Ninhursag was regarded as the Mother of all living things, including mankind, and Nanshe is said to care about men and women in their weakness: "Who knows the orphan, who knows the widow, knows one man's oppressing another, is mother to the orphan, and seeks justice for the poorest of people and who cares for the refuge and shelters the weak".4.8

B. EGYPTIAN GODS

The early and popular gods of Egypt had were often presented in groups of three: Father, Mother, and Son. In this way the believer felt himself to be a member of a divine family. The most popular Trinity was Osiris, Isis, and Horus, and when a person died he was referred to, not as the "late Neferte", but as "<u>Osiris</u> <u>Neferte</u>", for he was seen as having finally joined his eternal family. The stories of the love and faithfulness of both Isis and Horus to Osiris gave the Egyptians a "divine" model of a loving and happy family, and with such representation Osiris became the chief and most beloved of all the Egyptian Gods. Osiris was the God of the after-death existence, and according to Budge "No other god of the Egyptians was ever mentioned or alluded to in this manner, and no other god at any time in Egypt ever occupied exactly the same exalted position in their minds, or was thought to possess his peculiar attributes".4.6 Isis herself was in many places no less loved and prayed to than her husband, Osiris. Apuleius gives us an example of a prayer to Isis:

"O Holy and Blessed One, the perpetual comfort of human kind.
who by your bounty and grace nourish all the world; and whose
great affection, as a loving mother, is focused upon her children
who are in sorrow and tribulation. Without a moments neglect, day
and night you are there for them, bringing aid both to those on land
and those on the seas, lest the waves and wind destroy them....even
the gods in heaven adore you, and the lower gods bow down in
honor before you. For you control the heavens also; regulating its
rotation and giving light to the sun itself...Even in my poor estate,
I will perform the good acts that are appropriate to our devotion
to you. I will hold your presence always in my mind, and enclose
the image of your most holy godhead in my heart."4.7

The Father/Mother figure of intimacy by the Osiris/Isis marriage image
among those who worshipped this family Triad, was certainly a powerful
force and spiritual comfort on the deepest level of any type of religious
devotion. For more than 3,000 years were they worshipped and adored by
those who were seeking the joy of Embracing God and those who sought
the longed for eternal life. Even with the inroads of Christianity in Egypt
the Osirian faith survived until the jihads of Islam conquered and took
control of Egypt in the 7th Century AD.

C. HINDUISM

As mentioned earlier, the great God is Brahman, who is the One who
is so far beyond what man can think that he is seen as a totality of
perfection that can not be depicted or described in any way or be attached
to any concept of personality. However, the "lower" gods, especially the
Divine Triad of Brahma (Creator), Vishnu (Savior), and Shiva
(Destroyer) are given as a concession to man's limited way of thinking in
words, personalities, and actions that can be apprehended by the
anthropomorphic thinking person. They are representations of Brahman,
but not his essence, which is beyond thought or representation. These
gods as well as many others such as Durga, Lakshmi, Sita, Radha, and
Kali (the Universal Mother Goddess) are given anthropomorphic
personalities and feelings for the plight of mankind. Vishu himself, has
on at least 9 occasions, become incarnate to show man, who had lost his

way, back to the proper way of living (Dhamma or Dharma) that man will be put back on the correct path that will lead him to eternal life, usually by means of several, and sometimes many, reincarnated lives. But the goal is clear, eternal life by the grace of the gods. Vyasa, who wrote the *Srimad Bhagavatam*, said that he was visited by Narada, who had lived before, but was reincarnated for the express purpose of teaching Vyasa the way, and it was from this discussion that Vyasa came to write the Srimad Bhagavatam. One of the worship prayers within his book, at the beginning of the Sixth Book, Chapter Two, declares that God, although far above men, still cares for them:

"O Lord, You are the most worthy of praise,
You need nothing for yourself, for You are infinite;
Yet You accept the adoration of your children,
 And You sprinkle mercy upon them.
 We lift up our insufficient praise, and sing to You.
 In humbleness we bow down at your Lotus Feet,
 for it is a dictate of wisdom.
 You are the Lord of the Universe,
 beyond any name or form:
 Who can describe You, You are beyond thought and word.
 Yet, we sing of Your glory and power,
 for your presence sends away all evil."

Also in the work, Book Eleven, Chapter One, Vyasa declared:

You are truly the Infinite Brahman,
 You have no form and are beyond characteristics,
 You are also the Father-Mother God, all powerful.

From these two passages one can see that even though Brahman is beyond attributes, nevertheless, Vyasa seeks to praise him, calling him Father-Mother God who appreciates the praise of his human children. The closeness of God in Hinduism is so intimate that one speaks of the union of both The Atman (another term for Ultimate God) and the atman, the soul of man. It is generally by means of the "lower" gods that Brahman expresses himself as a personal god, very intimately related to man's soul (atman). It is in this way that man understands himself in an embrace of Brahman who is the source of all and his care of humanity is expressed by means of the personalized lower gods, who are usually seen as only presentations of Brahman, who is all in all. Already in the Vedas, the God Visvakarman (Creator of the Universe) is referred to as the "Father who created us", and the Heaven and Earth Gods, are called Father and Mother respectively, and To Yama (ruler of the world of the departed from earth) prayers are made that in that new world those praying may be reunited with their own forefathers, and Vishnu is asked that the worshipper may attain to Vishnu's dear place where men are devoted to the Gods and praising them, experiencing the "well of sweetness". Longing to be eternal, longing to embrace God, and seeing the gods, even Brahman Himself, as the Father of All, and where all are his children, this longing is deeply embedded in Hinduism from its very conception. The prayer to Soma Pavamana asks: "Make me immortal in that realm where happiness, where joys and felicities combine..and longing wishes are fulfilled." Yes, even from the earliest Vedas of Hinduism, man was longing for the Eternal, for personal immortality, for the joy of living in that realm where Brahman was the Father of All.

D. PLATONISM

Plato pointed to God as the Good Beyond Being, much the way that the Hindus described the Ultimate Essence of God as being Brahman. Plato also, realizing that one must speak of the unspeakable being of God, made concessions for the sake of human communications. In the creation story found in the *Timaeus* God is called the Maker and Father of the cosmos, but to "discover" him, i.e. take off his cover, is such a task that it can seldom be done, for God himself, in actuality, is past being found out, but if one ever were able to find him out, to know him, it would be impossible to communicate him to another. So Plato makes concessions to human concepts and speech, and uses anthropomor-phisms such as: Father of the Cosmos, The Good Beyond Being, The Maker (POIETES) and Architect (DEMIOUGOS) and Constructor and Framer of the Cosmos, The Pilot of the Cosmos, The Divine Shepherd of Humanity, The First Cause of all that exists, Beauty Itself, The Mind or Intellect of the Cosmos (NOUS), the Beginning or Origin (ARCHE) of all that is and even The Best Soul--i.e. Best Living Being. Plato's God is a God who is Father of the Creation, Father of the Lower Gods (for the same of serving and protecting mankind), and the Father and Divine Shepherd of mankind, who delights in their virtue as He delighted in the completed creation. God also planted a DAIMON within the soul of each man that would create and longing love for Himself, and that journey of love can be found both in the Phaedrus and in the Symposium in the speech of Diotima. <u>Plotinus</u>, perhaps Plato's greatest follower, and known as the Second Coming of Plato, referred to heaven as "The Fatherland". "Let us flee then to the beloved Fatherland...The Fatherland for us is there whence we have come. <u>There</u> <u>is</u> <u>the</u> <u>Father</u>." (I.6.8) Plotinus begins his Fifth Ennead with these words: "What can it be that has brought the souls (of men) to forget the Father, God?" All subsequent Platonists taught God as Father and Shepherd of Mankind who planted in them the longing to come to him that their love of beauty would be fulfilled only in the presence of God, Beauty Itself. When one considers all the Christian literature written from Justin Martyr, through Clement and Origen, through Ambrose and Augustine, through Chrysostom, Boethius, and the Pseudo-Dionysius, through Roger Bacon and Bonventura, Anselm and Aquinas, the Renaissance Platonists of Florence, through Boehme and Eckhart, through Erasmus and Bucer, and the Cambridge Platonists, through Kant and Schiller, to A.N. Whitehead, Dean Inge, Benjamin Jowett, Schleiermacher and many others, one can see how deeply Platonism and its longing for the Eternal and the Absolute Beauty have lifted mankind to the full adoration of the Father, Maker, and Divine Shepherd of Mankind.

E. JUDAISM

As mentioned before, Early Judaism or Mosaic Judaism, did not believe in a life hereafter, but it always thought of God as their God and Israel as the children of Yahweh. According to a Psalm (86) written by Ethan the Ezrahite, David would cry out to God: "You are my Father, my God, and the Rock of my salvation" and God then "would make him the first-born, the highest of the kings of the earth". It is probably sometime during or after David that the idea of God's being Israel's Father appeared. Later, Isaiah foretold of the anointed one (messiah) perfect king who would represent God as a caring counselor, who would bring peace to Israel, and give continuing and fatherly love and affection to Israel, and he would sit upon the throne of David and establish the Davidic kingship over Israel forever. (Is. 9:1-7). A Psalm, attributed to David, speaks of God (ELOHIM) as a "Father of the fatherless and protector of widows" (68:5). Yahweh. Later when the Pharisees adopted the belief in life after death, the Fatherhood of God continued to be a force in such thinking. The intertestamental literature carried on and probably expanded the idea of God's being both Israel's and the individual's Father. In Sirach (Ecclesiasticus 4:10) it states:

> Be like a father to orphans, and instead of a husband to their mother,
> You will then be like a son of the Most High,
> And He will love you more than does your mother.

The Psalm of Solomon (17:30) stated: "He knows them, that they are all the sons of their God." And in the book of Jubilees (1:24-25), God declares that if "they will obey my commandments, I will be their Father and they shall be my children". From the above quotations one can see that nothing appeared before the time of David to indicate that Israel thought of itself as the child of Yahweh, rather Yahweh was their God and they were his people. By the time of some of the earlier Psalms the relationship between themselves and God, (Yahweh was often quite fearful to approach) became more tender and affectionate, and by the time of Jesus people as individuals and the nation of Israel thought of their God as a Father.

F. SOME STOICS

The Stoics are basically eclectics with a Platonic base, for Zeno of Citium in Cypress, studied at the Platonic Academy in Athens for many years. Diogenes Laertius declared that Zeno was a pupil of Crates, and also attended the lectures of both Stilpo and Xenocrates for ten years. His total years at Plato's Academy then exceeded ten years, and during that time he well absorbed the Platonism that was taught before he left to found his own school. He and his pupils walked up and down the Stoa Poikile, a public covered walkway in Athens, and had conversations and dialogues that constituted the teaching of Zeno. Since they were holding class in that Stoa, they became known as Stoics. But they, by in large, are difficult, if not impossible, to group into one framework of mind, and as the years passed, even though they kept their Platonic base, they became more eclectic and diversified. Therefore, it is always suspicious when someone says, "The Stoics taught....". For one must really ask which Stoic is he talking about. The views of God also were diversified. Often God is simply called God (THEOS), other times He is called Mind or Intellect (NOUS), or Reason (LOGOS), or Fixed Fate (HEIMARMENEN), and Dia (DIA) which is another name for God. Sometimes he is referred to as Zeus, and at other times He is the Living Soul of the Universe who gives life to all that is, and from that He is sometimes presented as the Universe itself presenting all beauty in an orderly, visible, and majestic fashion. From various mixtures above, the general ethic was to follow God, or Nature (the Universe), or Fate, or Reason, and in so following, one can find personal harmony, peace, and happiness. D. Laertius gives this general summary of Stoic theological belief: "The Deity, they say, is an immortal living being (ZOON ATHANATON), rational (LOGIKON), complete and noetic in happiness (TELEION HE NOERON EN EUDAIMONIA), who takes providential care of all that is within the world. He is not in human shape. But He is the maker (DEMIOURGON) and Father of all (PATERA PANTON)." What is of concern here is that He is called Father of all, and many Stoics declared him to be such and offered up both praise and prayers in the most personal way. Epictetus, who to me is the Prince of the Stoics, taught many deeply felt wisdom sayings and doctrines that men may be happy as they lived in the acknowledged presence of God. Below are some of them:

If a man should be able to assent to this doctrine as he aught, that we are all sprung from God in an especial manner, and that God is the Father both of men and of gods, I suppose that he would never have any ignoble or mean thoughts about himself. (Discourse I.3)

And yet God has not only given us these faculties (reason and the five senses): by which we shall be able to bear everything that happens without being depressed or broken by it; but, like a good king and a True Father, He has given us these faculties free from hindrance. (I.6)

(Man) has learned that the greatest and supreme and the most comprehensive community is that which is composed of men and God.

....for men only are by their nature formed to have communion with God, being by means of reason conjoined with--why should a man call himself, not only a citizen of the world, why not call himself a son of God...to have God for your Maker and Father and Guardian, shall not this release us from sorrow and fears? (I.9)

Nevertheless, He has placed by every man a guardian, every man's Daimon (Demon), to whom he has committed the care of the man, a guardian who never sleeps, is never deceived...When you have shut the doors and made darkness within the room, remember never to say that you are alone, for you are not; but God is within the room, and your Daimon is within also.(I.14)

These are but a few of numerous passages in which Epictetus lauds God for being such a kind and giving Father, and although he is well satisfied with the life he has been given (he was a slave for many years and finally became free after numerous beatings in which he became a cripple--but no complaints, he loved life), yet he would be additionally pleased if God would grant him a life beyond his coming death. But he asks timidly, because he does not want God to think of him as being ungrateful for his present life or for being greedy for more of God's kind love and providence. Epictetus is extremely uplifting to read as his humble piety and love glow in the words he has written: he has a communion with God and how could he ever complain when such is the case! Not all the Stoics are fixed on God as a Father that can give eternal life, but this one was. For to him, the entire creation is one great city, and it is full of friends--first God, and also humankind, whom God has bound by ties of kindred each to each other. This represents the Stoic Brotherhood of mankind and the Fatherhood of God.

Another Stoic, Cleanthes, who followed Zeno as head of the Stoic school in Athens. Wrote this beautiful hymn to Zeus, declaring mankind to be Zeus' children.

O God most glorious, called by many a name,
Nature's great King, through endless years the same;
Omnipotence, who by thy just decree
Controllest all, hail, Zeus, for unto thee
Behooves thy creatures in all lands to call,

<u>We</u> <u>are</u> <u>thy</u> <u>children,</u> we alone, of all
On earth's broad ways that wander to and fro,
Bearing thine image whereso'er we go.
Wherefore with songs of praise thy power I will forth show.
Lo! yonder Heaven, that round the earth is wheeled,
Follows thy guidance, still to thee doth yield
Glad homage; thine unconquerable hand
Such flaming minister, the levin brand,
Wieldeth, a sword two-edged, who deathless might
Pulsates through all that Nature brings to light:
Vehicle of the universal Word, that flows
Through all, and in the light celestial glows
Of stars both great and small, A King of Kings
Through ceaseless ages, God, whose purpose brings
To birth, whate'er on land or in the sea
Is wrought, or in high heaven's immensity;
Save what the sinner works infatuate.
Nay, but thou knowest to make crooked straight:
Chaos to thee is order: in thine eyes
The unloved is lovely, who didst harmonize
Things evil with things good, that there should be
One Word through all things everlastingly.
One Word--whose voice alas! the wicked spurn;
Insatiate for the good their spirits yearn:
Yet seeing see not, neither hearing hear not
God's universal law, which those revere,
By reason guided, happiness to win,
The rest, unreasoning, diverse shapes of sin

Self-prompted follow: for an idol name
Vainly they wrestle in the lists of fame:
Other inordinately riches woo,
Or dissolute, the joys of flesh pursue,
Now here, now there they wander, fruitless still,
For ever seeking good and finding ill.
Zeus the all-bountiful, whom darkness shrouds,
Whose lightning lightens in the thunder-clouds,
<u>Thy</u> <u>children</u> save from error's deadly sway:

Vouchsafe that unto knowledge they attain;
For thou by knowledge art made strong to reign
O'er all, and all things rulest righteously.
So by thee honoured, we will honour thee,
Praising thy works constantly with songs,
As mortals should; nor higher meed belongs
E'en to the gods, than justly to adore
The universal law for evermore.4.9

This hymn of Cleanthes and the passages from Epictetus should remove all doubt expressed by some that the Stoic Deity was impersonal and that all Stoics were pantheists.

G. THE ROMANS

The Roman Empire was full of religions, and contrary to what some overly zealous modern Christian apologists claim, there was indeed some religious expression available for every spiritual taste. The Roman religions that are most often attacked as cold and impersonal were the state religions, and while it is true that in many cases they were not tuned to the needs of the individual, they did much for the community to bring harmony and stature to the welfare of the Empire, an empire that brought peace within its borders for many centuries, which is certainly more than Christian Europe can claim for itself. The "Christian" United States in only two hundred years has waged wars of aggression against the native Indians of North America, fought against "Christian" England, "Christian" Mexico, "Christian" Spain, "Christian" Germany, subdued and repressed the move for freedom by the Filipinos, and the most brutal of all its wars against its "Christian" Southern Self by its "Christian" Northern Self. Let us simply be a little humble when we, as American Christians, overly promote our "religious" virtues in judging other present nations and those of the past. Such arrogance promotes rejection among other nations, and is an embarrassment to God, who loves all his children throughout the world. The state religion of Rome that promoted Jupiter as the Almighty Father, unfortunately did not promoted fatherly care for the individuals and their families, but there were many other options, mostly imported, to the average person. First of all, even among many who did not have any type of confidence of personal life after death, there was the common practice of either having an altar within the house or building one outside the house to welcome the Roman Gods on the property and to give them honors. But here the readers attention will be directed to the many personal gods that were worshipped among the Roman people.

Concerning the imported religions into Rome: to be a legal religion in Rome it was necessary to have been either an indigenous one of the Roman people or it had to have been imported into Rome from a conquered territory or people. When the Roman Empire conquered a people in order to expand its territory, the religions of that people at the time of their being conquered were declared legal religions (COLLEGIA LICITA), i.e. a legal college (also guild, political party, or religion). Rome did not dictate their indigenous religions onto others, but did demand that the Roman gods be sacrificed to as a show of imperial unity, much the way Americans salute or pledge to the flag. But just as pledging to the flag of the USA does not dictate what personal religion a man must have, so also sacrificing to Jupiter or to the Emperor's Honor did not dictate the personal religion of the people of the Roman Empire. So Rome had no problem adopting legality for the religion of those people whom it conquered. Also it avoided religious strife and civil unrest. However, if after conquering a people, a new religion arose, Rome, feeling very suspicious of such gathering activities, and fearing that those religions were created simply as a front for rebellious activities and patriotic uprisings against Roman control, banned any new forms of religions. They were not given the status of a *collegia licita.* Pompey conquered Jerusalem in 63BC, and from that time forward no new religion in Palestine would be tolerated. Jesus' ministry was probably from 27AD to 29AD, almost a century after Rome had taken control. It was also at a time when the unrest of the Jewish people was very high and was led by a patriotic party of Zealots on behalf of Jewish freedom from Rome. Jesus himself warned against such a rebellion, and that may have played in Judas' disappointment in Jesus. When the followers of Jesus started to break away from traditional Judaism, it faced the problem of being an illegal party subject to Rome's punishment. Matthew and Luke both were well aware of the problem, as Matthew worked for the Romans as a tax-collector and Luke was a well educated and traveled Gentile. It is for that reason that Matthew and Luke both traced Jesus' heritage at least to Abraham, and quoted the Hebrew Scriptures extensively to "show" that Christianity is an extension, a fulfillment, of the Jewish faith, and this expanded continuation of a *collegium licitum* had been anticipated by the Jewish prophets long before Rome controlled Palestine. Therefore, the Gospel writers claimed legality for the Christian faith. Christian apologists relied heavily upon this argument until Constantine issued a tolerance for Christianity and by 325 declared it a collegium licitum. By this time Christians were using such passages of "prophecy fulfillment" to "prove" the validity of their religion against the other religions, and even after becoming legal they continued to use such Hebrew Scriptures that way, even if it meant mangling the original meaning of those very same Scriptures. This diversion is to answer the often asked question in Bible classes why the Christians were persecuted by Roman officials and so many other "imported" religions were not. Now is the time to look as the vast amount of imported religions that were available for the Roman who was not happy with his own traditional gods. The initial greatest of Roman gods was Jupiter, and it is possible that even he was borrowed and just wore "Roman theological clothing". He was the Sky-God, the Father of All, who is a combination of Dyaus Pitar, Dies-piter, and Father Zeus (Zeus-pater sounds very close to Jupiter). He rose to be Supreme God of the Romans and was often referred to as Jupiter Optimus Maximus (Jupiter, the Best and Greatest), and for engraving it was simply IOM (J and I were the same). Later a Triad, as in many religions, was formed by Jupiter, Juno (his wife), and Minerva (comparable to the Greek Zeus, Dione, and Pallas). But whatever happened thereafter, Jupiter was always known as Father Jupiter, as He was the Father of Rome.

Sarapis was imported from Egypt, and, as mentioned above was based upon Osiris and Isis popularity mingled with the Egyptian god, Apis, and was initially called Osorapis, and later contracted to Sarapis, It alone with a separate cult of Isis gave an intimacy to the relationship between the Roman believers and God that the state religions did not give. Isis also gave to women throughout the entire Empire a god who could relate to women, as wife, as mother, and simply as being female. She was greatly loved and adored almost as much within the Roman Empire as she was in her ancient homeland, Egypt. The Sun God was also worshipped widely wherever the Romans established themselves. This Sun God too came from all other cultures: Aton in Egypt, Marduk of Babylon was originally a Sun-god, Shamash from Mesopotamia, Ahura

Mazda from Persia, and Helios was also a Greek Sun-god. Eventually the Sun God of Rome took on the character of a Sun-god that came from India through Persia called Mithras, and was known as the Unconquerable Sun and was the favored god of Constantine until he became a Christian and even then for many years the coins he issued as Emperor had Christian symbols on one side and Mithraic symbols (SOLI INVICTO COMITI) on the other. Both gods were honored because both had served him well in his political and military career by which he ended up as the Emperor of Rome.

Many of the more personal gods were gods that were called upon for a particular event, they were functionaries. The Lars Familiaris safeguarded the land upon which stood the house, and gave security to the family. The Numina were gods of agricultural benefit, helping with the plowing, the sowing, and the reaping of the harvest. Marriage was considered a dangerous period, for it was the mixing of two different families who might have gods who were in conflict with each other. When the bride entered into the groom's house, the house gods might attack her if she came in by her own power. But to show his household gods that she was his sexual companion to provide new life for the household, and was entering with his consent, he carried her over the threshold of the entrance door to his house. One does not want to rile up the household Numina.

There were other gods who appeared briefly at dangerous times during childbirth. Below they and their function are described, when their function is completed they quickly disappear causing the Germans to refer to them as Augenblickgoetter (gods present only during the blinking of the eye).

Alemona protected the fetus.
Nona and Decima cared for the fetus during growth.
Partula was responsible for parturition.
Lucina and others brought the child into the light.
Intercidona, Pilumnus and Deverra were called upon during the celebra-
 tion of the birth to drive away evil spirits that might harm the new
 born.
Vagitanus produced the first cry.
Rumina helped with the breast feeding.
Edusa and Potina were instructive to eating and drinking.

Fabulinus brought forth the first words.
Statulinus helped the child succeed in his first stand.

Now say again that the Romans had no personal gods! Many other gods
did the Romans accept: Tyche (Greek for "Chance" or "Fortune") whose
chief symbol was the wheel (of Fortune); the fertility gods of agriculture
and rebirth that were mostly from the Greeks: Kore, Persephone,
Demeter, and Dionysus; Cybele the Great Mother who had her ups and
downs with the Roman officials (she was run out of town on
pornography charges--it was a very sensual religion); as mentioned
before, Isis from Egypt; the Hermetics ascribed to Hermes Trismegistos;
Asclepius god of medicine and health; Celtic cults; Judaism; and finally,
after Constantine, Christianity. The Romans were religious, but for their
personal afterlife hopes they looked away from their indigenous gods and
sought others. For in general the inscriptions upon the tombs of famous
Romans show little hope for life after death. Of course the religion of the
Greek philosophers gave the Roman intelligencia their nourishment:
Platonism being foremost, and the offshoots of Platonism (Gnosticism,
middle and Neoplatonism, much of Stoicism, and much of Christianity).
Almost no religion survived for this purpose without some Greek
influence, and that mostly of Platonism: the exceptions were influenced
by Mithra and Osiris-Isis. As such, there is no one theological backbone
that is easily identified that would be designated as a purely Roman
religion that lasted long into the post Christian era, for men, by now, had
demanded that their God be a caring Father, and one who offered eternal
life.

H. GNOSTICISM

Gnosticism was pre-Christian in origin, a Platonically saturated faith
that utilized Platonism, and later in Christian form challenged the more
middle of the roaders of Christianity. Both the non-Christian and the
Christian Gnostics had some things in common: knowledge of the Truth
led to salvation, the Hebrew Scriptures and Yahweh must be discarded in
the quest for the True Father of the Universe, and attachment to the flesh
and fleshly desires are hindrances to one's ascent to the pure life and
truth. The Christian Gnostics were a powerful force in the early Church
and many discussions involved them, their doctrines, and their scriptures.

They were certainly not as bad as Irenaeus made them out to be, and not as holy and unattached to human fleshly desires as they proclaimed themselves to be. Yet, they produced much spiritually filled literature that is quite devotional, uplifting, and even enlightening. The works of both Marcion and Valentinus made dramatic impacts upon the Church at large. Marcion's basic thesis completely discards the Hebrew Scriptures as not only irrelevant, but as a hindrance, to the life of love and the joy of the Gospel. His writings, unfortunately, have been lost, but from his critics one can conclude, with some suspicion about the objectivity of his critics, some of the things he taught. His New Testament, the first "New Testament" to be developed by a theologian, appeared in the Second Century after Christ. He included only some of the writings of Paul and a partial segment of Luke. His two contributions was to make, in an honest fashion, the Church at large to think out the relationship of the Hebrew Scriptures and the Christian Writings. Myself, I am rather partial to his views rather than what the Church did later in tying together both for the sake of a "complete" Bible. As mentioned before, the Church at large was greatly motivated to become legal and make a claim as a very old religion that only now in the person of Jesus was being fulfilled. Marcion's arguments that Christianity was a completely separate religion, not only not depending upon Moses, but in rejecting any allegiance to Yahweh and Moses as being, not only a hindrance, but a misdirection of one's quest to experience life after death and the presence of the True God. Yahweh's creation of the earth secretly under the cover of his mother Sofia, was against the will of the higher heavens and the True God, and Yahweh's jealousy of worshipping the True God was to be rejected. Valentinus, a contemporary of Marcion, was held in high esteem by his Gnostic church in Rome, and he is considered the most influential Gnostic by many, almost acquiring the leadership of the Church at Rome. If one were to seek out the relationship of Gnosticism and Platonism, I would recommend my book *Plato's Gift to Christianity,* and for other and broader aspects of Gnosticism: The *Nag Hammadi Library* edited by James M. Robinson; *Gnostic Religion* (second edition) by Hans Jonas; *The Gnostic Gospels* by Elaine Pagels; *Gnosis* by Kurt Rudolph; *The Other Bible* edited by Willis Barnstone; and Walter Scott's, *Hermetica.* Below are some passages from the Gnostics that show their devotion to the True God. From the Hermetica of Walter Scott:

'That Light,' he said, 'is I, even Mind (NOUS), the first God, who
was before the watery substance which appeared out of the darkness; and the Word (LOGOS) which came forth from the Light
is the Son of God. (Libellus I.6)

But Mind (NOUS) the Father of all, he who is Life and Light, gave
birth to Man, a Being like Himself. And He took delight in Man, as
being his own offspring; for Man was very goodly to look on, bear-
the likeness (EIKONA) of his Father. (I.12)

Therefore with all my soul and with all my strength did I give
praise to God the Father, saying:
  "Holy is God the Father of all, who is before the first beginning.
  Holy is God, who wills to be known, and is known by them
  that are his own.
  Holy are You, who by your Word has constructed all that is;
  Holy are You, whose brightfull nature has not darkened;
  Holy are You, of whom all nature is an image." (I.30-31)

There are many such passages in Gnostic literature, but without doubt
they proclaimed God as a loving Father, who was delighted with his
creation of man, and who wanted to draw near to them and lift them to
the True and Eternal Realm. Yes, there are still some Gnostic Churches
today.

I. CHRISTIANITY

No other religion has emphasized the Fatherhood of God as much as
has Christianity. Prepared for by the Platonic view of God's love for his
creation, his loving care by planting a good daimon (demon) into the
hearts of men to prod them to focus on their return to the eternal home
with the Father and Maker of the creation as well as by posting guardian
lower gods (angels) over them that none of them should be neglected,
Christianity prospered in such a setting, and Jesus consummated in his
life and teachings such a relationship with God, whom he often called his
father, especially in the Gospel according to John. However, he taught
just as much that God was the Loving Father of all people, both
corporately and individually. In his Sermon on the Mount, Jesus referred

to God as man's Father 17 times, and the New Testament Canon, following his lead refers to God as Father 260 times. When one compares the shortness of the New Testament (The Canonized Greek Christian Scriptures) with the lengthy canonized literature of other religions and the fact that God is referred to 260 times in such a brief work, indicates that that is certainly the main theme of those scriptures. The Father knows our needs (Mt 6:8), one is to begin a prayer by addressing God as "Our Father who art in heaven" (Mt 6:9); he is forgiving and gracious, and therefore no need to be anxious, and is always accessible in prayer (Mt 7:11). According to the Gospel of John (20:17ff), some of Jesus' very last words, spoken to Mary Magdalene as she hugged him after the resurrection, were: "You must cease holding me, for I must yet ascend to the Father. But, go, tell my brothers of me, for I must ascend to my Father and to your Father, to my God and to your God." Departure from this earth was to ascend to the Heavenly Father, who was the God of all. Martin Luther, in his explanation of the first article of the Apostles, speaks of all that God has given to man: creation itself, sustenance for all bodily needs, clothing and shelter, protection from danger and evil, and God does "das alles aus lauter vaeterlicher, goettlicher Guete und Barmherzigkeit" (does it all out of pure fatherliness, Godly goodness and a compassionate heart). Evagrios the Solitary reminds us that "He who loves God is always communing with Him as his Father" (One Prayer, 55). August Sabatier in the chapter entitled "The Essence of Christianity" in his work *Outline of a Philosophy of Religion* stated:

> The Father who lives in me lives equally in my neighbour; He loves him as much as He loves me. I ought therefore to love Him in my neighbour as well as in myself. This paternal presence of God in all human souls creates in them not only a link but a substantial and moral unity which makes them members of one body, whatever may be the external and contingent differents which separate them. From the Fatherhood in heaven flows the brotherhood on earth.

> Those who, with Jesus, make it in the arms of the Heavenly Father, accomplish it with strength and joy.

Adolf Harnack in his work What is Christianity? stated that the three main teachings of Jesus, as he sees it, are:

> Firstly, the kingdom of God and its coming.
> Secondly, God the Father and the infinite value of the human soul.
> Thirdly, the higher righteousness and the commandment of love.(51)

Harnack, speaking of the second of the three, stated: "But the fact that the whole of Jesus' message may be reduced to these two heads--God as the Father, and the human soul so ennobled that it can and does unite with him..." (p.63) And he further adds:

> Moreover, the genuineness, nay the actual existence, of religious experience is to be measured, not by any transcendency of feeling nor by great deeds that all men can see, but by the joy and the peace which are diffused through the soul that can say, "My Father". (p.66)

J. ISLAM

There are 99 names of Allah, Allah being one of them. However, Father is not one of them, which to me keeps Islam from developing the human kindness one to another and the feeling of nearness to God. I understand that Allah is seen far beyond any anthropomorphism, yet to reject the symbolic name "Father" because Allah has no consort and no son, seems to me to be overly fearful of anthropomorphic expressions which are necessary for human communication, and a concession for this need ought to be made. After all, many of the 99 acceptable names for Allah are just as anthropomorphic as father is: the King, the Guardian of Faith, the Protector, the Forceful, the Creator, the Judge, and the Nourisher--to name just a few of them. Even the Sufis do not, at least in the writings I have read, use the name Father for God; and, of course, it does not use the name Mother either. One will search in vain for God the Father in the Koran.

K. The Northsmen

In the *Deluding of Gylfi* by Snorri Sturluson the first name of the Highest God is All-Father, and "His greatest achievement, however, is the making of man and giving him a soul which will live and never die, although the body may decay to dust or burn to ashes".4.10 The place, at least for dead warriors, of heaven was in the Asgard level of existence where the incomparably large hall of Valhalla was located, and it became the new home of those who passed from the middle level of existence, the earth called Midgard. The warriors themselves seemed to be privileged in "heaven" to carry on their favorite activity of war through-out eternity, waging war and battle during the day and healing of all the wounds took place during the night, so that the next day the festival of war could continue. Next to Valhalla is Gladsheim (Home of Gladness) and Odin presides there and in joyous festivities welcomes the slain warriors to join him in the festival. There will be a cataclysmic destruction of heaven and earth, but with its renewal good men will live again in Gimli in heaven. Norse theology and eschatology are not either systematic or dogmatic. But Norse theology does see some type of great destruction of the world, and a joyous renewal of life afterward. As to the Father, Odin is constantly designated as such. But the highest Trinity is Odin as foremost, Thor and Freyr. Odin, sometimes called Wuotan, especially among the Germans. In fact Odin's supremacy is so Great in every area where the Norse gods are honored, that Jacob Grimm saw a type of monotheism involved in which all the others were lower gods, and if not actually developed, Norse religion was headed in that direction. He stated in his work *Teutonic Mythology*,

> There is one more reflection to which the high place assigned by the Germans to their Wuotan may fairly lead us. Monotheism is a thing so necessary, so natural, that almost all heathens, amidst their motley thong of deities, have consciously or unconsciously ended by acknowledging a supreme god, who has already in him the attributes of all the rest, so that these are only to be regarded as emanations from him, renovations, rejuvenescences of him.4.11

One can charitably dismiss J Grimm's phrase "motley thong of deities" and still find much truth in what he says. The point of these references is to show that the Chief God of the Norsemen, Odin (Wuotan) was the Father of all, and man was his chief creation and was given an eternal soul by the kindness of the Wise One, Odin.

This chapter ends then having presented man as longing for eternal life, and he came to believe that man too had an immortality within his nature and that it was given him by the kindness of God, who came to seen as a loving Father that wanted his children to enjoy him forever. This longing was probably there from the beginning of man's understanding of himself, but it only slowly began to be expressed, not only as a longing, but as a teaching of the leaders of each religion presented in this chapter. Plato and others following him stated bluntly that man had been made by the Father and Maker for the very purpose of eternal existence and had planted a spirit or soul or demon within man from the very time of his being born as a fleshly human being. This implanted demon reminded each person that he was a child of God and his future was way beyond the limitation of his material existence he was experiencing in his present life form. Such developments had taken or were taking place in both the Indian and the Egyptian religions also. Man's nature partakes, without doubt, of the desire to live forever, and additionally to embrace with joy the Father-God who had made him in the first place. Those religions that teach and convince their followers to believe such give to their adherents a joy and love of God that is beyond the scope of any other human emotions, because it answers the existential dilemma as does nothing else, and gives man a deep spiritual peace.

CHAPTER FIVE

MAN'S ASCENT TO THE ETERNAL

I. THE LONGING FOR THE ETERNAL

From the beginning of mankind he has sought to lengthen his days as much as possible, to retain life, and to avoid death, as much as possible. The yearning for life, especially at the time of death, was very clear in the earliest of human documents that spoke of the human fate. In the Babylonian Gilgamesh Epic, Gilgamesh, after the death of his loved and close friend, Enkidu, sets out to find the antidote to death and the gateway to immortality. Gilgamesh mourns:

> He who with me underwent all hardships--
> Enkidu, whom I loved dearly,
> Who with me underwent all hardships--
> Has gone to the fate of mankind!
> Day and night I have wept over him.
> I would not give him up for burial--
> ...
> Since his passing I have not found life,
> ...
> Let me not see the death which I ever dread.5.1

After fruitless adventures in quest of immortality, hope is given up and Gilgamesh realizes that he is going to die. "Thereupon Gilgamesh sits down and weeps, his tears running down over his face."5.2

Zarathushtra prays for both a long happy life and immortality afterwards:

> And so to such a man will be given
> the best of all possessions...bliss.
> By means of Truth and Your Most Bountiful Spirit
> grant, O Mazda, enlightenment
> and the full measure of the Good Mind

so that each may enjoy unlimited bliss
all the days of his long life (Yasna 43.2)

Answer me faithfully that which I ask You, O Ahura.
How may I obtain, through Truth,
that promised reward
...
so that Perfection and Immortality may be mine, O Mazda?
(Yasna 44.18)

May the Creator of Life
lead us through the Good Mind
to that fulfillment of existence for which we long.(Yasna 50.11)

The Hindus yearned also for the eternal and such evidence is very early in the life of their religious literature. In the Khandogya Upanishad, the Eighth Prapathaka, the Third Khanda, and the Fourth paragraph: (Khandogya Upanishad 8.3.4) it states:

Now that serene being (Self) which, after having risen from out of this earthly body, and having reached the highest light, appears in its true form, that is the Self, thus he spoke. This is the immortal, the fearless, this is Brahman.

In the Aitarey Upanishad, the Second Aranyaka, the Sixth Adhyaya, and the Eighth paragraph (Aitarey Upanishad 2.6.8) it states:

He (Vamadeva), having by conscious self stepped forth from this world, and having obtained all desires in that heavenly world, became immortal, yes, he became immortal. Thus it is, Om.

Even the very earliest of Hindu writings, the Vedas, show the longing that men had to be with the gods, eat with them and their own ancestors, and there to enjoy, in highest heaven, the life of the spirits. Book Ten, Chapter 14 of the Vedas speak thus, in what may be a funeral oration:

Honour the King with thine oblations, Yama, Vivasvan's Son,
who gathers men together, Who travelled to the lofty heights

above us, who searches out and shows the path to many. Yama first found for us a place to dwell in: this pasture never can be taken from us. Men born on earth tread their own paths that lead them whither our ancient Fathers have departed...There shalt thou look on both the Kings, enjoying their sacred food, God Varuna and Yama. Meet Yama, meet the Fathers, meet the merit of free or ordered acts, in highest heaven.(10.14.1-8)

May they ascend, the lowest, highest, midmost, the Fathers who deserve a share of Soma. May they who have attained the life of spirits, gentle and righteous, aid us when we call them.(10.15.1)

To meet one's ancestors in the highest heaven in a pasture that can never be taken away, and above all to meet Yama (the God of that eternal realm) face to face, what bliss! They have returned home having left behind all imperfection and have partaken of Soma in the presence of God. Yes, the prayer of another pleads to Vishnu, "May I attain to his (Vishu's) well-loved mansion where men devoted to the Gods are happy, where men devoted to the Gods are exulting" (1.154) For humanity very early did his soul become the summum bonum. In early Egypt, Third Millennium BC, the average Egyptian saw in the legend of Osiris and his resurrection that for which he and all others longed: life after death. It is hardly by accident that Osiris became the most worshipped God of all Egypt, and the one who was praised with the hopes of eternal life longer than any other god anywhere in history.

Among the Greeks it was Plato who well established the doctrine of the soul and its quest and desire to come to the eternal realm of joy, harmony, and the presence of God. Plato was not the first Greek to teach the quest for eternal life, but it seemed to have come first from either the disciples of Pythagoras or the followers of the Orphic Mysteries, for both taught that immortality was the goal and the joyous fate of the soul of man. In Plato's works there are many references to the soul's longing and its attaining eternal life: these following dialogues speak of it extensively; *Phaedo, Phaedrus, Symposium,* and the *Timaeus.* The longing element of the soul is the love of beauty that God has planted in the soul for the express purpose of driving man back to him, for God Himself is Absolute and Everlasting Beauty, and man will never be fully happy until he meets God face to face and experiences what Christians call the beatific vision. Earlier I summarized the speech of Diotima (as put into the mouth of Socrates by Plato) in which the love seeks out beauty at the lowest level first, i.e. the love of a beautiful body. But then moves to the beauty of all the bodies of humanity, as one is incapable of showing forth all such beauties. Then to step up again, he, by reason, looks upon the soul or the mind (the thinking soul), the true man within, and sees the glory of a beautiful soul, and then again, the souls of all men point him even higher. The fifth step involves beauty in a different light, such as an institution that mends the body so that the suffering becomes well, and then that which gives light to the soul, and to harmony giving laws and then, yet higher, to sciences and mathematics, for they represent in thought the absolute beauty of harmony, balance, symmetry, and with mathematics the truth within its laws never change or fades. Then "Diotima" brings her speech to Socrates with this long climatic statement:

> He who has been instructed thus far in the things of love, and who
> has learned to see the beautiful in due order and succession, when he
> comes toward the end will suddenly perceive a nature of wondrous
> beauty (and this, Socrates, is the final cause of all our former toils)
> --a nature which in the first place is everlasting, not growing and
> decaying, or waxing and waning; secondly, not beautiful in one
> point of view and foul in another, or at one time or in one relation
> or at one place beautiful, at another time or in another relation or
> at another place foul, as if beautiful to some and foul to others, or in
> likeness of a face or hands or any other part of the bodily frame, or
> in any form of speech or knowledge, or existing in any other being,
> as for example, in an animal, or in heaven, or in earth, or in any
> other place; but beauty absolute, separate, simple, and everlasting,
> which without diminution and without increase, or any change, is
> imparted to the ever-growing and perishing beauties of all other
> things. He who from these ascending under the influence of true
> love, begins to perceive that beauty, is not far from the end. And
> the true order of going, or being led by another, to the things of
> love, is to begin from the beauties of earth and mount upwards for
> the sake of that Other Beauty, using these as steps only, and from
> one going on to two, and from two to all beautiful forms, and from
> beautiful forms to beautiful practices, and from beautiful practices

to beautiful ideas, until from the beautiful ideas he arrives at the
idea of Absolute Beauty Itself, and at last knows what the essence
of beauty is. This, my dear Socrates, said the stranger of Mantineia,
"is that life above all others which man should live, in the contemplation of Absolute Beauty; a Beauty which if you once beheld, you
would seek not to be after the measure of gold, or garments, beautiful
young people, whose presence now entrances you; ...But what if man
had eyes to see the True Beauty--the Divine Beauty, I mean, pure
and clear and unmixed, not clogged with the pollutions of mortality
and all the colours and vanities of human life--looking towards, and
beholding converse with the True Beauty Simple and Divine?
Remember how in that communion only, beholding Beauty with the
eye of the mind, he will be enabled to bring forth, not images of
beauty, but realities (for he has hold not of an image but of a reality),
and bringing forth and nourishing true virtue to become the Friend
of God and be immortal."(Symposium 210-212)

That love implanted in the soul that drives man up this ladder of beauties
until the soul reaches God Himself, that Absolute Beauty, was given and
implanted by God himself, to draw, even drive, all men back to himself.
For man could not find peace or rest, until he reached, with his mind, the
beatific vision of God Himself. Plato describes this strong longing of the
love in our soul in various places, especially the four dialogues
mentioned above. Western man's theology has never been the same since
Plato, as Alfred North Whitehead declared a century ago, "All Western
philosophy is but a series of footnotes to Plato."

    That Platonic yearning for the Absolute Beauty shows itself, as does
much Neoplatonism in the Sufi teachings, except that the Sufis,
following Islamic doctrine, do not proclaim God as the Beautiful Father,
yet they do hold on to Plato's doctrine of God's being Absolute Beauty
Itself and to which they long to go. Rumi's words were: "The Lord of
beauty enters the soul as a man walks into an orchard in Spring, and says,
'Come unto Me.'". Robert Frager in his Heart, Self, & Soul describes one
of the states of spiritual development with these words:5.3

    LOVE, YEARNING, INTIMACY, AND SATISFACTION--we
    have one major desire, to love God, to yearn for and feel God's
    presence, to be satisfied only by God's love and to desire nothing else.

The Hindu <u>Shankara</u> born 686 AD and died after a short life of only 32 years, yet in them helped to bring some consistency into the entire lore of Hindu philosophy (actually, because Hinduism's open and liberal respect for different views, an impossible task). In his very youth, after his father died, he wrote of family and all earthly experiences: "All are fleeting, all must change. Know this and be free, enter the joy of the Lord." To him that which is real is only the Eternal that can not change. For nothing, no knowledge, can be truly real if its existence is temporary. One must make a quest to the unchanging and eternal, Brahman. This concept is exactly like Plato's of Absolute Beauty. It is possible that there was some Platonic influence upon Shankara, but not necessarily. Alexander had marched all the way to India and had established Greek culturally centered cities even to the footstep of India, and the Greeks are mentioned several times by the <u>Edicts</u> <u>of</u> <u>Asoka</u>, of the Third Century BC. Today's city in Pakistan called Kandahar was established or changed into a Greek cultured city, and the name Kandahar is their pronunciation of the name Alexander. At any rate there was at one time a mixture of the two cultures in the area, although Indian Hindu culture remained dominant, but sporadically challenged by Buddhism, until its confrontation of the invading Muslims about one millennium later. The longing for God and immortality had from the foundation of Hindu thought in the Vedas was always there, but it probably was influenced some and refined by changing thought patterns both within and without.

<u>Plotinus</u> described this longing for that which is above as a natural function of the way man and the heavenly hierarchy are made in their very being. Each level of existence looking upward and longing for the next level until it has reached the Ultimate One. In that context he wrote: "The Soul (3rd highest being) turns itself to the Intelligence (2nd highest being) as the Intelligence contemplates the One (The Highest Being)...The Begotten always longs for the Begetter and loves It...But when the Begetter is the Highest Good, the Begotten must be so close to it that its only separateness is its otherness."(Ennead V.6). Plotinus' great proclamation to mankind was that it should flee to the Fatherland above, seek out the Absolute Beauty, for he who does not "He is the true unfortunate...and he alone". "Let each one become godlike and beautiful who would contemplate the Divine and Beautiful...so ascending the soul will come..." (V.8-9). Plotinus in a letter written to Flaccus said:

I applaud your devotion to philosophy: I rejoice to hear that your
soul. has set sail, like the returning Ulysses, for its native land--
that glorious, that only real country--the world of unseen truth. To
follow philosophy the senator Regatianus, one of the noblest of
my disciples, gave up the other day all but the whole of his patri-
mony, set free his slaves and surrendered all the honors of his
station...The wise man recognizes the idea of the Good within
him...The infinite, therefore, cannot be ranked among its objects.
You can only apprehend the Infinite by a faculty superior to reason,
by entering a state in which you are your finite self no longer--in
which the Divine Essence is communicated to you. This is ecstasy.

A Platonic Christian work by the name of Pseudo-Dionysius presented man with the same spiritual unrest and a longing for the Eternal.
In his work on *The Divine Names* (593c-d), the author, after describing
the "super-essential Being of God--transcendent Goodness" goes on to
declare: "It is at the center of everything and everything has it for a
destiny. It is there 'before all things and in it all things hold together.'
...All things long for it." Not only mankind, but all the living things, long
for the "super-essential Being of God". The author, speaking of the the
Good who emanates rays down from above bring men to a rational
consciousness of both reality and God himself. Those rays

...abide in the Goodness of God and draw from it the foundation
of what they are, their coherence, their vigilance, their home. Their
longing for the Good makes them what they are and confers on them
their well-being. Shaped by what they yearn for, they exemplify
goodness (696a).

And again he stated: "And so it is that all things must desire, must yearn
for, must love, the Beautiful and the Good...to will whatever it is they do
and will because of the yearning for the Beautiful and the Good...The
divine longing is good seeking good for the sake of the Good. That
yearning which creates all the goodness of the world preexisted super-
abundantly within the Good." (708b-c). The Good who then planted that
yearning in all his creatures to drive them back to the Beauty and
Goodness of Himself. Throughout the works of Pseudo-Dionysius the

Platonic theme is constantly there, that God planted in all things a yearning to come to Him and there find their everlasting fulfillment.

Anselm, in his *Proslogium*, expressed personally his own yearning and longing to be with God and enjoy the eternal realm. In his very first chapter he declared:

> Speak now, my whole heart! speak now to God, saying, I seek thy face; thy face, Lord, will I seek. And come thou now, O Lord my God, teach my heart where and how it may seek thee, where and how it may find thee. Lord, if thou art not here, where shall I seek thee, being absent? But if thou art everywhere, why do I not see thee present? Truly thou dwellest in unapproachable light. But where is unapproachable light, or how shall I come to it? Or who shall lead me to that light and into it, that I amy see thee in it? Again, by what marks, under what form, shall I seek thee? I have never seen thee, O Lord, my God; I do not know thy form. What, O most high Lord, shall this man do, an exile far from thee? What shall thy servant do, anxious in his love of thee, and cast out afar from thy face? He pants to see thee, and thy face is too far from him. He longs to come to thee, and thy dwelling-place is inaccessible. He is eager to find thee, and knows not thy place. He desires to seek thee, and does not know thy face. Lord, thou art my God, and thou art my Lord, and never have I seen thee. It is thou that hast made me, and hast made me anew, and hast bestowed upon me all the blessings I enjoy; and not yet do I know thee. Finally, I was created to see thee, and not yet have I done that for which I was made... From a native country into exile, from the vision of God into present blindness, from the joy of immortality into the bitterness and horror of death...Restore thyself to us.

John of the Cross, laments in his *Dark Night of the Soul*, the fact that he is living in the dark night within and yet longs for the Light to shine in and lift him to God. He hopes that "by means of true mortification" he may "attain to living the sweet and delectable life of love with God" and therefore leave the dark night of his soul and enter`` into the Light of God. For even in the soul's darkest night, the superior part of the soul feels the "keenness of the thirst of love" that he has for God. For it is in "the yearnings of love whereof the soul becomes conscious".

Thomas Browne in his *Religio Medici* wrote this prayer:

Teach my indeavours so Thy works to read,
That learning them in Thee, I may proceed.
Give Thou my reason that instructive flight,
Whose weary wings may on Thy hands still light.
Teach me to soar aloft, yet ever so
When near the Sun, to stoop again below.
Thus shall my humble Feathers safely hover,
And, though near Earth, more than the Heavens discover.
And then at last, when homeward I shall drive,
Rich with the Spoils of Nature, to my Hive,
There will I sit like that industrious Flie,
 Buzzing Thy praises, which shall never die,
 Till Death abrupts them, and succeeding Glory
 Bid me soon in a more lasting story.5.5

In the work *The Imitation of Christ* the following counsel is given to a young believer:

I know your desire, and have heard your many groanings. Already
you will to be in the glorious liberty of the sons of God; already do
you light in the everlasting habitation, and the heavenly country
which is full of joy: but that hour is not yet come.(Chapter 49).

In Kabir's first song, God asks the believer "Where do you seek Me?" and then God declares that He is right there beside the believer. Kabir's second song declares that spiritually there really is no difference among the castes, for they all seek God: "For the priest, the warrior, the trades-man, and all the thirty-six castes, alike are seeking God". Occupation and sexual gender are irrelevant, for all seek after God. Kabir declared in his 29th song: "I brought with me the thirst for the Infinite" and in his 31st song, again he exclaimed, "I long for the meeting with my Beloved".

Meister Eckhart in a sermon expressed this thought: "Know that, by nature, every creature seeks to become like God. If there were no search for God, the heavens themselves would not be revolving...Whether you like it or not, whether you know it or not, secretly all nature seeks God and works toward him."5.6 Soren Kierkegaard laments for the person who feels that he does not need God, for "to be in need of God is no shameful embarrassment, but precisely the perfection of human life,"5.7. Again he stated that the happy man who meets his responsibilities and gives God the credit for enabling him to do such, is not shamed when others then accuse and mock him for being impotent when left on his own, but rather he "in whose heart joy always conquers because he jubilantly, as it were, throws himself into the arms of God in unspeakable wonder."5.8

Auguste Sabatier stated in his *Outlines of a Philosophy of Religion* that humanity naturally seeks God for the sake of ending his limitations, one of which, is mortality."Man cannot know himself without knowing himself to be limited. But he cannot feel these fatal limitations without going beyond them in thought and by desire."5.9 The desire is fulfilled in a reciprocal affection between himself and God. "What can they (men) have in the shape of life superior to the life of perfect and reciprocal affection,--God giving Himself to man (in Jesus Christ) and realizing in him His paternity, and man giving himself to God without fear, and realizing in Him his humanity?"5.10 Man will long for until he receives his fulfillment and rest in his relationship with God; it is in his nature to demand it. Nikolai Berdyaev states of the longing for eternity and God in these words: "Keen yearning is possible in the very happiest moments of life. There is deeply inherent in man a yearning for the divine life, for purity, for paradise, and no happiest moment of this life answers to that yearning."5.11 Longing for the eternal is certainly justified by the fact that for the individual all else passes away, and only that that has ultimate reality can plant an ultimate concern and longing.

Finally, Pierre Teilhard de Chardin in his *Hymn of the Universe* cries out to God:

Receive, O Lord, this all-embracing host which your whole creation, moved by your magnetism, offers you at this dawn of a new
day (in man's history)...In the very depths of this formless mass
you have implanted...a desire, irresistible, hallowing, which makes
us cry out, believer and unbeliever alike: "Lord, make us one."p.13

II. PATHS TO THE ETERNAL

In many people and religions sometimes the paths to the Eternal are simply called The Way, The Path, The Journey, or The Word among many other descriptions of the course that people take to reach the fulfillment of their spiritual longing. Below are seven paths of The Way to arrive at paradise everlasting: Personal Commitment that includes surrender, conversion, and faith; Meditation and Contemplation that includes prayer and devotion; Mysticism that seeks some type of union of the personal soul with the spirit of God; Asceticism as a form of self-denial, denial of earthly pleasures, and a spiritual non-attachment to the earthly realm; Ethics that are based on the IMITATIO DEI, i.e. the effort to imitate God as much as possible in virtue; A Love Relationship between God and the believer, and this sometimes overlaps with much of Mysticism and the Ethical quest; and finally Knowledge.

A. PERSONAL COMMITMENT, SURRENDER, CONVERSION, AND FAITH

For Christians, Jesus is the Way, the Truth, and the Life, and the Gospel of John is foremost in directing his readers to Jesus as the Word of God, the Light of the world that shines into the hearts of men, the Good Shepherd, the True Vine, the Door, the Messiah, the Savior of the world, the Son of the Heavenly Father, the True Bread from Heaven, the Resurrection and the Life, "The Way, The Truth, and The Life--no one comes to the Father, but by me". Commitment to Jesus means committing oneself to following the Way that he has established. "Follow me" means more than a verbal proclamation that Jesus is Lord. It means to commit totally to his way of life; to sell all to purchase the Pearl of Great Price; to put secondary mother, father, sister and brother; to turn the other cheek; to take up the cross; to love others as he has loved them; to obey all the commandments that he has passed on to mankind; "...he who believes in me will also do the works that I do"(J 14:12); seeking first the kingdom (Mt 6:33); being a peacemaker (Mt 5:6); being willing to lose one's life to save it (Mt 16:26 & Mk 8:36); a complete mindset that puts away old garments and old wineskins (Lk 5:36); for "No one who puts his hand to the plow and looks back is fit for the kingdom of God"(Lk9:62). Obviously more people would become

Christians if they actually could find one. But the Way is narrow. Faith means commitment, surrender, a total conversion of thought, desires and action, and sincerely trying to follow the example of Jesus, and only in that way is one saved by faith. Saving faith without works does not exist. It is what Dietrich Bonhoeffer called "cheap grace"; for it very little value in the quest to please God and justify his grace.

Krishna is no less demanding of his followers: for the one who wants to know the difference between good and evil must surrender all his actions unto Krishna, and worship him alone ("he worships me alone") (Bk 11, Chapter 5 of the Srimad Bhagavatam). If one wants the salvation of Krishna he must "take refuge in me and perform the duties of life without attachment" (Bk11.4) --like Jesus' "sell all and purchase the Pearl of Great Price. One frees himself from his evil deeds by "chanting the name of God and surrendering himself at his Lotus Feet" (Bk6.1). Yes, "The path of God is hard to follow"(Bk4.1). The believers are to trust God as their Beloved Companion, and honor him as the most Honorable of all Teachers, and they must bow down humbly and worship Him (Bk3.4). His conversion must be so complete he is considered a new creature, born again, a second birth: "A man is called dwija, or twice-born, when he receives his birth from above" (Bk11.11) Words without a committed life to the new Way of seeing things, a Way inspired by God, will not bring salvation of liberation from one's sins. For, in Shankara's words, "A sickness is not cured by saying the word "medicine". You must take the medicine. Liberation does not come by merely saying the word "Brahman". Brahman must be actually experienced" 5.12

The Sufis, Neoplatonists in Islamic clothing, a splendid and wonderful group of people who are deeply concerned with honorable lives to please the One who gives life to all, often were outcasted and even murdered by the conservative followers of islam. From Idries Shah's book *The Way of Sufi* are the following words:

Mansur el-Hallaj was dismembered while still alive, and is the greatest Sufi martyr. But can you name the person, who cut him up? Suhrawardi was murdered by the law (Islamic), but what was the name of his executioner? Ghazali's books were thrown into the flames, but by the hand of whom? Nobody remembers these people's names, for the Sufis decline to remember the names of the infamous.

Everyone knows the names of Ghazali, of Mansur, and of Suhrawardi. Idries Shah continues and reminds his readers that it is not enough to remember these Sufi martyrs' names, but to remember what they taught, and to commit to such a life of beauty and faith as did the martyrs themselves. Cheap religion is throwing out honorable names, without knowing what they meant, what they taught, and without following their teachings and examples. 5.13

There have been numerous Christian martyrs, that is, those that tried following in a committed way the life and teachings of Jesus. At first, for three hundred years, they suffered sporadically under the Roman Empire, and then, believe it or not, they suffered for many centuries under the church authorities themselves who tried to control the lives of those who did not believe everything the authorities told them to believe. For years the Christian has to admit, "The enemy was us". So much has been written on this, the sufferings of the pious followers of Jesus, that it will not be discussed at length here. The main purpose of this writing is to remind Christians today that faith means following Jesus, not just going to church, giving money, confessing his name and loving our children. It is more radical than that, i.e. it goes to the very root of one's existence (radical is from the Latin word RADIX, meaning root). All committed believers are radical, for all has changed, the way he looks upon life, the way he treats others, the way she shows kindness and mercy upon another, and the way all goals and hopes are shaped. In that way Jesus is the Way for the Christians, and the medicine must be taken, not only spoken. Hegel, in proclaiming that one must enter into faith with his heart fully committed, and not just test the waters with his toes, refers to an anecdote from the ancient Greeks work called PHILGELOS (A Lover of Laughter) in his statement that "This is the same...as the one in the familiar anecdote in which a Scholastic declares that he won't go into the water until he has learned to swim."5.14 The path to spiritual fulfillment is found in committing oneself spiritually, talking only about it does not make one proficient in spiritual swimming. For the "elevation of the human being to God", declared Hegel, is the union of feeling and faith. "Religion is for everyone" and it is "the manner and mode by which all human beings become conscious of truth for themselves".5.15 Again Hegel declared: religion "poses the demand that one should remove oneself 'from finite things' and elevate oneself to an infinite energy for which all other bonds are to become matters of indifference."5.16

Soren Kierkegaard encouraged his readers to turn themselves towards God and to take a step in His direction, that would be the beginning of a spiritual and religious life that would change him forever. God will even help him make that first single step:

> So then, go with God to God, continually take that one step more, that single step that even you, who cannot move a limb, are still able to take; that single step, that even the prisoner, who has lost his freedom, even the one in chains, whose feet are not free, is still able to take: and you are committed to the Good. Nobody, not even the greatest that has ever lived, can do more than you.5.17

William James in his *The Varieties of Religious Experience* described the radical conversion of the mind from a non religious outlook to a religious one this way:

> To be converted, to be regenerated, to receive grace, to experience religion, to gain an assurance, are so many phrases which denote the process, gradual or sudden, by which a self hitherto divided, and consciously wrong inferior and unhappy, becomes unified and con-sciously right superior and happy, in consequence of its firmer hold upon religious realities.5.18

But to experience such a religious uplifting, one must personally take that one step, take and consume the medicine, approach the Being of God. To simply read about religion for the sake of mental knowledge is not enough. Aldous Huxley in his *The Perennial Philosophy*, reminding that to enjoy a landscape or a country site, one must in person go there, simply finding the location of such a place on a map and expecting to then appreciate the beauty of the land is foolish. He stated:

> To suppose that people can be saved by studying and giving ascent to formulae is like supposing that one can get to Timbuctoo by por-ing over a map of Africa. Maps are symbols, and even the best of them are inaccurate and imperfect symbols. But to anyone who really wants to reach a given destination, a map is indispensably useful as indicating the direction in which the traveller should set out and the roads which he must take.5.19

To have the way pictured, mapped or simply described will not give the religious experience, one must get on the road, travel the Way, view the beauties within the trip, and then arrive to realize for oneself the joy of the journey. Such always necessitates a step to be taken, a decision to be made, an effort, and most of all a commitment fortified by faith.

Karl Jaspers declared that Jesus did not prescribe medicine or commitment that he himself did not take. He stated:

> The life of Jesus seems illumined by the Godhead. At every moment he is close to God, and nothing has meaning for him but God and God's will. The idea of God is subject to no condition, but the norms it imposes subject everything else to their condition. It gives knowledge of the simple ground of all things...The essence of this faith is freedom...By believing, man can become truly free...The certainty of his faith in God made possible for Jesus an attitude of soul which in itself is incomprehensible...This independence amid immersion in the world is the source of Jesus' wonderful serenity...He broke free from every practical order in the world...Besides the commandment to follow God into the kingdom of heaven, all other tasks... become meaningless.5.20

That is why I call such a faith a radically necessitated commitment to God and His will, for the sake of the love of God and the hopes of the life immortal. Jaspers then declared that Jesus is the helper of those who seek to follow him, even against the traditional religious policies: "He is invoked by the 'heretics' who take their radicalism seriously." In another work *Way to Wisdom*, Jaspers has a chapter entitled "The Unconditional Imperative" in which he speaks of those radical believers that broke with their overlords and tradition to make real "the purest moral energy in their faith". He refers to others, who like Jesus, paid the greatest price for their radical commitment to the Way that would lead them to God. They knew both how to live and die their faith. He points to Socrates, to Thomas More, to Seneca, to Boethius, and to Bruno. Socrates could not go against his conscience, and drank the hemlock; More bared his neck to the sword; Seneca died at the command of Nero; Boethius like More was executed after a long imprisonment; and Bruno accepted death at the stake rather than betray his personal faith. This section is about faith and commitment: it is not about saying a creed in a church and feeling fulfilled.

Rudolf Bultmann in his *Jesus and the Word* stated: "Jesus knows only one attitude toward God--obedience. Since he sees man standing at the point of decision." Man is confronted by Jesus to make a choice, to believe and be committed and follow the way, or not to do so. Bultmann stated in his *Jesus Christ and Mythology* thus: "Belief in the almighty God is genuine only when it actually takes place in my very existence, as I surrender myself to the power of God who overwhelms me here and now."5.21 Paul Tillich in *The New Being* in talking about the conversion and commitment process that is involved in faith stated: "But faith means being grasped by a power that is greater than we are, a power that shakes us and turns us, and transforms us and heals us. Surrender to its power is faith."5.22

B. MEDITATION, CONTEMPLATION, PRAYERS, AND DEVOTION

Man has always participated in some form of prayer or devotion to powers beyond himself, even when he had no idea as to how he should pray, for it was a natural expression calling out either for help in time of danger, or for fertility in time of draught, for a child to help the parents in old age, for protection from the weather, enemies, or the flesh eating beasts. Man has always fallen to his knees in humility before the natural powers and the infinite sky in either fear or hope of blessing or to express gratitude for being spared another day to live again tomorrow. Some of the earliest prayers and praises in the form of hymns come to us from the Indian Hindu Rig-Vedas. The very first hymn of the First Book in the Rig-Veda calls out to Agni, "the dispeller of the night, O Agni, day by day with prayer, bringing thee reverence, we come:..Be to us easy of approach, even as a father to his son: Agni, be with us for our welfare". The prayers throughout ask for strength and well being, daily assistance, help for the warrior who protects, protection from the evil man, for wealth that brings delight, abundance of livestock and cattle, for the fair fruits of the earth, for friendship, and for children. The earliest prayers seem to be limited to the basic needs of the earthly life, and only later for much more than a long life, that is, for some type of immortality, and then for eternal bliss within the presence of God himself. Of course, when men meditated on and contemplated about his life, and then about its brevity, it was natural to expand the desires of his prayers. To become devotional and mindful of God at all times then became a natural result of such meditation about man's basic being and needs, and then about his highest hopes. By the time of the Upanishads the Hindu had indeed raised his level of concern about his mortality to bring it into his prayer life and his devotion to a certain god was directed in the hopes of passing through death into another form of existence, even if he must undergo many attempts by living many lives, he sought immortality. In the Upanishads, the hymns to the various gods and their temporal benefits are replaced by a search for the ultimate reality that is behind, beyond, or in support of all that is temporal. Focus is put upon the spiritual inner journey of the soul that man might come to self-realization, an intimate relationship with God on a permanent basis, that he might experience and even become part of the Eternal Order. His longing ascends to the ever upward until he becomes himself immortal. The Katha Upanishad (II Adhyava, 6 Valli) his thoughts start at the basic five senses and then move upward, step by step, to immortality:

Beyond the senses is the mind,
Beyond the mind is the highest (created) Being,
Higher than the Being is the Great Self,
Higher than the Great Self is the highest Unborn,
Beyond the Unborn is the Person,
 the all-pervading and entirely imperceptible.
Every creature that knows Him is liberated,
 and obtains immortality.
His form is not to be seen,
 no one beholds Him with the eye.
He is imagined by the heart,
 by wisdom, by the mind.
Those who know this gain immortality.
...
He is the One who is.

A prayer from the Brihadaranyaka Upanishad (I.3.28) reads:

> Lead me from the unreal to the real.
> From darkness lead me to light.
> From death lead me to immortality.

The unreal means death or temporality, and the real means immortality, and likewise, darkness means death or temporality and light means immortality. The longing for the eternal was definitely, not only there in the hearts and minds of men, but explicitly stated in their prayers. The blessed Path that leads to immortality is the goal of the following prayer from the Srimad Bhagavatam (Bk 4, Ch.5).

> To Thee, O lord, we bow down!
> Thou dost charm away
> Life's long dream of sorrow;
> With thy holy name on his lips,
> Meditating with the heart,
> Upon thy divine attributes,
> Man walks thy blessed Path.

Prayer and Meditation are definitely Paths by which man can honor God. The Srimad Bhagavatam (Bk 8, Ch 2) states that "God is to be worshiped with whole-souled devotion and to be meditated upon with focused mind. Feel his living presence, and make obeisance unto him with the following sacred prayer." One of those prayers reads:

> Thou art the compassionate Father,
> Thou art the loving Mother,
> Thou art power, and thou art knowledge:
> Lord of all beings, we salute thee.

A prayer of Zarathushtra reads (Yasna 50):

> May the Creator, as Charioteer,
> teach me how to follow the directives of the Good Mind
> by guiding the path of my tongue through His wisdom.

...
With hands outstretched in adoration,
And with fervent prayer in measured verse welling up from the heart.
...

May the Creator of life
lead us through the Good Mind
to that fulfillment of existence for which we long.

<u>Jesus</u> taught his disciples to pray in this simple but personal fashion:

Our Father, the One who is in the heavens,
Let your name be holy.
Let your kingdom come (among us).
Let your will be generated on earth,
   as it is in heaven.
Our daily bread, give to us this day.
Forgive us our debts, even as we forgive our debtors.
Do not put us to the test, but deliver us from that which is evil.
(Mt 6:9-13)

Jesus further encouraged his disciples to feel free and comfortable when praying to God, for if they as humans know how to lovingly listen to the requests of their own children, how much more would the Perfect and Heavenly Father be willing to hear their prayers, and to grant them their needs (Mt. 7:7-12). As indicated above, God does require that we ourselves exercise the grace of forgiveness to others before we ask God to forgive us, and Mark added "And when you are standing and praying, forgive anything that you might have against anyone, that also your Father in the heavens may forgive your trespasses" (Mk 11:25-26). In another passage Jesus tells his disciples that if someone has a just complaint against them, they should go, settle justly, make reconciliation, and be friends again, and then come and offer a gift to God the Father (Mt 5:23-24). Because of this, prayer to Jesus seemed to be a purifying experience, for man had to cleanse his life and conscience of ill actions he had brought against others. His soul had to put on the proper garments to be invited to the banquet of God's loving presence. Not that God does not forgive more from his gracious nature than because of our worth, but because part of his answer to our prayer and the benefit for which we are praying is that indeed we cleanse our lives of the burdens we load on others and any damage we may have caused them. Thus in faith, which is courageously and trustingly following the path of correctness or righteousness, we can ask God to cleanse and purge us of any spiritual defect, and then we can be lifted up in spirit as though we were clothed in white heavenly garments. God's forgiveness is always real, but we pray that it would be made real in our own hearts and minds, and then the peace of the Lord is with us. Jesus wanted us to get the maximum from our prayers, and that included, not only friendship with God, but with our human brothers--his other children.

As a Platonic-Stoic Cicero spoke of the joy and uplifting of the spirit that comes from philosophic meditation. He describes those who come to Delphi to discuss and meditate the oracles of Apollo given there and contemplate day and night on the meaning of such, that each would know his own mind (know yourself), and from such meditations come the feeling of union with the divine mind, "the source of its inexhaustible joy". For when one contemplates the glory and nature of the gods, he too experiences a fire in his heart that is passionate about becoming also, like the gods, immortal. The soul contemplating the unity and harmony of the heavens, is convinced that a Divine Reason and Intelligence supports the universe and renews it eternally. Therefore, he himself, the meditator, is convinced that his own life can not be limited to this brief span upon earth. As he gazes upward and views such a glorious spectacle and how serenely it appears, he reconsiders his entire being and existence.5.23

Anselm encouraged his readers to meditate upon God, and separated from the world and all its activities, simply to think on God alone, and then the benefits will be great: "Yield room for some little time to God; and rest for a little time in him. Enter the inner chamber of thy mind; shut out all thoughts save that of God, and such as can aid thee in seeking him; close thy door and seek him."(Proslogium, Chapter One). Meditation can bring a soft, silent, and warm joy to the person who has shut all else out of his mind. St John of the Cross described it this way:

All things I then forgot,
My cheek on Him who for my coming came.
All ceased, and I was not,
Leaving my cares and shame
Among the lilies, and forgetting them.5.24

Bernard of Clairvaux, in his *The Steps of Humility*, listed the following as the fruits of contemplation: understanding of the truths of oneself and other creatures, perfect joy, and a type of justice that harmonizes one's will with God's will. The combination of these three: truth, joy, and justice are the rational soul's beatitude. Francis de Sales, in his *Introduction to the Devout Life*, recommended that one find a place of tranquillity, where one will be undisturbed, and daily come to meditation of God in Christ, in order to imitate his life and be uplifted to that height of serenity. Meditation, to him, was the spiritual daily bread that a man must consume in order to live spiritually. Immanuel Kant believed that the only purpose of prayer was to instill in one's heart the burning desire for a greater purity of life, a moral deepening of the soul, and a spirit that is more capable of imitating the beauty of God. His are the following statements from his *Lectures on Ethics*:

Pray is unnecessary, in either the objective or in the subjective sense, where the object is not to induce a moral disposition.

Thus the purpose of prayer can only be to induce in us a moral disposition; its purpose can never be pragmatic, seeking the satisfaction of our wants. It should fan into flame the cinders of morality in the inner recesses of our heart; it is a means of devotion, which in turn is a practice the object of which is to impress the knowledge of God upon our hearts with a view to action. Prayers are devotional exercises...(if one subtracts our self centered wants from prayers)... what remains? Only the spirit of prayer, the sense of devotion, the guideline leading the heart to God by way of faith, by way of the trust we place in Him that He will complete the imperfection of our morality and make us partakers of blessedness.5.25

Obviously more prayers would be "answered", if one took Kant's advice. But many, on a much lower level, still pray for things, even what team is wanted to win a football game. "Good mercy!" Kant would cry out if he saw someone crossing himself before entering the batter's box in baseball, hoping that God would find his success at swinging the bat at this time would be a significant event in the spiritual growth of humanity. Hegel found the most significant thing about meditation is that it brings together, in one's mind, both man and God, and that is the very essence of religion. "Knowledge of God is in principle mediation, because here there obtains a relation between myself and an object, God, who is something other than I am."5.26   Ralph Waldo Emerson expressed views that were similar to those of Kant. He stated in his *Essay on Self-Reliance:*

> Prayer that craves a particular commodity,--any thing less than all
> good,--is vicious. Prayer is the contemplation of the facts of life
> from the highest point of view. It is the soliloquy of a beholding and
> jubilant soul. It is the spirit of God pronouncing his works good.
> But prayer as a means to effect a private end is meanness and theft.
> It presupposes dualism and not unity in nature and consciousness.
> As soon as a man is one with God, he will not beg.5.27

Dr. Charles Mayo, a surgeon at the Mayo Clinic at Rochester, Minnesota, and a son of the founder, declared that in contemplation of the beauty of the universe, the process of evolution, and the continuing increase in knowledge in every field of human study has convinced him of Divine Guidance. "Knowledge of evolution, and of other refinements which have occurred progressively throughout history, makes me more keenly aware of the wonder of all things and more conscious of a feeling of Divine Guidance."5.28

The wonderful miracle in prayer is that it can change the person doing the praying, for he comes to know more about himself when he, in solitude, is alone before God, especially when he expressing a confession. It gives him a time, apart from the crowd and unattached by daily living, in which his inner self is humbly speaking and seeking the truth about himself and his relationship with both God and others. Soren Kierkegaard stated in his *Purity of Heart*:

> The prayer does not change God, but it changes the one who offers
> it. It is the same with the substance of what is spoken. Not God, but
> you, the maker of the confession, get to know something by your
> act of confession. Much that you are able to keep hidden in darkness,
> you first get to know by your opening it to the knowledge of the all-
> knowing One.5.29

Kierkegaard further protests that all people tend to hide behind busyness in order to avoid being alone, lest they find themselves alone with God. Even the clergy arrange a full day's worth of meetings so that they do not accidentally find themselves in church alone with God. He stated:

> Oh, that this talk, far from detaining anyone who sincerely wills the Good, or calling anyone away from fruitful activity, might cause a busy man to pause. For this press of busyness is like a charm. And it is sad to observe how its power swells, how it reaches out seeking always to land hold of ever-younger victims so that childhood and youth are scarcely allowed the quiet and the retirement in which the Eternal may unfold a divine growth.5.30

Thomas Merton made the following comments about the nature and purpose of meditation:

> The distinctive characteristic of religious meditation is that it is a search for truth which springs from love and which seeks to possess the truth not only by knowledge but also by love...and makes our quest for truth a prayer full of reverential love and adoration striving to pierce the dark cloud which stands between us and the throne of God...Let us never forget that the fruitful silence in which words lose their power and concepts escape our grasp is perhaps the perfection of meditation..The proper atmosphere of meditation is one of tranquillity and peace and balance. The mind should be able to give itself to simple and peaceful reflection. Intellectual brilliance is never required. The will should find itself directed toward the good and strengthened in its desire for union with God. It does not have to feel itself enkindled with raptures of ardent love. A good meditation may well be quite "dry" and "cold" and "dark".5.31

Man can stand alone before God, directly and personally. What a rich thought for us! No mediators are needed. This is a point driven home by Karl Jaspers when he declared:

> This reality is accessible to existence through the orientation toward God that lies at its source. Hence faith in God, springing as it does

> from the source, resists any mediation. This faith is not laid down
> in any definite articles of faith applicable to all men or in any
> historical reality which mediates between man and God and
> is the same for all men. The individual, always in his own histor-
> icity, stands rather in an immediate, independent relation to God
> that requires no intermediary.5.32

Meditation, contemplation, prayer, and devotion are terms that express an individual's conscious act of separating himself from all others, all human activities, and all human desires and passions, so that he or she may be alone before God in silence and tranquillity in order to see himself or herself more deeply, more spiritually, and as part of a greater whole in a context that is within his personal relationship with the Creator and Lover of his soul. To find himself alone before his Heavenly Father lifts him up above all hindrances into a state in which he finds his greatest dignity and identity as a human being. It can be a sobering state, a joyous one--even an ecstatic one, a humbling one, or simply a serene one in which all else at the moment seems irrelevant. Without such a personal activity religion loses it glory and power and beauty, and the soul never truly finds himself within his brief experience of life in the flesh. A more intense form of meditation is found among those who have been classified as mystics, and it is now time to turn to them and to explore the heights to which their spiritual quests have taken them.

C. MYSTICISM

The entire realm of mysticism is certainly one of the most intellectually vague, criticized by many of the more dogmatic minds, beyond logic and therefore a suspicious field of inquiry to the logical, thought to be self-induced visions of euphoria by some in psychology, and, in general, thought to be a break-down of normal representations of spiritual experiences and in consequence only exaggerated feelings, and finally thought to be and declared to be "heretical" by the fundamentalists of all religions--because the mystics seem to break down the barriers that separate religions, and that is seen as a gross evil to the fundamentalists of those desiring to claim their symbols of faith to be the only valid paths to God. Nevertheless, based on the works of love and the gentleness of spirit of many of the mystics, one must be open minded enough to give them a fair hearing. Jesus himself said that if one does not believe his words then judge him by his works: "Believe me that I am in the Father and the Father in me; or else believe me for the sake of the works themselves" (J 14:11). For the mystics, religion is not a code or heavy laden theological statements, but a personal insight into reality and a subsequent experience caused by that insight that itself causes a new and more beautiful vision of life accompanied by a more humane and gentle life of virtue, including love and grace practiced on a grand scale. William James in his book *Varieties of Religious Experience* proposed that the basic ingredient to judging the validity of a religious experience is the life that is lived afterward in regard to its beauty and social value. For instance, if a man were to declare that he was God or Napoleon, but had to be committed to a psychiatric ward because he could not make life work for himself and was a dangerous burden to society, that would invalidate his claim to be God or Napoleon, or even to have been selected as a spokesman for either. However, if a person claimed a vision or embrace of a divine sort, and afterwards lived like Francis of Assisi, Dag Hammersjoeld, or Albert Schweitzer with a cause for the benefit of others that was approached in a spirited, kind, committed and rational way and that resulted in some great service to humanity, then how is it possible to declare his mystical experience to be a fraud, and therefore, not to be honored or respected. And how much worse for the Church to declare such a one a heretic and burn him or her at the stake! Jesus again declared that by one's works (fruits) one will know what kind of person a man is, and it is by that that he is to be judged (Mt 7:20). For a healthy tree (person) brings forth good fruits, but a sick tree (person) does not bear good fruits. The results of the mystical experience then are the following: the person has a new vision of life, has a more devout and kindly character, has a mission that betters the lot of at least a portion of humanity, is open to all people without the artificial barriers that custom has created, has an inner peace, power and joy that display themselves in a happy countenance. To speak even briefly of the many mystics that have graced mankind is impossible, but a few shall be mentioned along with some of their words. Richard Maurice Bucke was one of the first to speak of mystics and their *Cosmic Consciousness* and published his book by that name in 1900. The people he mentioned who claimed to have such experiences included: Gautama the Buddha--the enlightenment under the Bodhi Tree (called Bo Tree), Jesus the Christ--The Forty Days in the Wilderness, The Transfiguration and many passages in the Gospel of John (I and the Father are One), Paul of Tarsus (the experience on the road to Damascus, where only he among his company "heard the voice"), Plotinus (ascended up the scale of spirituality even passing the Intellect--the NOUS, until he had communion with God and experienced the touch of primeval Being Itself), Dante who will be discussed later, John Yepes, often called John of the Cross, who spoke of an illumination while he was in prison, and many others did he speak of. In each case a great spiritual experience was felt, and in each case the person returned to society with a new spiritual power to serve others and to lead others. There are many Christian mystics, both in the West and the East, and, in the West both men and women--about equally divided, and all seemed to follow a similar pattern of a more fruitful and more loving life after their proclaimed experience. The best way to let them have their say, is simply to read what they did and what they wrote. Mystics also are present in Hinduism, Judaism, and even Islam (the Sufis). Sometimes they seem to express their experiences with God in a way that offends the conservative mind--Teresa of Avila seemed to clothe her experience with Christ in words that symbolized a sensual love affair (Ruysbroek and John of the Cross did likewise), but it is necessary to remember that they are to be understood spiritually or allegorically (as most people interpret the Song of Solomon in the Hebrew Scriptures).

Here I would like to present the basics of mysticism according to four authors in chronological order: William James from his *The Varieties of Religious Experience*; Evelyn Underhill from her *Mystics of the Chruch*; F.C. Happold from his *Mysticism*; and a book edited by Barry W. Holtz called *Back to the Sources: Reading the Classic Jewish Texts*. According to William James there are four basic marks of mysticism: ineffability, noetic quality, transiency, and passivity. It is an experience then that is indescribable, a high state of knowing, momentary, and most often the person is passive and receives the vision or illumination from above. Evelyn Underhill makes the following statements about mysticism.

Mysticism, according to its historical and psychological definitions, is the direct intuition or experience of God; and a mystic is a person who has, to a greater or less degree, such a direct experience--one whose religion and life are centered, not merely on an accepted

belief or practice, but on that which he regards as first-hand personal knowledge. In Greek religion, from which the word comes to
us, the mystae were those initiates of the "mysteries" who were
believed to have received the vision of the god, and with it a new
and higher life...It is found in experience that this communion
(with God), in all its varying forms and degrees, is always a communion of love.5.34

Not only the act of contemplation, the vision or state of consciousness in which the soul of the great mystic realizes God, but many
humbler and dimmer experiences of prayer, in which the little
human spirit truly feels the presence of the Divine Spirit and Love,
must be included in it.5:35

F.C. Happold listed seven characteristics to the mystical state of being:
ineffability ("it defies expression in terms which are fully intelligible to
one who has not known some analogous experience"); a noetic quality,
that is, the depth of the experience causes the mind to take on a new
pattern of thinking; transiency, the experience is very limited in time and
one finds himself quickly back to normal life; passivity, the experience
seems to happen to him; consciousness of the Oneness of everything, and
for the theistic experience, God seems to be in everything; a sense of
timelessness, the consummation of the experience blots out everything
else even a sense of time; and, finally, especially among the Hindus the
individual ego (the small self) seems to end and be absorbed into the real
Self, the Atman, and this greater Self is divine.

In an article by Lawrence Fine "Kabbalistic Texts", included in the
edited work of Barry H. Holtz, *Back to the Sources: Reading the Classic
Jewish Texts*, Fine lists five tendencies that define, in a narrow way,
mysticism.5.37

1. "Generally speaking, mystics seek intimate knowledge of the
   divine that goes beyond intellectualization and rational thinking."
2. "Mystics tend to find in *themselves* something in common with
   the divine."
3. (Mystics) "tend to look upon the world of nature as a whole, as
   an opportunity for discovering the sacred. God is often construed
   as being *immanent* in all of nature".

4. "Mystical religion almost always involves a specially *disciplined* way of life."
5. "This special discipline involves using various kinds of techniques of meditation or prayer."

For the Christian mystics, the works of Evelyn Underhill are excellent, although somewhat dated. For a more general study that includes mystics of all kinds, including all religions, I would recommend the work by F.C. Happold, *Mysticism*. One can also read Book Seven of Augustine's *Confessions* for an account of his personal experience. Dante ends his great work *The Divine Comedy* with the Thirty Third Canto of the Paradise section, the last Canto of the entire work with the following:

> Then they turned me to the Eternal Light into which
>   we must not think any mortal vision,
>   however clear, can ever penetrate so deeply.
> And I who drew near to the goal
>   of all desires, ended, as I ought,
>   within myself, the ardor of my longing.
> ...
> For my sight, growing pure, penetrated
>   ever deeper into the rays
> of the Light which is true Itself.
> ...
> In that Light we become such
>   that we can never consent
>   to turn from it for another.

This was part of the way in which Dante expressed his "Beatific Vision" of the Eternal Life that moved the entire universe in gentle harmony by the power of His love. In closing this section on mysticism, I should like to quote William James' words about the subject because they reflect my own station and feelings towards mysticism.

> "Whether my treatment of mystical states will shed more light or darkness, I do not know, for my own constitution shuts me out from their enjoyment almost entirely, and I can speak of them only at second hand. But though forced to look upon the subject so extern-

ally, I will be as objective and receptive as I can; and I think I shall
at least succeed in convincing you of the reality of the states in
question, and of the paramount importance of their function.5.33

That is in the same spirit that I have presented this very brief section on
mysticism. Many have found it to be a valid, spiritual, uplifting path to
experience the Eternal One, who is beyond human logic and greater than
the human symbols (words) can express. May the mystics continue to
experience God so intimately and then continue to bring their newly
enhanced spiritual lives back into the human community and shine some
of their light upon us all.

D.   ASCETICISM, SELF-DENIAL, RENUNCIATION, AND NON-ATTACHMENT

In his book *The Philosophy of the Upanishads*, Paul Deussen reminded his readers that asceticism, as a practice for spiritual enhancement,
was first practiced by the Indians and was evidenced in the Vedas. He
stated:

> It is a tribute to the high metaphysical capacity of the Indian people,
> that the phenomenon of asceticism made its appearance among them
> earlier and occupied a larger place than among any other known
> people.5.38

Veda X.109.4 speaks of some who practiced "severe devotion". Veda X.
154.2 speaks of those (rishis) who have advanced to heaven by means of
"tapas" (tapas is a word that incorporates religious fervour, asceticism,
austerity, self-denial and abstracted meditation). Veda X.136 speaks of a
muni practicing munihood in which an austere ascetic life is practice:
having long hair, dirty clothes stained yellow, put up with the wind with
nothing else on but his natural body, travels the desert path, and working
with things that are most hard to bend. Their faith was made flesh in their
asceticism and it is that faith expressed in asceticism that wins for them
immortality. To them it was impossible to attain knowledge of the Atman
in any other way than by means of asceticism, since spiritual work could
only bear fruits by such.

The <u>Srimad Bhavagatam</u> states that true love of God and non-attachment can only by reached by certain means, and of those means are:
devotion to spiritual practices, shunning the association of the worldly,
learning to love solitude, overcoming the passions, and not speaking
against other religions.5.39 <u>Shankara</u> stated: "The scriptures declare that
immortality cannot be gained through work or progeny or riches, but by
renunciation alone. Hence it is clear that work cannot bring us liberation.
Therefore, let the wise man give up craving for pleasure in external
things, and struggle hard for liberation...Let him rescue his own soul
which lies drowned in the vast waters of worldliness...give up all worldly
activities and struggle to cut the bonds of worldliness." 5.40   But the
Hindus were certainly not the only ascetics, all religions that believed in
a life after death and the hope of immortality, had many within that tried
to show that they would give up everything that was temporal for the
eternal, which, to a man of strong faith, was obviously wise. But the
percentage of those who actually lived the ascetic life were few
compared to all the adherents of a particular religion, even if it protested
that life was short and eternity long for the believer.
    Many <u>Sufis</u> felt the need to be as nothing, as least when appearing
before God in prayer, and there seemed to be, at least to the giver of the
humorous story that follows, a little too much boasting about being
nothing. The story goes this way:

> There was a sheikh who in his solitude while in a mosque, feeling
> the majesty of God as well as his own smallness, cried out to God,
> "O God, You are everything and I am nothing. I am just a small
> piece of dust before You." A student of the sheikh heard the anguish
> and humility expressed by his master, and deeply impressed by such
> lowliness of heart also cried in a like manner: "You, O God ,are the
> power and the glory, everything revolves around You, and I who
> am before You am nothing, and can do nothing without You." A
> beggar who was passing by the mosque heard the cries of the two
> of them and himself felt the same smallness, and came into the
> back of the mosque and tearfully cried out loud, "O God, I am
> nothing." Surprised by the third voice, the student turned and when
> he saw the beggar, he said to his sheikh, "Who does he think he is,
> calling himself nothing!"

Kabir rejected asceticism and proclaimed that man should dance and rejoice in the beauty of this life. He was truly a joyful mystic, and love and life were his paths to God, not asceticism. One of his songs reads:

Dance, my heart! dance today with joy.
The strains of love fill the days and the nights with music,
    and the world is listening to its melodies:
Mad with joy, life and death dance to the rhythm of this music.
The hills and the sea and the earth dance.
The world of man dances in laughter and tears.
Why put on the robe of the monk, and live aloof from the world in
    lonely pride?
Behold! my heart dances in the delight of a hundred arts;
    and the Creator is well pleased.(XXXII)

This is a translation by Rabindranath Tagore whose translation of Kabir's songs are available in the book simply titled *Songs of Kabir*. The reason I mention this is that it shows that mystics and ascetics, although sometimes traveling the same way and share certain routes, are not the same. I also mention it because the *Songs of Kabir* is a joy to read.

During the Middle Ages there were many ascetics in the Christian Church, and, of course, coming out of the Middle Ages, each, such as Saint Brendan, was associated not only as one who practiced a very ascetic life, but also was "renowned for his powers as a miracle worker". It was said of Cuthbert, that even when very young, "put his neck to the yoke of monastic discipline" and later embraced the life of a hermit, and even ceased talking. Evagrios The Solitary wrote:

Do you desire, then, to embrace this life of solitude, and to seek
out the blessings of stillness? If so, abandon the cares of the world,
and the principalities and powers that lie behind them; free yourself
from attachment to material things, from domination by passions
and desires, so that as a stranger to all this you may obtain true stillness. For only by raising himself above these things can a man
achieve the life of stillness. Keep to a sparse and plain diet, not
seeking a variety of tempting dishes...With regard to clothes, be
content with what is sufficient for the needs of the body.5.41

The words of <u>Francis of Assisi</u>: "I am going to marry a bride, one nobler and fairer than any you have ever seen, one that will be outstanding for beauty and will impress everybody else...Lady Poverty."5.42 In the Imitation of Christ attributed to <u>Thomas A Kempis</u> one can see immediately the contempt of the vanities of the world, even other humans. It states: "The greatest of saints avoided, when they could, the society of men, and did rather choose to live to God, in secret. A certain one hath said, 'As oft as I have been among men, I returned home less a man I was before'." 5.43   The author did not identify "a certain one" but the quotation came from a letter of <u>Seneca's,</u> listed as his Seventh Letter. The author also stated, and one can here remember the Sufi story above, "Your unfathomable judgments, O Lord; where I find myself to be nothing else than Nothing, and still Nothing! O weight unmeasurable! O sea that cannot be passed over, where I discover nothing of myself save only and wholly Nothing!" Indeed, to be nothing seemed to be something big among the mystics, well, at least some of them. Of course Jesus did teach that man had to put the worldly matters secondary in his quest for the Kingdom of God, as he made clear in the story of Mary and Martha, the parable of the Great Pearl, and leaving all to follow Him. Yet, he did so more on the mystic level than the ascetic level, for he was always among people, loving people, and serving people in every possible way he could: as teacher, advisor, as physician, and as comforter. Jesus went to weddings and talked about dinners and feasts of joy in times of celebrations. He was not a John the Baptist, the one obvious ascetic in the Gospels. Jesus was even accused of wine bibbing while he was in the company of harlots, sinners, and even tax collectors. I do not judge the sincerity of the ascetics of any religion, but it does seem that some seek to "outdo" even the founders of their religion. I personally could not be an ascetic, but for those who find that this helps them to focus their lives and their loves towards God, then for them this path is helpful and can even be admired. <u>Immanuel Kant,</u> to me, has a more balanced approach when warning of the dangers of being worldly attached:

> The more dependent we are on such pseudo-necessities, the more is our contentment at their mercy. Man must, therefore, discipline his mind in regard to the necessaries of life. If we wish to make a classification of needs, we may call excess of pleasure and amuse-

ment luxury, and excessive self-indulgence in comfort effeminacy. Luxury makes us dependent upon a multitude of enjoyable things. Man becomes dependent upon a multitude of pseudo-necessities; a time comes when he can no longer procure these for himself and he becomes miserable, even to the length of taking his life; for where luxury prevails, suicide is usually common. The prevalence of luxury limits the range of our welfare.5.44

Ralph Waldo Emerson in his essay *The Over-soul*, likewise has a balance of the soul's priority to seek out the Eternal Beauty, leave behind the unnecessary elements of the world's order, and yet see the beauty in the works of God. Some excerpts follow:

Such a thought is the love of the Universal and Eternal Beauty. Every man parts from that contemplation with the feeling that it rather belongs to ages than to mortal life....and instantly we come into a feeling of longevity. See how deep, divine thought reduces centuries, and millenniums, and makes itself present through all ages. Is the teaching of Christ less effective now than it was when first his mouth was opened?....The things we now esteem fixed shall, one by one, detach themselves, like ripe fruit, from our experience, and fall....The landscape, the figures, Boston, London, are facts as fugitive as any institution past, or any whiff of mist or smoke, and so is society, and so is the world. The soul looketh steadily forwards, creating a world before her, leaving worlds behind her....After its own law and not by arithmetic is the rate of its progress to be computed. The soul's advances are not made by gradation, such as can be represented by motion in a straight line; but rather by ascension of state, such as can be represented by metamorphosis....This is the law of moral and mental gain. The simple rise as by specific levity, not into a particular virtue, but into the region of all the virtues....For whoso dwells in this moral beatitude already anticipates those special powers which men prize so highly....and the heart which abandons itself to the Supreme Mind finds itself related to all its works, and will travel a royal road to particular knowledges and powers. In ascending to this primary and aboriginal sentiment, we have come from our remote station of the circumference instantaneously to the center of the world, where, as in the closet of God, we see causes, and anticipate the universe, which is but a slow effect.5.45

Our soul can make progress without attachment to the worldly things and the worldly order, but to negate them and even more to despise them are probably less helpful than enjoying them without deep attachment to them. One can find helpful beauty in every aspect of life and the creation, and such can, and usually does, enhance one's ascent to the Spiritual and Eternal Realm. Strict asceticism, frankly, is for the very few as a viable path to the joy of the Eternal, and the embrace of God.

E. ETHICS, IMITATIO DEI, VIRTUES, AND SERVICE TO HUMANITY

There is no religion in which good works, virtue, imitating God, and doing beneficial services to others do not play a major role in procuring for the believer an eternal life: basically, it is a sine qua non, an absolute essential for salvation. While some segments of the Christian faith claim it is true, such segments have combined the forensic atonement theory of Anselm of Canterbury with a strict Calvinism, and that view will be discussed after the presentation of the teachings of Jesus. The two oldest religions that taught that man was made for immortality, Hinduism from the East (India), and the various faiths, especially Osirian worship, from Egypt. In Hinduism, following the Way (Dharma or Dhamma) and within that Way to present a life of virtue (Karma) was the entire basis of stepping forward towards immortality, In Egypt one's works were presented before the judge who balanced one's evil deeds against a feather to determine if one were to enter the eternal realm of Osiris or not, and that in connection with his confession of purity in which he denied not doing any evil: the so called "negative confession" required him to deny doing any of the 40 possible sins presented, e.g. "I have not committed a sacrilege", "I have not committed adultery", etc. In ancient Israel salvation was directed to the nation and an individual's earthly well being, and not the individual for the sake of immortality. Sin would call down punishment from Yahweh for the covenant was to be kept, and a breaking of it by an individual or the nation called for punishment.

Repentance and Yahweh's loving kindness would bring forgiveness and welfare to both or either the nation or the individual. Salvation, as Israel described it, depended upon the works of the covenant being kept.

Hindu teachings stress good works as the very key to one's future and good works are constantly emphasized: "Do not swerve from Dharma"; "Do not neglect the duties to the gods"; "Treat your mother, father, teacher and guests as gods" (like Jesus' whatsoever you have done unto these you have done unto me), therefore, one is to treat others as gods; "imitate the good works and devotion of the Brahmins"; "This is the rule"; "This is the command of God, and this you should observe." The Srimad Bhagavatam reminds its readers that the real goal is making the man good so that his deeds will be good automatically without any thought of merit when he does them, then karma becomes his. "Thou shalt go beyond both good and evil. Good actions will proceed from thee without any thought of merit, and thou shalt desist from evil actions naturally and not through a sense of evil".5.46 The Bhagavad Gita throughout is somewhat a lecture by Krishna to Arjuna to do the works appointed to him by heaven, for unless one listens to Krishna and comes to him in obedience his soul will not fulfill its purpose and his entrance into heaven will be delayed by another reincarnation. For Arjuna is told to use his mortal powers for worthy work, and such an one is honorable. And

> "Do your allotted task!
> The body's life does not proceed if it lacks heavenly work.
> There is a task of holiness to do...
> You shall do the heavenly purpose and do it well" (Bhagavad Gita, 3)

One must present a right life (one that has followed the sacred path-- Dharma), and then peace comes to the dying.

> "Right life! And, in the hour when life is ending,
>   With mind set fast and with trustworthy piety,
> Drawing still breath within and being calm,
>   In happy peace that faithful one does die,--
> In glad peace passes to Purusha's heaven.
>   The place which they who read the Vedas name
> Aksharam, "Ultimate;" whereto have striven

Both saints and ascetics--their road is the same" (BG, 8)

Krishna will come to those who are constantly true in every good action, with humble devotion worship Krishna as the One, and to the him who has a good mind and is happy within his deeds of goodness (BG 12)

Zarathushtra spoke of purity in both words and deeds, and it is in that purity that one gains immortality:

Through Your Spirit of Benediction,
and Your Supreme Mind,
You will grant Perfection and Immortality to him
 whose words and deeds are in harmony with Truth,
 with the Sovereignty of Mazda
 and the Devotion of Ahura. (Yasna 47.1)

He will have proclaimed the Laws of Mazda if he has bettered material existence through his good deeds, upon which he can ask for salvation. (Yasna 51). Also Yasna 53 proclaims that those who have understood and practiced "the words and deeds of the Good Religion" and have established in their lives the straight paths of the Religion of Ahura, they will receive the God's blessing. When the soul reaches the day of judgment, he will present his good deeds which have come from good thoughts and good words, and it is by means of such acts of virtue that the soul claims his right to be blessed with immortality.

Although Mo Tzu has no real theology and no eschatology, he does teach that Heaven loves mankind and mankind in turn is to love all within humanity. Therefore, to obey Heaven, one is to love all people equally and to work for their benefit without partiality or hatred to any. He taught a universal love, for to obey Heaven was to imitate it, and Heaven loved all people. Mo Tzu does seem to confine the blessings of Heaven upon mankind to blessings received within this present life. Nevertheless, the blessings are gained by imitating Heaven's love for all people.

In the Christian Scriptures works also seem to be the advocate for those appearing before the throne of God. Jesus spoke thus: "Not every one who says to me, 'Lord, Lord,' shall enter the kingdom of heaven, but he who does the will of my Father who is in heaven."(Mt 7:21); and again "For whoever does the will of my Father in heaven is my brother and sister and mother."(Mt 12:50); "Then the King will say to those at his right hand, 'Come, O blessed of my Father, inherit the kingdom prepared for you...for I was hungry and you gave me food, I was thirsty and you gave me drink, I was a stranger...I was naked and you clothed me..etc. Then the righteous will say, 'Lord when did we see you hungry and feed you, or thirsty...or a stranger...or naked and clothe you?...And the King will answer them, 'This is true, I say to you, when you did it to one of the least of these my brothers, you did it to me.'"(Mt 25:31-46). The passage makes it clear that the King will judge men on what they did to the least of Jesus' human brothers. "For those who are accounted worthy to attain to that age and to the resurrection of the dead..."(Lk 20: 35). Many will be invite to a banquet, but those not having on the proper garments (that is clothed in virtue) will be dismissed from the banquet. "Do not marvel at this; for the hour is coming when all who are in the tombs will hear his voice and come forth, those who have done good, to the resurrection of life, and those who have done evil, to the resurrection of judgment"(J 5:28-29). "I very seriously tell you, if one obeys my word, he will never see death"(J 8:51). "We must work the works of him (God) who sent me, while it is day; night comes, when no one can work"(J 9:4). In this passage Jesus includes himself "we must" and later the book of Hebrews declared that Jesus fulfilled his task, his obedience to God, and in that he perfected the way of salvation, and those who obey him and his words, will also come to eternal salvation. "Although he was a Son, he learned obedience (Mt 26:39) by means of what he suffered, and, when he was made perfect, he became the source of eternal salvation to all who obey him" (Heb 5:8-9). If one reads the Sermon on the Mount then one will get a good idea of what one does in order "to obey him". The rich young man who eagerly sought what he must do to inherit the kingdom of God was told to obey the basic commandments of the natural law. But when he thought he had obeyed them to perfection, Jesus asked him to sell his possessions, donate the proceeds to the poor and then follow Jesus. Nowhere did Jesus tell him just to believe something, for in Jesus' teaching only the tree that bears fruit is saved, and only the man who invests his talents receives more. However, Jesus was happy with the scribe who said that there is only One to worship, and to love him with all one's heart, mind, and strength and to love one's neighbor as oneself was greater than offerings and sacrifices. "And when Jesus saw the wisdom in his answer, he said to him, 'You have very little distance between you and the Kingdom of God"(Mk 12:33-34). Jesus also declared that whatever happened in the future his commandments will stand and are to be obeyed, "Heaven and earth will pass away, but my words will not pass away"(Mk 13:31). Within Luke's account of the Sermon on the Mount, Jesus lets them know that their perseverance, their love, their being treated poorly, and their good works will be remember-ed and they shall receive their reward in heaven. In the parable of the Sower Jesus declared that the seed that prospered by falling on good soil represented those who have a beautiful and good heart and upon hearing the word, grasp it and hold it fast to themselves, and with endurance bear good fruit. They are the good soil who have a good and beautiful heart, and it is that good and beautiful heart that determines what they do with the word when they hear it. They were clothed in virtue to begin with, before the word ever came. A beautiful and good heart (EN KARDIA KALE KAI AGATHE) received the word (LOGON) and clutched it like the "pearl of great price", and in endurance (HUPOMONE) bore good fruit, i.e. works of virtue.(Lk 8:15). Those are the people who follow Christ and can call themselves Christians--"Pick up the cross and follow me" is not "salvation by belief alone".

<u>Chrysostom</u>, warned the people of his church that in order to feel confidence in the final judgment, they were to prepare for it with good works, yes, works like the products of the angels themselves.

> Therefore, considering these things,
>   Let us cast out that venom in us,
>   Let us end our quarrelings,
>   Let us make prayer that we may become as we should.

> Instead of living like beastly devils,
>   Let us become as mild as angels;
> And where we have suffered from others and have been injured,
>   Let us consider our own actions,
>   And the reward appointed us for this commandment, and soften
>   our anger towards those who have hurt us.
>   ....
> And so doing we will go through life more peacefully,
>   And when we depart from earth to go towards heaven,
>   May we find our Lord to be as merciful to us as we have been

to others.

...

And where we have slipped into sinfulness,
   Let us be extra forgiving to those who have sinned against us.
For by acting kindly and gently towards others,
   We will deposit much mercy for ourselves when we come to
      Judgement.5.47

Gregory Palamas in his *The Triads* declared that man must produce works of virtue during his life that are in keeping with the Divine will in order to experience heaven. "Such a divine and heavenly life belongs to those who live in a manner agreeable to God, participating in the inseparable life of the Spirit...Such a life always exists, subsisting in the very nature of the Spirit...(and then quoting Symeon Metaphrastes, he contiues)...The glory which even now enriches the souls of the saints will cover and clothe their naked bodies, after the resurrection, and will elevate them to the heavens, clad in the glory of their good deeds and of the Spirit."5.48 Meister Eckhart said that man can only become a "son of God" by means of walking the paths of justice. He used two Platonic themes that one will rise up to God by means of being like God in purity and by the power of love of God. "Likeness and love hurry upward like flames, to bring the soul to its origin, in the One that is our Heavenly Father. So I say that likeness of the One leads the soul to God, for he is One, unbegotten Unity." (*Book of Divine Comfort*, 2). The visible deeds of goodness are the evidence that there is within the soul an inner process of virtue, and that inner process of virtue is from God and is divine, and thus the visible works are the natural expression of the necessary inner virtue. This inner virtue drives man back to God, and is from God in the first place, and expresses its longing for God by deeds that are in keeping with His nature. "Know that, by nature, every creature seeks to become like God. If there were no search for God, the heavens themselves would not be revolving...Whether you like it or not, whether you know it or not, secretly all nature seeks God and works toward Him" (*The Sermons*: 15 "Into the Godhead"). Immanuel Kant also accepts this Platonic doctrine that man is to become like God, even in nature and motive. Man's nature is to be brought to a state of purity where one never has to think about doing good or find a motivation for doing good or do good because one is obligated by law or custom, but simply does it because he is good in essence, just as God does it by his very essence."God's acts are necessarily moral, but not from obligation. We do not say that God is obliged to be true and holy". Kant declared that it is only since the Gospel of Christ that the imperative of a moral law has been shown in its full purity and holiness, and this moral law is laid upon us all. For Kant, to merely profess a belief and expect salvation from that confession, is against every moral law and against the essential nature of God himself. Yet if man is falling short of the law as given in the life of Christ, he will be able to seek aid from God who is indeed a nourishing, forgiving, and loving Father. When man is weak "he must look for divine aid to make up for the deficiency". For "religion has two constituents" honoring God with our deeds of purity and loving God. For "there is the universal duty which devolves upon man of so ordering his life as to be fit for the performance of all moral duties." "The basis of religion must, therefore, be morality. Morality as such is ideal, but religion imbues it with vigor, beauty, and reality." All quotations above are from Kant's *Lectures on Ethics (Eine Vorlesung Kants ueber Ethik)*.

GWF Hegel in his *Phenomenology of Spirit* ties man's identity to the Spirit that has consciousness by means of reason, and therewith man becomes an ethical being. Basically he is saying that Spirit must create "the beauty of ethical life".

> "But as immediate consciousness of the being that is in and for itself, as unity of consciousness and self-consciousness, Spirit is conscious-ness that has Reason...Finally, when this Reason which Spirit has is intuited by Spirit as Reason that exists, or as Reason that is actual is actual in Spirit and is its world, then Spirit exists in its truth; it is Spirit, the ethical essence that has an actual existence. Spirit is the ethical life...as it is the immediate truth--the individual that is the world. It must advance to the consciousness of what it is immediate-ly, must leave behind it the beauty of ethical life...The living ethical world is Spirit in its truth."5.49

Leo Tolstoy when asked what he believed stated:

> I believe the main thing we must know is what we ourselves must not be doing and what we must be doing, to create the Kingdom of Heaven on earth, and that we all know. And if every one of us will

begin doing what we ought to do, and stop doing what we ought not to do, using the light of God we have in us, only then will we reach the Kingdom of Heaven. Every human being in the depths of his heart strives to reach this goal. Christianity leads the way to self-improvement. I believe that moral laws are so simple that people cannot excuse themselves by saying that they do not know the law. They should not renounce their wisdom, which is what they are doing. 5.50

Again Tolstoy wrote in his *The Kingdom of God is Within You*:

According to Christ's teachings it (the true life) consists in the great-approach to the divine perfection, as pointed out to every man and inwardly felt by him, in a greater and ever greater approach toward blending our will with the will of God, a blending toward which a man strives,...Divine perfection is an unattainable finiteness of the human life, toward which it always tends and approaches, and which can be attained by it only at infinity.5.51

From the above examples one can see that the overwhelming consensus of the world's great religions and their greatest representatives believe that the imitation of God's nature, the highest concepts of virtue, the essence of the Golden Rule, social service, and the lifting of the burdens of others while not being a burden oneself, all being based upon a new, spirited, and divine nature within, are the indispensable elements to true religion and the Way of salvation, the Tao, the Dharma, and the truth of the Spirit and the great expression of the man that has a spiritual mindset in his head and a longing for God and Eternity in his heart.

F. KNOWLEDGE

Most religions have some type of code of ethics that have been handed down through the generations, and most of them trace their origin back to either the founder of the religion or those close to the founder and are made sacred by the teaching that they initially were received by God directly or by the inspiration of his Spirit. Their purpose is to give the followers knowledge of good and evil, so that they can choose the good and thus please the gods or the God in question. In some religions there were many gods, that is, immortals, and many of them were not too "good" themselves, and thus some followers were rather skeptical about the verity of the revelations as they were handed down, yet they did believe that God himself was the measure of all things. Socrates was such a skeptic and his dialogues was quest for the truth, i.e. the true knowledge of good and evil. The problem with Socrates himself is that his skeptical nature could not be satisfied with any definition of good or of a particular virtue, and this was man's dilemma: in order to please the One God he had to be good, but he did not know what was good nor how to come about knowing the truth about the essence of ethical living. When his student, Plato, taught that man had an obligation to imitate God, who was the perfect Good, the problem remained, for knowledge of God himself was just as difficult to grasp as knowledge of the Good, that was God. He was the Good beyond essence and existence, and, in Plato's own words, beyond finding out. So the problem remained for Plato and his followers. Finally Plato taught that one could come to a certain correct belief that was not knowledge itself, but did not betray knowledge by turning it over to emotive influences. The quest must be taken rationally with as perfect as possible a dialectical and rational task. This called for a new way of thinking that brought man beyond the limitations of thinking only in the material realm and the thoughts that were planted in the visible world. Man must rise above the visible by a super mathematical logic that was always true and never changing with one's life setting or culture or age, as the truths of mathematics itself never changed. Plato devised a scale of thinking in which a man started at the bottom with the most simple concepts of truth and worked his way up until he found himself seeing things only with a rationally purified mind, and as he went from the seen to the unseen (that which is seen by the mind only), he had made a great step towards knowledge. He had stepped across a line that divided visual truth from mental truth, he had gone up the divided line. Plato believed that there was a world of truth, and ideal world of forms: that is, each virtue, like justice, had a form, and each concept/idea had a form. The visible things one sees are modeled after their perfect forms: for example, one can see with one's eyes many horses, some more perfect or beautiful than others, but one can visualize the perfect horse with the mind, and the perfect horse is the original one made by God in the world of forms, it the first, the ARCHE, and only knowledge of the ARCHE is sufficient to know what the perfect horse is like. The diagram below will visualize the way of Plato's thinking.

Form of Bit	NOESIS (pure know- Ledge)	ARCHAI (original)
	EPISTEME -----> (knowledge)	<------- NOETA (mind in state of EPISTEME)
Understanding of bit's function	DIANOIA (understanding)	MATHEMATICA

The bit	PISTIS (belief)	ZOA (living things)
	DOXA --------> (opinion)	<-------- DOXASTA (mind in state of opinion)
Painting of a bit	EIKASIA (Imagin- Ation)	EIKONES (images)

Let us start with the bit (for a horse). The lowest level of reality is a painting of the bit. One goes up a step and he has the made bit that can function to control the horse and this is a higher knowledge of the bit than just the painting of it. Then one takes another step upwards and crosses into the realm of the mind to the one who understands the bit's function and is able to make a bit, for he is not only a user of it, but one who grasps the idea of the bit. The final step up is the form or idea of the bit in the world of ultimate reality, the original bit formed by God. Those who see only the visible bit, functional or merely painted, are in the realm of DOXA, opinion, and have no real knowledge of the bit, for they have no mental understanding and live in the world of the visible bit. But one who goes above the divided line has DIANOIA, that is, an understanding of the bit, enough knowledge to create one that functions, but not to create one that is eternal, never wears out, and functions absolutely perfectly. For he does not have pure knowledge of the heavenly bit. Therefore man can come to enough knowledge in order to make a bit that will function, and in the same way in every other field of human endeavor, he can have enough knowledge to be functional, yet not have perfect knowledge of the eternal virtue or discipline. When he has an understanding of things and virtues he lives above the divided line in the invisible world of the mind. But when he lives below the divided line, he lives only in the visible world and has no perception of reality, the best he can have is correct opinion (ORTHO DOXA), but he cannot lay claim to understanding and even much less to pure knowledge itself. Therefore, it is the quest of the lover of wisdom (PHILOSOPHOS) to see above the divided line by the power of the mind and to teach his perception of truth and wisdom to others that they may know what virtue is and what evil is. It is then by that knowledge that man can live in accordance to the true knowledge and thus please God. To Plato knowledge is not possible below the divided line and men will only live by his own opinions of things and will only with luck or chance become good. To imitate God is to know him as much as possible, and this is done by traveling up the divided line by rational dialectic until one "sees" (with his mind) the Absolute Good and Beautiful, God himself. To then explain it perfectly is impossible, and therefore, each must make his own journey to seek out the nature and goodness of God before he can presume to imitate God in his life. It is in this way that Plato taught that knowledge is the key to goodness, and all those philosophies and religions that are based upon Platonic thought will have this inclination to desire GNOSIS, knowledge. Both the Christian "Gnostics" and the pre-Christian Gnostics follow this strong desire to know God. The mystics of all religions desire the same, and all Western mysticism is grounded in Platonism by means of Neoplatonic thought that shines most brightly in Plotinus and in Christian form first with Gregory of Nyssa the Capadocian Father. The Pseudo-Dionysius carried such thought into the Middle Ages, and the Sufis carried Neoplatonic thought into Islam. The deep desire to know God as much as possible was for the purpose of knowing his nature that one might be able to imitate his goodness as much as possible.

Among the Hindus also there are statements indicating the importance of knowledge in the quest to become immortal. The Sankhya philosophy stresses knowledge as the best way to realize the Supreme Spirit and the very brief *Isa Upanishad* states that it is he with knowledge who will win immortality. Likewise the *Mundaka Upanishad* states that it is by the peace of knowledge that one's nature is purified and he who knows is liberated and goes to the Heavenly Person, than the high. He who knows the supreme Brahman, becomes also the very Brahman.

In the Hermetic literature, a part of the Gnostic movement-- there is really no unifying principle that unites all Gnostics, except certain trends of thought, and one of those trends is the claim to attain GNOSIS, knowledge. In the *Corpus Hermeticum*, in the First Libellus there is the statement that "This is the Good, this is the consummation, for those who have attained GNOSIS (knowledge). And in the Sixth Libellus it is stated that "if you seek knowledge of God, you are also seeking knowledge of the Beautiful. For there is one road alone that leads to the Beautiful, and that is piety joined with knowledge of God." The greatest evil man can have is ignorance, and the greatest of ignorance is the ignorance of God. The Tenth Libellus expresses the same thought: "And this alone, even the knowledge of God, is man's salvation; this is the ascent to Olympus; and by this alone can a soul become good." Libellus XIII states that one of the irrational torments is ignorance (AGNOIA).

The Greek mystic Evagrios the Solitary in his work *On Prayer: One Hundred and Fifty-Three Texts* stated number 86 this way: "Spiritual knowledge has great beauty: it is the helpmate of prayer, awakening the noetic power of the intellect to contemplation of divine knowledge." Leibniz, however, reminds us of the Platonic teaching that man cannot have absolute knowledge, especially of God, and declares that Metaphysics is a "sort of knowledge of God", and further states that normally knowledge comes from experiments, but that would be impossible in the quest of knowledge of God, unless God should see fit, out of love, to send us a miraculous vision-- and Leibniz does not encourage anyone to sit around and wait for one. Emanuel Swedenborg wrote *Divine Love and Wisdom*, and in the work stressed that both must work together to be of value, for man can love foolishly and he can be wise without love, and neither situation is helpful for man in his attempt to imitate God. "But so as a man does from love what wisdom teaches, he is an image of God".5.52 He also taught that if these two capacities, love and wisdom, were taken away from man, "all that is human would perish". In his *Education at the Crossroads*, Jacques Maritain says much the same: "Thus the prime goal of education is the conquest of internal and spiritual freedom to be achieved by the individual person, or, in other words, his liberation through knowledge and wisdom, good will, and love."5.53 Arthur Clutton-Brock wrote:

> Education ought to teach us how to be in love always and what to
> be in love with. The great things of history have been done by the
> great lovers, by the saints and men of science and artists; and the
> problem of civilization is to give every man a chance of being a
> saint, a man of science, or an artist.5.54

While most of us today understand that to excel in any field like science, literature, history, medicine, music, and archaeology knowledge is an absolute necessity, and to excel in any field one must love the knowledge of that field and devote himself to it. Unfortunately in the field of religion, theology, and ethics people tend to distrust knowledge and almost pride themselves in their ignorance of any serious study in the field in which they say is the most important of their lives. Whether this is blindness, laziness, or hypocrisy, I do not know, but certainly before they condemn the quest of those religious ones who devote much time to the academic study of their faith, the history of it, the beginning of it, its weaknesses and strengths, and the benefits it can offer to the initiated and what the believer then can bring to others, they must ask themselves if their own simplicity is really such a basis for honest faith or, much worse, the judgment of others. As mentioned above, especially in the field of religion, one must love knowledge and wisdom: "You shall love the Lord God with all your heart and with all your soul and with all your understanding"(Mt 22:37). This statement by Jesus is not to be confused with Deuteronomy which stated: "You shall love the Yahweh your God with all your heart, and with all your soul, and with all your might (Dt 6:5). Jesus replaced might with understanding. Jesus used the Greek word DIANOIA, which is generally translated understanding (RSV has "mind"): but what it means is that which goes through your intellect or mind. That is, that everything that goes is to be flavored with the love of God. Mind, Intellect, and understanding are words that point to knowledge and wisdom of spirit. Do not let God go through your mind without thinking about it. You shall love the Lord your God with all your DIANOIA. While this passage at first would remind one of Moses, it should be well understood that Jesus rejected Moses' call to strength in facing the Canaanites, with the Platonic mental exercise of thinking about the Good, the Beautiful, and the Eternal with all one's intellectual powers. Knowledge is to be used as a path to God, as are all the other paths.

G. LOVE

This classification of Love as a path to God is not for the purpose of limiting love to being a path, for it is also the goal and climax of religion to love God and to be loved by God. But since love is also a path to God and to harmony with one's fellow human beings, it is proper to present the subject here.

Mo Tzu lived between the death of Confucius 479 BC and the birth of Mencius in 372 BC, and he probably did his writing and teaching in the latter part of the Fifth Century BC, which makes him a contemporary of Socrates and an elder contemporary of Plato. If this is accurate, then his doctrine was the first to clearly spell out universal love to all humanity even though it had been mentioned earlier by Hesiod and then Empedocles. Without doubt Mo Tzu was the first from China to spell it out in detail and demand it of his followers. His attacks upon the greater nations for conquering the lesser ones, tribal or nationalistic hatred of others, and all forms of partiality made him an object of ridicule by the Confucians, especially Mencius. To Mo Tzu the good man's purpose of living was to promote love and things beneficial to all humanity and to try to eliminate all hateful and destructive acts. All partiality must give way to universality. It is the Golden Rule that Confucius had taught, but instead of within a small group of friends or within the tribe, the Golden Rule was to be universalized. To love all as one loves his father or his own child was the high aim of the truly good man. The truly good ruler will think as much of his subjects as his own child: feeding them when hungry, clothing them when naked and cold, tending to their needs when they are sick, and honoring them in burial. Man's life is quick and passes as quickly as the glimpse one has through a crack in a wall as he is riding along. This is not, in Mo Tzu's mind, a wild fantasy, but rather a workable plan to bring harmony to all mankind, for if out of kindness one gives you a plum, you are likely to share a peach with him. One who loves others will be loved in return. It is true that Mo Tzu did not visualize the gaining of immortality through such love, but his message nevertheless established a path for "heaven on earth", if all men were to follow it during their brief existences.

Among the Greeks it was <u>Hesiod</u> who first wrote of love as being the first born among the gods, for it was the necessary basis of happiness even for the immortals. <u>Empedocles</u> taught that during strife it is love that can bring all things together again; the elements, the gods, and men themselves. Love is the great unifying power of all, and makes them desired by one another, driving out strife and hate. The goddess of love, Aphrodite, blesses mankind by giving them love, as well as blessing the other gods and goddesses with her power of love. Love unites, hatred divides. But it is in <u>Plato,</u> especially his Phaedrus and his Symposium where the power of love attracts humans together, gives society harmony, drives men towards the beautiful, and finally leads mankind to God, who is Beauty Itself. Plato's views of love have been previously laid out in full and will not be repeated here. But chronologically one must respect his place as the great foundation of love seeking beauty in all its forms in the Western World.

In <u>Hinduism</u> also love is seen as the foundation of religion and the quest of knowing God. It is the Karma supreme that lifts man's soul to God and raises the entire level of humanity to a type of divinity.

> The highest religion of man is unselfish love of God. If one has
> this love, one attains to truly divine wisdom. Fruitless is the know-
> ledge which is not love. Vain indeed is all struggle for spiritual life
> if in one's heart there be not love.5.55

In the <u>Christian</u> <u>Scriptures</u> love is also evidence of the one who is a follower of Jesus and the one who honors God. Jesus, it seems, gave only one commandment, at least what he called a commandment, and that was that his disciples love each other: "A new commandment I give to you, that you love one another; even as I have loved you, that you also love one another. By this all men will know that you are my disciples, if you have love for one another"(J 13:34-35). Unfortunately his "followers" have not done a very good job with that commandment, but have given it up for heresy hunting, witch burning, wars of mutual slaughter, amidst much greed, hatred, and envy. Nevertheless, it is by love that all will show if they are followers of Jesus. All other claims to being "Christian" will be rejected by him, for this is the "new commandment" he gives to his followers, and the only one in the form of a commandment. And no one comes to the Father but by him (that is, his way of life, living out his precepts). A "sinful" woman who wept at Jesus' feet and anointed them with ointment, was, despite the Pharisee Simon's complaint, forgiven because of her love. "She was forgiven much because of the fact that (HOTI) she loved much." (Lk 7:47). Paul's exhortation in I Corinthians 13 is well known by most Christians. It puts forth love as the binding force of all other qualities, for man may have faith, knowledge, gifts of prophecy etc., but if he does not have love, then all other qualities and gifts lose their significance. Love is the greatest of these, and will abide forever. Only by love can man imitate God, for God is love (I J 4:7-8). One cannot know God if he does not have love (I J 4:7-8). If a man says he loves God, but hates his brother, he is a liar (I J 4:20). Peter likewise declared love to be essential: "Having purified your souls by your obedience to the truth for a sincere love of the brothers, from the depths of your heart, love each other (I P 1:22).

   The Sufis also see love as an essential feature of the spiritual life. Ibn el-Arabi of Spain stated:

   My duty is the debt of love. I accept freely and willingly whatever burden is placed upon me. Love is as the love of lovers, except that instead of loving the phenomenon, I love the Essential. That religion, that duty, is mine, and is my faith. A purpose of human love is to demonstrate ultimate, real love. This is the love which is conscious. 5.56

The Sufi Kabir, speaking of God as his Lover, proclaimed: "Who will unite me with my Lover? How shall I find words for the beauty of my Beloved" For He is merged in all beauty." (Song 118) This love of God will be found throughout all of the Sufi writings.

Throughout the ages of <u>Christianity</u> there also have been mystics who have reached out to God in the deepest recesses of their souls with ardent and flaming love to be ultimately united with God. <u>St</u> <u>John</u> <u>of</u> <u>the</u> <u>Cross</u> in his work *Dark Night of the Soul* presents a ladder of love in which one may step up the ten steps to reach the climax of human love for God. The first step feels the longing for God, the second one's seeking of God without rest, and the third step of the ladder of love is expressed in the passion for work for others. The fourth step is that of perseverance during suffering that will not permit man to cease his loving of God, and the fifth step begins with heightened anticipation of the love, he tries to comprehend the fulness of God. The sixth step is the act of constantly touching God at all times during one's thinking hours, and the seventh step presses on rather boldly to see God, and the eighth step is one in which the soul feels for and grasps at union with God, holding firmly that no separation takes place. The ninth step is the experience of a burning and passionate sweetness within the soul, and in the final step the soul becomes mentally wholly assimilated to God, all one's being feels united with God so that the ego fades away, and then his ascent is completed. These steps, or variations of them, are taken by most Western Christian Mystics as they are the content of the path or way to God, each step increasing the love of the believer in his quest to feel at one with his beloved God.

<u>St</u> <u>Hesychios</u> <u>the</u> <u>Priest</u>, in a similar way of thinking stated:

Just as the richness that comes from moving closer to God is
evident in the angels, so love and intense longing for God is
evident in those who have become angelic and gaze upwards
towards the divine.5.57

Likewise, <u>St</u> <u>Maximus</u> <u>the</u> <u>Confessor</u> said: "The whole purpose of the Saviour's commandments is to free the intellect from dissipation and hatred, and to lead it to the love of Him and one's neighbour. From this love springs the light of active holy knowledge."5.58 In the Imitation of Christ there is a long oration about the beauty of love in the Fifth Chapter of the Third Book, and part of it reads:

Nothing is sweeter than love, nothing stronger, nothing higher, nothing wider, nothing more pleasant, nothing fuller nor better in heaven or earth; because love is born of God, and cannot but rest in God, above all created things...'My God, Object of my Love , Thou art all mine, and I am all Thine.'

John A T Robinson argued in his work *Honest to God* that love so consumes the nature of man and is so in control of the heart that no other ethical standards are necessary: "Nothing prescribed--except love... (and then after summarizing Joseph Fletcher--approvingly--stated)...It is a radical 'ethic of the situation', with nothing prescribed--except love".5.59 While this might seem up front as a wild overstatement, one must remember that God is Love and therefore, since God certainly does not need any ethical standards imposed upon him from the outside, the person consumed by the Love of God, and living to imitate Him as much as possible, may reach that point also when he can live the perfect ethic simply by following the power of love within him that has come from God, and this is not too far from what some of the mystics have been saying for a millennium. Daniel Day Williams in his *The Spirit and the Forms of Love* speaks of the love of Francis of Assisi in a similar way:

But for St Francis and his followers the spirit of love leads to radical nonconformity amid the patterns of culture with their structures of power and privilege. Love must take form in human service and its source is personal union with the spirit of Jesus.5.60

When a person has a "personal union with the spirit of Jesus" then no external demands of culture are necessary, for the love that is grounded in the spirit of Jesus is beyond such and will need no ethical compulsions. Soren Kierkegaard put it this way:5.61

Only the Good (God) is one thing in its essence and the same in each of its expressions. Take love as an illustration. The one who truly loves does not love once and for all. Nor does he use a part of his love, and then again another part. For to change it into small coins is not to use it rightly. No, he loves with all of his love. It is wholly present in each expression. He continues to give it away as a whole, and yet he keeps it intact as a whole, in his heart. Wonderful riches.

Man has a deep longing for the Eternal, and seeks the embrace of God who gives him both that longing and that hope. There are many ways in which man, throughout the ages, has sought to come to God and fulfill his longing in the hopes of becoming, like God, immortal. There are seven general avenues by which man seeks to come to God. The first is by a faith that experiences commitment, a change in mindset (conversion of priorities), and a surrender of the self to attain the goals end. The second is personal devotion, prayer, meditation, and contemplation by means of which he can stay focused on his path and the goals he hopes to attain. The third is an exclusion of all other values for the sake of immortality and the joy of embracing God, and in this spiritual state all controversies, human problems, doctrinal technicalities, and human vanities are completely set aside as being irrelevant and a hindrance to one's following the path. The mystic focuses totally on God and the joy that is his in the hopes of the beatific vision, even while in the confines of the present material life. The fourth is a way of self-denial and non-attachment to the to the material world to the utmost that is possible, utilizing only those things that are absolutely necessary to keep the body alive. The fifth way is to live fully this present life, but to live it with deep care and respect for all others who are also traveling this path towards eternity. Here one enjoys life and makes every effort to make life beautiful for all others that his life can reach. He tries to imitate the virtues of God and gives himself to the service of his fellow humans and even to all living things. He is ethically charged and rejoices in doing good. The sixth way is the path of knowledge, for it is in knowing that one can distinguish between good and evil, and once the separation is made, then he too can be assured that his ethics are proper and good, and in that sense, he seeks to travel the ethical path as do the people of the fifth way. Finally, the seventh way seeks to unite all the previous ways by being saturated, purified, and directed by the emotion of love. But love is in need of knowledge, of focus, of commitment, and of meditation, but once those are acquired love lifts up the devotee to the highest spiritual and psychological level permitted the human experience, and in this he feels he shares a unity with God, who is Love, and embraces also eternity for love itself never ends. None of the paths can be completely separated from the other paths, for they, indeed, do overlap. But different people choose to make a backbone of their spiritual lives out of one of the seven and use the other in aiding their desire to follow their preferred path to

God and to eternity. Love, in a sense stands alone, and yet every other path must have love embedded in its particular essence. For commitment, meditation, prayer, the mystical longing and quest, self-denial and non-attachment, works of kindness and a high ethical standard, and knowledge gain their vitality and power when fueled with love. This Fifth Chapter has presented the ways in which one comes to embrace God, and the next and final chapter will present the results and joy that one experiences in embracing God.

CHAPTER SIX

THE FINAL EMBRACE OF GOD: FRIENDSHIP
AND UNION WITH THE ETERNAL

This final chapter presents the climatic mental, emotional, and spiritual experiences that occur in reaching the final goal of the longing that
humanity has in its heart for immortality and the embrace of God:
enlightenment that brings a deeper understanding of self, a type of peak
experience, a state of peace and joy, a deep feeling of friendship and love
of God, a sense of union with God in which the self loses its
self-consciousness and its being merged with the majesty of God, the
abandoning the physical and passing through death, and the final and
eternal embrace of God.

I.   ENLIGHTENMENT AND A DEEPER SPIRITUAL
     UNDERSTANDING

     Enlightenment can be an experience that seems a simple mental
concept that is brought to light and understood well for the very first time
to a mental vision that communicates a thought or concept from outside
one's normal thinking nature that brings a much deeper understanding of,
not only the concept, but the entire way a person thinks about himself or
life itself. In this second way of defining enlightenment, the person feels
a definite difference within his soul and heart, because the mental
perception of being has so enlarged his thought patterns that he would
consider any return to his pre-enlightenment mindset to be an intolerable
diminishing of his personal being and of his awareness of reality. This
can be seen in the rational movement of Western society that happened
to man's awareness of himself in what is generally called the Enlightenment of the Eighteenth Century, for ever since that time it would
unthinkable for philosophical thought to go back to the time before the
Enlightenment. The Western mind would feel robbed of its rational
identity if forced to do so, as a society and as individuals. A religious

enlightenment demands for those who experience it the same validity in the spiritual growth of men who, afterwards, are asked to become pre-enlightened once again. Unfortunately, in scientific matters the church in the West did ask that of some of the rationally enlightened people of the Eighteenth century and, as a result, brought upon itself a disrespect that harmed its status and identity. But for the person who has mentally and spiritually dwelt upon certain complexities (or mysteries) of his religion and then comes upon a mental breakthrough as to his own reality and the meaning of the mysteries, he is, in fact, a new being. When one generally speaks of "Enlightenment" in a spiritual sense, one thinks of Siddhartha Gotema, who under the Bodhi tree, found the answers to his questions concerning suffering and death, and thus he became the "Enlightened" one, and therefore could never return to his pre-enlightenment state of mind.

Yasna 43 is the Yasna that speaks of Zarathushtra's Enlightenment and speaks of the bliss and happiness that comes from such an enlightenment:

> And so to such a man will be given
> The best of all possessions...bliss.
> By means of Truth and Your Most Bountiful Spirit,
> grant, O Mazda, enlightenment
> and the full measure of the Good Mind
> so that each may enjoy unlimited bliss
> all the days of his long life.

Then Zarathushtra testifies:

> When the full force of the Good Mind took
> possession of me,
> O Mazda,
> then I realized You as Mighty and Bountiful.

Zarathushtra also confessed that his enlightenment now required him to speak the truth he had come upon to others, for that was to do what was best for mankind. One of the necessary ingredients of receiving the enlightenment was the commission to bring that enlightenment to mankind: Zarathushtra, Buddha, and Socrates all felt that God had called them to this mission in order to lift up their minds and behold the truth that they mind find happiness.

The Taittiriyaka Upanishad also declares the mental breakthrough that brings about new spiritual consciousness of oneself and how one relates to all about him. He finds his identity in his being, in his eating, in his breathing and in all his mental understanding. Max Mueller's translation put it this way:

> He who knows this (that is has been enlightened), when he has
> departed this world (become unattached to the material realm),
> after reaching and comprehending (longing for and understanding)
> the Self (Brahman) which consists of food, the Self which consists
> of breath, the Self which consists of mind, the Self which consists
> of understanding, the Self which consists of bliss, enters and takes
> possession of these worlds, and having as much food as he likes, and
> assuming as many forms as he likes, he sits down singing this
> Saman of Brahman: Havu, havu, havu (an expression of extreme
> wonder)! (Taittirivaka Upanishad 3.10.5)

The enlightened one's complete life-view changes as he finds bliss and fulfillment in eating, in thinking, in the bodily and imaginary forms he takes on, and even in his act of breathing. For in all aspects of living he finds his "self" united with "Self", his being or soul united in the bliss of Brahman. And of this "spiritual" food there is no end "having as much food as he likes", and this phrase may remind some Christians of the sayings of Jesus who proclaimed himself to be the "Bread of Life" who has come down from heaven (J 6), or the "Water" which if man drinks he will never thirst again. Plato often spoke of the mental enlightenment of the world of reality which men could experience by means of rational thought that took the form of dialectic. Man comes out of the darkness of the cave in which he dwelt all of his life by means of rational dialectic and comes to the surface of the earth and beholds the day light, the sun, the beauty of colors and the manifold loveliness of nature. And as above, in Plato, the man is required to return to the cave and bring his enlighten-ed mental capacity to those still "dwelling in darkness". The Jewish people felt they had received, with an understanding of the Torah, a spiritual breakthrough in knowing Yahweh and his laws, and also felt a need in their earlier history to bring forth this enlightenment to those who dwelt in darkness. For their light would shine upon people who formerly dwelt in darkness, and this would bring the nations great joy, and one could declare: "The people who walked in darkness have seen a great light; those who dwelt in a land of deep darkness, on them the light has shined." (Is.9:2). For Yahweh's justice, the Law, would be a light to the peoples (Is 51:4).

In the Gospel of John it is declared that Jesus, that is, his life and teachings are the light of the world, whether or not the world understands that it is so. For his life was the light of men...for in Jesus, "the True Light" that enlightens everyone was coming into the cosmos (J 1:9).

The Greek Christian mystic, Gregory Palamas, spoke much of contemplating the Light of God, which also made its appearance in the life of Jesus. Some of his words are:

> So, when the saints contemplate this divine light within themselves, seeing it by the divinising communion of the Spirit....the mind becomes supercelestial...and contemplates supernatural and ineffable visions, being filled with all the immaterial knowledge of the higher light...it is made beautiful by the creative and primordial Beauty, and illumined by the radiance of God...they are initiated into Him (Jesus), for He is Himself deifying light.6.1

Isaiah the Solitary described the enlightenment of the intellect this way: "If your intellect is freed from all its enemies and attains the Sabbath rest, it lives in another age, a new age in which it contemplates things new and undecaying".6.2   John of the Cross declared that when the light of God illumines an angel, it enlightens and kindles him in love because the angel is already a pure spirit, but when God illumines man he must first realize that he is presently in darkness for "this enkindling and yearning love (of man for God) are not always perceived by the soul". Therefore, man must come to experience the "light" for himself, that is, the awareness of his longing and love of God. Upon being "enlightened" man then is raised to a new life of understanding, of love, and his own longing for the Good and the Eternal within.6.3   In the *Imitation of Christ* a prayer for mental illumination starts out with the simple plea: "O good Jesus, enlighten me, with the clear shining of an inward light, and remove away all darkness from the habitation of my heart"(23.3).

Sometimes, especially in antiquity and during the Middle Ages, the mystics described their mental enlightenments as elaborate visions from above, and a prime example of this is Dante's Canto 33 of the final section, Paradise, of his *Divine Comedy*. For people of antiquity and the Middle Ages, visions were a view of reality, but for us, apart from the mental perception gained, they are, at least scientifically, if they are thought to come from the outside, unreal. But all people are different, and it would do us well today that we try to understand the mental breakthroughs that they did experience, without being so skeptical of the "visions from above" that we negate the validity of the spiritual experience that they did actually have. And even in this modern age, we ought not to be so skeptical that we deny the possibility of God's giving someone a direct enlightenment. Hegel put it this way:

> Among the ancient Athenians the death penalty was exacted if one
> did not allow another person to light his lamp from one's own, for
> one lost nothing by doing so. In the same way God loses nothing
> when he communicates himself.(*Lectures of 1827: Part One, the
> Concept of Religion: 279*).

For the life changes and new views of reality did come with the experiences that they had. For one can not doubt Augustine's conversion and subsequent life, nor the beauty of the life of Plotinus, nor the open love that the Sufi's share with humanity. The beautiful lives of many in the realm of Western Christianity that follow a proclaimed vision or enlightenment cannot be doubted: Eckhart's works of kindness, Francis of Assisi's love for mankind, for all animals, for all nature are the wonderful responses of his spiritual enlightenment, for Kabir's experience of love that made his life a life of love without limits. John Smith, the Cambridge Platonist, declared:

> Goodness and virtue make men know and love, believe and delight
> in their immortality. When the soul is purged and enlightened by
> true sanctity, it is more capable of those divine irradiations, whereby
> it feels itself in conjunction with God. It knows that almighty Love,
> by which it lives, is stronger than death. It knows that God will never
> forsake His own life, which He has quickened in the soul. Those

breathings and gaspings after an eternal participation of Him are but the energy of His own breath within us.6.4

Leibniz when viewing the wonders and joy of Christmas saw it as an enlightenment in man's soul so that "with us on Christmas Eve water is changed into wine". I also like the words of Richard Maurice Bucke that appear near the beginning of his book *Cosmic Consciousness*:

> Along with the consciousness of the cosmos there occurs an intellectual enlightenment or illumination which alone would place the individual on a new plane of existence--would make him almost a member of a new species. To this is added a state of moral exaltation, an indescribable feeling of elevation, elation, and joyousness, and a quickening of the moral sense, which is fully as striking and more important both to the individual and to the race than is the enhanced intellectual power. With these come, what may be called a sense of immortality, a consciousness of eternal life, not a conviction that he shall have this, but the consciousness that he has it already.6.5

Enlightenment is a word that denotes an understanding, mainly of the mind, but also with the heart, or the whole being. Jack Dean Kingsbury, in commenting on the parables of Jesus in the Gospel of Matthew puts it this way:

> True understanding takes place when what is heard (or "seen") [5:28; 13:13] and therefore grasped by the mind touches the heart of the individual (13:19), i.e. his complete inward being (15:18), which comprises both the emotional (5:28; 6:21; 15:19) and the rational self (9:4; 12:34; 24:48). When this occurs, the individual undergoes a spiritual renewal, and the necessary result (cf. "Indeed", 13;23c) is that he does (cf. POIEI, v. 23c) the will of God, i.e. He "bears fruit" pleasing to God (13:23; 7:16, 20). Hence, according to Matthew the concept of understanding describes the nature of the Christian man.6.6

II. PEAK SPIRITUAL EXPERIENCE

Enlightenment and understanding, although permeating the entire person, are more an activity of the mental or rational capacities of man, whereas the peak spiritual experiences are either more intensely emotional or simply beyond the rational explanation or understanding. It often is a happening so far beyond the normal functions and activities of man that it must be handled in a special, or at least, a different, section. The peak experiences of men have been discussed in Chapter Five to a partial degree, but more as a classification of the characteristics of the experience rather than the experience itself. This section will attempt to present the fulness and nature of the experience itself.

Augustine of Hippo had such a momentary vision or experience, as all such peak experiences seem to be quite momentary, experienced briefly like the flash of brilliant lightning that fills and enlightens the entire sky with a majestic power and beauty, and then quickly is gone. In his *Confessions* (Bk 7.17) he speaks of the wonder of briefly feeling a love for God that brought the full beauty of God to him as a magnificent vision in which he received great joy. "Then indeed I clearly saw your invisible things, understood by the things which are. But I was unable to fix my gaze upon them. In my frailty I was struck back, and I returned to my former ways. I took with me only a memory, loving and longing for what I had, as it were, caught the odor of, but was not yet able to feed upon." Another "peak experience" of Augustine was the reading the words of Plotinus which changed his life forever. Peter Brown stated of the event: "It was a reading which was so intense and thorough that the ideas of Plotinus were thoroughly absorbed, 'digested' and transformed by Augustine."6.7 Augustine, while contemplating some theological questions, also "heard" the voice of a child in a sort of chanting in which the voice told him, in a constantly repeated refrain, "Take it and read it, take it and read it", and as he picked up the scriptures the first thing he read was Jesus command to the young man to "go home and sell all that you have" as a prerequisite to following Jesus and attaining eternal life.

Abraham H Maslow in his book *Religions, Values, and Peak-experiences* refers to such experiences in many religions (unless one calls Confucianism a religion: lacking, as it does, personal links to God). He stated: "The very beginning, the intrinsic core, the essence, the universal nucleus of every known high religion...has been the private, lonely, personal illumination, revelation, or ecstasy of some acutely sensitive prophet or seer." But such an experience need not be limited to prophet or seer, but to any "acutely sensitive" believer. Maslow believed that people in general can be divided in the "peakers" and "non-peakers", the former consisting of individuals who are private in their deepest spiritual endeavors and the latter who are more organizational and community oriented in their religious expressions, often bound to liturgy and creeds and other theological formulas. He classifies this difference this way: "The cleavage between the mystics and the legalists." But admitted that often the legalists instead of merely "tolerating" the mystics went to the efforts of persecuting them, for something they themselves did not believe in because they were simply, by their own chosen nature, incapable of experiencing. This is rather sad on two accounts: for the peakers they are persecuted and condemned for the deepest and most joyous experiences of their lives and for the non-peakers they themselves never have the great high spiritual experiences that the total embracing of God offers. Maslow sorrowfully sums it up this way:

> To sum it up, from this point of view, the two religions of mankind tend to be the peakers and the non-peakers, that is to say, those who have private, personal, transcendent, core-religious experiences easily and often and who accept them and make use of them, and on the other hand, those who have never had them or who repress or suppress them and who, therefore, cannot make use of them for their personal therapy, personal growth, or personal fulfillment.6.8

John of the Cross speaks of such experiences as "the purest spiritual sweetness and love" in which the soul "is purged from the affections and desires of the sense" and "obtains a liberty of spirit". He further mentions that, although the experience is indescribable, it deepens and stimulates one's faith and love. Meister Eckhart describes these elements of the peak-experience: "the soul looks at God without anything between; here it receives it being and life and draws its essence from the core of God, unconscious of the knowing-process, or love or anything else. The it is quite still in the essence of God, not knowing at all where it is, knowing nothing but God."6.9 John Wesley spoke plainly about his experience in Aldersgate Street when he felt his "heart strangely warmed" when he heard the preface that Martin Luther had written to his exegesis of the *Book of Romans*. But most peak-experiences happen when one is alone before God: Moses on Mount Sinai, Buddha under the Bo Tree, Paul (even though in a group) alone had the experience on the road to Damascus, and Jesus in the Desert. Kierkegaard, in his verbal assault on the Danish Christendom of his day, accused the priests of loading themselves with such a full schedule of meetings and events (for which they complained about for being overworked) so that they would not find themselves alone in the church for fear of actually meeting God there and not having any group to hide in.

For those who do seek a solitary place and set aside time for God, they are the ones who most likely have the deepest spiritual experiences, of which some may be so intense that their lives are ever captivated and changed by those brief moments. For in those brief moments of spiritual euphoria one breaks the bonds and limitations of normal life, and finds himself liberated from creedal concerns, from human dilemmas and problems, from the terrors of societal life. He is completely separated in thought and feeling to experience the Eternal. Religion becomes full of vitality and joy because it becomes totally personal--I and Thou--and a sacred, momentary, bonding takes place between God and man, which is the supreme religious experience. Most of us, at least to a small degree, do have such momentary experiences, even if they are not as long lasting and dramatic as those experienced by others, but they are real, and they are a blessing that comes with the embrace of God.

III. PEACE AND JOY

A third benefit received from the embracing of God is the pacific feeling of a joyous peace within, a longing for such being satisfied. It is personal and it is deeply embedded in the heart, mind, and soul of the individual who experiences it. The joy comes from the expelling of the restlessness and empty striving that formerly occupied and even tormented the inner most parts of one's being. The Svetasvatara Upanishad (4.11) states: "If a man has discerned Him, who being One only, who rules every element, in whom all things come together and in whom all things dissolve, who is the Lord, the bestower of blessings, the Adorable God, then he passes forever into that peace." Embracing God is acknowledging that God is the desire and ruler of every heart, and this embrace liberates one from all the evils that plague man's mind and soul, and thus gives a calm peace to the believer. "Your lovers contemplate your blissful form, and lose themselves in the joy thereof" *(Srimad Bhagavatam* Bk 2.3). "Blessed are those who know You as their very own, for they shall be at peace" *(Srimad Bhagavatam* Bk 4.5). The 20th Century Hindu scholar, Sarvepalli Radhakrishnan, stated the results of the embrace of God this way:

> The tension of normal life disappears, giving rise to inward peace,
> power and joy...The Hindu term "santi" or peace, which is a posi-
> tive feeling of calm and confidence, joy and strength in the midst
> of outward pain and defeat, loss and frustration. The experience
> is felt as profoundly satisfying, where darkness is turned into light,
> sadness into joy, and despair into assurance."6.10

Abraham H Maslow makes this generalized statement of the peace and serenity that accompanies the peak-experience, and refers to it as the "plateau-experience": "This is serene and calm, rather than a poignantly emotional, climatic, autonomic response to the miraculous, the awesome, the sacralized, the Unitive."6.11

The Christian Canonized Scriptures are full of such expressions that proclaim the peace and joy of God that comes to those who commit to the Gospel Way of Life. John presents these words of Jesus to his disciples: "I leave you peace, my very own peace I give you. This is not peace as the world knows it, for it will not let your heart be troubled or live in fear"(J 14:27). Jesus then told them that the basis of this peace and joy is the Love of the Father which he has brought to them. "If you keep what I have commanded you, you will reside in my love, even as I have kept my Father's commandments and remain in his love. These things I have spoken to you that my very own joy will be in you and your joy may be filled with mine. This is that commandment, that you love each other as I have loved you"(J 15:10-12). Jesus had told them earlier in the Sermon on the Mount "Therefore, do not be anxious asking your-selves what you shall eat or drink or where you will get necessary clothing, this is what others do, for your Heavenly Father knows what you need. Simply seek first to be in the Kingdom of His Righteousness, and all these needs will be given you"(Mt 31-34). Paul reflects the same thought as Jesus when he encouraged the Christians at Rome with these words: "For the Kingdom of God is not comprised of eating and drinking, but of righteousness and peace and joy in the Holy Spirit"(Rm 14:17). And the fruits of the Spirit are "love, joy, peace..."(G 5:22). To the Philippians he gave this advice, "Do not be anxious about anything, but in everything, by prayer and petition, with thanksgiving, let your requests be made known to God. Then the peace of God, that which surpasses all understanding, will guard your hearts and thoughts and keep them in Christ Jesus"(Php 4:6-7).

Augustine, after his much searching for spiritual peace, and finding it in his Platonic Christian faith stated at the beginning of his *Confessions:* "You have made us for Yourself, and our hearts are restless, until they rest in You." He states later in his confession the joy that comes from resting in God: "There is a joy, not given to all, but to those who love You for Your Own Being, whose joy You Yourself Are. This is the happy life, to have joy before You, of Your Being, and for Your own pleasure. This is the happy life, and there is no other"(Bk X). Anselm confessed in his *Proslogium*, "My God and my Lord, my hope and the joy of my heart...I have found a joy that is full, and more than full. For when my heart, and mind, and soul, and all the man, are full of that joy, joy beyond measure will still remain"(Ch 26).

The Koran speaks of the serene joy one has when one is pleasing to God (89:27-30). It is a spiritual serenity, a far step away from our usual emotions, and is a spiritual achievement of ultimate reality, and is content with whatever God brings to us in our lives, and it is rooted in the love of God. Rumi, the Sufi, sees God as the Music Master of the universe, and brings this spiritual music into our hearts: "We rarely hear the inward music, but we're all dancing to it nevertheless, directed by the One who teaches us, the pure joy..."(Rumi, *The Music Master*). Rumi also spoke of his sinking into the Infinite God with the following words:

As salt resolved in the ocean
I was swallowed in God's sea
Past faith, past believing,
Past doubt, past certainty.

Suddenly in my bosom
A Star shone clear and bright;

All the suns of heaven
Vanished in that Star's light.

Flowers every night
Blossom in the sky;
Peace in the Infinite;
At peace am I. 6.12

In *Song LXX* of Kabir, he declares this of the one who has experienced the vision of God, "He who has seen Him and touched Him, is freed from all fear and trouble...his work and his rest are filled with music: he sheds abroad the radiance of love."

Friedrich Schleiermacher in his *Christmas Eve: Dialogue on the Incarnation* puts into the mouth of Agnes these words:

For I do not know how to describe with words how deeply and ardently I then felt that all radiant, serene joy is religion; that love, pleasure, and devotion are tones making up a perfect harmony, tones which fit in with each other in any phrasing and in full chord.

One can conclude that peace and joy are of the higher experiences of embracing God in mind and heart. Religious people from different ideas of "correct theology", when they put aside such doctrinal concerns and the personal quest to embrace God is taken to heart and exercised with all spiritual energy, then the embrace of God is no longer hindered by conflicting concepts and the embrace plants deeply into each heart the serenity and joy that is really beyond words, not possible to be communicated to another, but must be personally experienced. Those who experience this joy and peace do not see much value in using their energies to engage in conflict with those of a different theological mind, especially when one realizes that the other person also has embraced God and lives in that same spiritual peace and joy.

IV. THE FRIENDSHIP AND LOVE OF GOD

All humans desire among themselves to have love and friendship, for without them there is mutual consensus that life would hardly be worth living. They fill every void and bridge every separation, and it is only natural that humanity in its longing for the Eternal, desires the love and friendship of the Eternal God, and the embrace of God that is clothed in love and friendship is, for most religious people throughout the world, the ultimate goal and bliss that can be attained. For who could possibly want more? Hesiod himself declared Love to be the first born of creation, and for us that would mean that it was in Love that the creation took place in the first place. For God, who is Love, sought to create existence outside of himself in order to share his love. God's great universe was born of his own love, and that is why we exist. Empedokles who followed Hesiod refers to the Goddess Love as that Being who, in the midst of chaos and strife, brought creation together in harmony. This Goddess of Love was not only in the creation, unifying it with harmony and perfection, but She also was within the hearts of men that they might be unified within and also united by good deeds of kindness to their fellow men:

> And Love in their midst...Observe Her with your mind; do not sit
> with dazed eyes. She it is who is known as inborn in mortal limbs,
> through whom they think friendly thoughts and do well-fitted deeds,
> calling her Joy and Aphrodite.6.13

In the *Srimad Bhagavatam* Sri Krishna teaches that it is love that binds himself to his followers: his love for them and their love for him. Krishna states: "As gold smelted by fire gives up its dross and becomes pure, so all evil is charmed away from my devotee by the power of my love" and also "Those only who have pure love for me find me easily. I, the Self dear to the devotee, am attainable by love and devotion."(Bk 11.8). Also in Book 11, Third Chapter, the confession is made by a certain Pingala: "Near me is my God, who is eternal, who is the True Lover, in whom are delight and satisfaction, and in whom is all true wealth." Asoka, who was influenced by the Greeks and converted to Buddhism, in his edicts to bring peace to the people of his domain in India he refers to himself as one beloved of the Gods: *Deyanampriyah* literally means friend of the Gods or beloved of the Gods (it is the same with the Greek word, popularized by Plato, THEOPHILOS, and the name given to the unknown recipient of Luke's two works in the Christian Scriptures (Lk 1:3 and Acts 1:1--he wrote his works to one who was a friend of God and one loved by God). Even Mo Tzu who speaks of "Heaven" is a rather vague way still refers to the fact that "Heaven" loves mankind. "How do we know that Heaven loves the people of the world? Because it enlightens them universally...If Heaven did not love the people of the world, then why would it send down misfortune simply because one man kills another? Thus I know that Heaven loves the people of the world"(Part One, Section 26). Here Mo Tzu declares that every individual on earth has the loving care of Heaven, and if one is killed, it will be misfortune for the killer; for love must prevail among the created mankind.

Plato presented God as a loving Father who created the universe and mankind because he wanted to share existence with others. He was never jealous of any situation concerning men, for there is no competitor for man's love in Plato; Plato has no devil or satan or any type of personalized evil. There is only God, his helpers (the lower angels who individualize his care for each person--"that none should be neglected"), and the material world made after his own blueprint of perfection (the world of forms). Plato sees God as one who desires friendship and love with humanity, not only during man's brief earthly existence, but in eternity because he gave man an eternal soul that it might enjoy him forever. Plato used the term THEOPHILOS (friend of God, or the beloved of God) twenty times in his later dialogues. In his *Symposium* he speaks of the union of mankind and God in the union of man's love for the Beauty of God. For God instilled in man's soul this love that longs for God, and since He is the God of Love, or Love itself, it is then to be understood that an imitation or emanation of God himself dwells in man that longs for the fullness of love itself, God. The same is attracted to the same, from the lesser to the greater, from mankind to God. For "Love is the oldest and noblest and mightiest of the gods, and the chiefest author and giver of virtue in life, and of happiness after death" (Symposium 180b). Later in the Symposium, Agathon declares, "The previous speakers, instead of praising the God Love, or unfolding his nature, appear to have congratulated mankind on the benefits which he confers upon them. But I would rather praise The God first, and then speak of his gifts; this is always the right way of praising everything"(195a).This is similar to Jesus' saying that one is to seek first the kingdom and then these other blessings will naturally come. God loves us, and he is delighted when we love him back, and even lovingly forgives us when we pray for things first without thought of expressing our love. From God's point, in Plato, the relationship of mankind with God is one of love, initiated by God himself, who is not only the source of love, but is Love Itself.

The <u>Christian</u> <u>Scriptures</u> speak much of God as both the source of love and love itself. Jesus was particularly concerned that the love that he brought to the disciples would remain in them after he had left them. He prayed: "I made known to them Your Name, and I will make it known, that the love with which You have loved me may be in them, and I in them"(J 17:26). Bringing knowledge of God's love to humanity was the great call of Jesus, the Good News from above--God is the source of all love and He loves you. For God loved the cosmos so much that he sent his only Son so that whoever believes and accepts his message will not perish, but have eternal life. For it was not to condemn the cosmos that God sent his Son into the world, but that the world would be lifted to salvation by his message and acts by which he brought the love of the Father to it. For Jesus was the Word made flesh: the Way, the Truth, and the Life, and all were vesselled in Love (J 1-3).

> Beloved (AGAPETOI), let us love each other, because love is out
> of God himself (HE AGAPE EK TOU THEOU ESTIN), and every-
> one who loves has been generated (GEGENNETAI)out of God him-
> self, and therefore knows God...because God is Love (HO THEOS
> AGAPE ESTIN). God manifested his love to us by the act of send-
> ing his one begotten Son into the cosmos in order that we might live
> the life (of love) through him (I J 4:7-9).

Since God is love, when one is born out of God, he is born into love from love, and is likened to God in nature. His one special Son brought this love to us to show us the love of God and also to show us how such love should function in human form. But all men too are the children of God because they are begotten out of God by his love for them. So man can say (ESMEN TEKNA THEOU) "we are the children of God" (Rm 8:16), and nothing in all creation will be able to separate us from the love of God (Rm 8:39). Yes, not even death, for the final embrace of love between God and man will be forever. That is why love is the greatest of all the virtues man can have, because it is having a spark of God within us, for God is Love.

Augustine lamented that perhaps his love was not only too late but too little to fully enjoy the embrace of God:

> Give me yourself, O my God! Restore yourself to me! Behold, I love you, and if it be too little, let me love you more strongly. I cannot measure so as to know how much love may be wanting in me to that which is sufficient so that my life may run to your embrace, and not be turned away, until it be hidden "in the secret of your face (*Confessions* Bk 13.8).

Augustine was undoubtedly too sensitive about his own failures here, for his concern over the power of his own love is needlessly magnified, for the embrace of God comes from God himself and from the love that God has for mankind. It is God who is Love and God who initiates love among men, and to humbly receive it is to love God back. To pass such love on to others is to validate its power and the fact that the love of God is within us. We do love back, but only because He loved first. Augustine then takes rest in the goodness of God for that is accepting the Gospel. "In your gifts do we rest, and there we have joy in you. Our rest is our peace. Love lifts us up to it, and your good Spirit lifts up our lowliness" (*Confessions* Bk 13.9).

Diadochos of Photiki stated that love shared with God is a state above that of faith because it brings a new reality of God to the heart: "We should know, moreover, that a person energized by God to such love rises, at that moment, even above faith, since by reason of his great love he now senses consciously in his heart the One whom he previously honoured by faith."6.14 For with love, (EROS), one goes out of himself (EKSTASIS) and from the material world into the arms of God. For that EROS is the intense longing one has for Beauty Itself, and only when Beauty itself has been "seen face to face" or, one could say, embraced, is EROS fulfilled. This, of course, is a Platonic doctrine that had great influence with the mystics of both the Western and Eastern Church, but especially with those of the Greek Orthodox Church. Among the mystics the Platonic view of EROS is that it exceeds both PHILIA and AGAPE in its intensity in desiring union with God. Theodorus, the Great Ascetic, spoke these words: "There is no form of virtue through which a man may become akin to God and united with Him that is not dependent upon love and encompassed but it; for love unites and protects the virtues in an indescribable manner."6.15 Maximos the Confessor likewise declared:

> God is said to be originator and begetter of love and the erotic force. For He externalized them from within himself, that is, He brought them forth into the world of created things...which signifies the erotic force. For what is worthy of love and truly desirable is God himself. Because loving desire is poured out from him, He himself, as its begetter, is said to be in movement, while because He is what is truly longed for, loved, desired and chosen, He stirs into motion the things that turn towards him.6.16

In the Teutonic myths Frigg is the highest ranking female god because she was consort of Oden the Highest God, yet among the people, Freya, as the goddess of love, was more honored. Love was central to life itself and among the Teutonic hierarchy Freya, at least among the common people, leap-frogged Frigg in being honored in their hearts. Freya and her worshippers bonded in her love. It is always the God or Goddess of love that binds people of religion with their God.

The Sufis, also greatly influenced by Platonism and Neoplatonism, taught almost a romantic embrace with God, such was the intensity of God's love shared with them. Union, both with the Sufis, and some Western mystics also, was expressed very physically, for God was the Beloved, in whom the lover experienced a complete loss of self while becoming enraptured and embraced by the Love of God. When love binds God with the worshipper, the worshipper loses a sense of self. Baba Kuhi, the first Sufi poet of Persia, declared his lost of self with these words: "But when I looked with God's eyes - only God I saw. I passed away into nothingness, I vanished, and lo, I was the All-living -- only God I saw."6.17 Kabir spoke this way of his love shared with God, and he sounds like one approaching a beautiful and perfect woman of whom he feels himself completely unworthy.

> Now I am greatly afraid.
> So high is my Lord's palace, my heart trembles to mount the stairs:

Yet I must not be shy, if I would enjoy His love.
My heart must cleave to my Lover;
I must withdraw my veil, and meet Him with my body.
Mine eyes must perform the ceremony of the lamps of love.6.18

Rumi put his union of love with God this way. "When one is united to the core of another, to speak of that is to breathe the name *Hu*, empty of self and filled with love."6.19

Meister Eckhart speaks of love as a certainty and an intimacy that bind man with God, and "a man discovers that God is his Friend, and he knows what is good for him and all that belongs to his happiness"(The Talks of Instruction, 15). Eckhart pleaded with his parishoners to open up to God's love and come to him which is really very easy, because of God's great love for his children. "Nobody ever wanted anything as much as God wants to bring people to know him. God is always ready but we are not ready. God is near to us but we are far from him. God is within, we are without. God is at home, we are abroad."6.20 Eckhart then invited his people to come home where God is and to come into the dwelling for no other place is so pleasant or lovely. John of the Cross (John Yepes) taught that God resided happily in man's soul and there embraces the inner being of man. Frederick Schiller in his beautiful *Ode to Joy*, speaks of man's great joy in acknowledging God's loving wings lingering constantly over him, and recommends that man in his festival of joy make a toast to honor God: "Drink to Him whose love abounds, Him whose praise through stellar spaces like a seraphs' chorus sounds, Drink to Him whose love abounds, Praise Him by your joyous faces". How very descriptive of the Embrace of Love and Friendship that man and God share, joy that can only burst out in dance and song, giving a toast to God with one's joyous face.

V. THE EMBRACE'S ULTIMATE MYSTERY
OF UNION WITH GOD

This section is beyond the understanding of many people, as they are hesitant to imply that the great distance between the Creator and the creature does not always exist in some very clear line of distinction. There is, of course, a distinct I-Thou between the Being of God and the being of man and the entire 'created universe'. But there are some who are so deeply in love with the Creator who is seen as their constant friend and companion, and enjoy a friendship with Him that is so intense, that they feel they are like an alter-ego to God himself. Man often speaks of his most intimate mate as the alter-ego or "better half" or "significant other" or some other phrase that implies a merging of their innermost selves and their sharing of such a deep love and fellowship, that they speak of the relationship as an union of being. This can also mean, in the utter delight of the loved one's presence, a certain unawareness of oneself. Often one is so caught up in a beautiful sunset, an exquisite animal giving birth, or a happening of great joy, that for that brief moment the individual is so enraptured that he losses all thoughts about himself. Such an experience as these happens when a person of deep religious intensity feels the nearness of God in his life, heart, and emotional state. This merging of oneself is called the mystery of union that the soul experiences. The <u>Hebrew</u> <u>Scriptures</u> speak of man and wife becoming one, when in physical actuality there is no loss of individuality, yet there is a connotation that is valid. A group of protesters can become as one when they are united in a cause, and feel that they share the same spirit among themselves. Jesus said he was one with the Father, and prayed that his disciples would become one with him and one with each other, for the spirit would unite them in God. The mystical union takes place in many liturgical churches when the "body and blood" of Christ are consumed by the believer, and the Eastern Church often refers to the sacraments as the mysteries (Sacrament being a Latin term, and Mystery being a Greek term). The following passages in this section are to be understood as a mystery or at least a metaphor of a spiritual reality that does happen to the one who is being lifted up in his act of adoration. I hope the reader will gain some encouragement from their testimonies and have a positive feeling rather than to be skeptical and critical of another's deep religious experience.

The <u>Hindu</u> <u>Upanishads</u> often speak of this union that comes from devout meditation of a man as he with his heart and mind constantly adores his God. The <u>Mundaka</u> <u>Upanishad</u> (3.2.5-8) expressed this conviction:

When they have reached Him (the Eternal Self), the sages become satisfied through knowledge, they are conscious of their Self, their passions have passed away, and they are tranquil. The wise, having reached Him who is omnipresent everywhere, devoted to the Self, enter into Him wholly...Their deeds and their self with all his knowledge become all one in the Highest Imperishable One. As the flowing rivers disappear in the sea, losing their name and their form, thus a wise man, freed from name and form, goes to the Divine Person, who is greater than the great.

In Hindu thought it is only by means of illumination that unites us to God do we really become his children, born into in his likeness. It is in realizing our oneness with God that one finds peacefulness and such closeness to God that his personal ego is forgotten in that moment. That moment of illumination is called *samadhi* in Hindu and represents a stage of such union with God that the individual loses himself. It sounds much like the declaration of Jesus that the person who tries to save his self will be lost, but the person who loses himself will the saved. In the words of Swami Prabhavananda:

All cravings leave him. Only one desire remains: to love God and live in complete self-surrender to his will. This pure and selfless devotion is followed by absorption in God, and ultimate union with him Love, lover, and beloved become one.6.21

While this might sound extreme to some Christians, these are the same Christians who sing <u>Fanny</u> <u>J</u> <u>Crosby's</u> hymn "I am Thine, O Lord", in which this union with God is implied, hoping to lose one's will that it might merge with God's will.

I am Thine, O lord, I have heard Thy voice,
And it told Thy love to me;
But I long to rise in the arms of faith,
And be closer drawn to Thee.
...
Let my soul look up with a steadfast hope,
And my will be lost in Thine
...
When I kneel in pray'r, and with Thee, my God,
I commune as friend with friend.

To lose one's will is to lose one's self, and to replace one's will with God's will is to lose oneself and merge with God. When the Hindu states that Brahman is my self within the heart, he is saying with Fanny Crosby, let my will be lost in Thine.

The Greek schools of philosophy, especially the Pythagoreans and the Empedocleans speak of a unity brought about by EROS and its child DIKE, and the spiritual union brought about applies not only to man's relationship with other men, but also with the gods, and all of nature. For the Spirit or Soul of the universe permeates all things, and therefore brings about a natural unity. This is a major theme of the Stoics who see all living beings participating in the "World Soul" or "Cosmic Life". In Heracleitus the mystical union of all is produced by the Logos that orders all and unifies all into a cosmic harmony. The Pythagoreans probably exerted the most influence upon mystical Greek thinking, but certainly the Orphic and Dionysian cults played major roles in extending the thought that all values are brought together into divine unity in the person of God. Plato himself absorbed such thinking into his teachings on the nature of God. Therefore, it is not surprising that it was the Neo-platonists of the West that formed the basis for both Christian Mysticism and Islamic Mysticism (i.e. the Sufis). Plotinus, in discussing the One and the Beautiful speaks this way about "finding" the One, the Beautiful.

> Not in a place, it is found in that multitude of beings capable of receiving It as if it were divisible--quite as the center of the circle remains in Itself while each of the points of the circle contains it and each of the radii touches it. Thus we ourselves, by one of our parts, touch the Supreme, unite ourselves to It, and are suspended from It. We establish ourselves in It when we turn towards It.(5.1.11)

Let us take a look at some of the Christian Mystics who sought a type of union with God by loss of their own will or loss of their self-consciousness because they are absorbed into God during the time of extreme adoration. Meister Eckhart stated:

> A really perfect person will be so dead to self, so lost in God, so given over to the will of God, that his whole happiness consists in being unconscious of self and its concerns, and being conscious,

instead, of God, in knowing nothing and wishing to know nothing except the will and truth of God, or "knowing God".6.22

To Eckhart such happens when "he is wrapped up in God's love". From his Tractate II he stated: "O wonder of wonders! When I think of the union of the soul with God! He makes the soul to flow out of herself in joyful ecstasy, for no named things content her."

Jaroslav Pelikan in his book *Jesus Through the Centuries* has a chapter on mysticism entitled "The Bridegroom and the Soul". In it he makes the following statements: "By a working definition, mysticism may be identified as 'the immediate experience of oneness with Ultimate Reality.'" And again: "the monastic commentary's object is rather God's relations with each soul, Christ's presence in it, the spiritual union realized through charity." Also: "And after purification and illumination will come union". He then refers to John's relating Jesus as saying, "Abide in me, and I in you." The mystical union took the form of Bridgroom and bride, i.e. Christ and the human soul. He also warns that there is a danger of expressing this love in terms of sensual eroticism, which was often done, but such must be taken as a metaphor. As I mentioned Fanny Crosby's words above, Pelikan reminds his readers of the gospel hymn I Come to the Garden Alone..."and the Son of God ...He tells me I am His own, and the joys we share as we tarry there, *None other has ever known*." One can read more of this along with its relationship to the eroticism of the troubadours in Denis de Rougemont's *Love in the Western World*.

John of the Cross, in his work *The Living Flame of Love* stated: "Love unites the soul with God, and the more degrees of love the soul has, the more profoundly does it enter into God and the more is it centred in Him." John taught that the Divine Embraces that took place between man and God were always based upon a union created by an intense love between the two of them. Intensity and love must come first, and without them, there will be no ecstatic embrace and no union of soul with God.

The Sufis also use very intimate language in describing their "love affair" with God. "My Lord who ravishes my eyes, has united Himself with me." So were the words of Kabir.6.23 Rabindranath Tagore says the following about Kabir: "...the moments of intimate love..is here seen balanced by his lovely and delicate sense of intimate communion with the Divine Friend, Lover, Teacher of the soul...Union with Him is the one thing that matters to the soul, its destiny and its need...and this union, this discovery of God, is the simplest and most natural of all things, if we would but grasp it." 6.24 The Sufi Hakim Jami spoke of the Embrace of and subsequent unity with God in these words: "Love becomes perfect only when it transcends itself--becoming One with its object; producing Unity of Being."6.25 Robert Frager puts it this way in softer words: "At such times, we may feel that the veils between us and God have suddenly lifted. We sense God's presence far more deeply than usual, often in the form of profoundly experiencing God's attributes such as love, compass-ion, beauty, or unity."6.26 It is well to mention here that the line between God and man is clearly remembered by the Sufis as well as the Christian mystics, for God's Being always remains absolutely transcendent in Essence, and He is inexhaustible and man's ascent to "know" Him will, even in eternity, be endless, joy and love will be lifted ever higher without ever actually knowing the fullness of God. He is Wholly Other than his creatures in Essence and Being. Plato would be quick to remind us that God Himself is actually beyond Being and Essence, untouchable in reality, and beyond our understanding as we understand essence and being, yet to seek him and to know Him face to face is the basic quest of our being human, for the daimon within will never be satisfied until it has seen Beauty face to face. Yet, as Gabriel Marcel reminded us, love is beyond perception and "As soon as one loves or is loved by another being, an awesome solidarity comes into being between the two."6.27 For there are some things greater than knowledge, and Pierre Teilhard de Chardin in his *Hymn of the Universe* stated: "...like the monist I plunge myself into the all-inclusive One; but the One is so perfect that as it receives me and I lose myself in it, I can find in it the ultimate perfection of my own individuality."6.28 In this way, perhaps, one can say that it is in loving God with all one's heart, soul, and mind that one comes to a merging of the Spirit in which one finds his true self. To know oneself one is to know God. Eva Mary Grew and Sidney Grew in their book about Johann Sebastian Bach, made the following statement:

But there was something operative in or upon him as a creative artist that was superior to his mind and intellect. It was a rapture essentially emotional in kind, a "possession" literally *enthusiastic,* that brought him face to face with God and filled him with a sense of the closeness of God. When this rapture seized him...it lifted him to the production of music that is holy...He was the universal man... And he became the artist before whom one would bow, were it not that he takes us by the hand and bids us stand upright and calm in the presence of insoluble and otherwise terrible mysteries.6.29

Ralph Waldo Emerson remarked that "Ineffable is the union of man and God".6.30 Leo Tolstoy encouraged us to take a greater effort toward "blending our will with the will of God, a blending toward which a man strives." For it was, in his mind, the only way in which mankind could rise above the life of violence and unhappiness in which he now lives. The union with God can happen to any who is totally committed and in love with God, and, while it does not mean a union of essence, it is a union of the essential, the will and the mind of men, so that one feels that God lives within his own soul and is embedded in his own heart. As Paul stated: "Not I, but Christ who lives in me."

VI. PASSING THROUGH DEATH

After man has union with God and bathes in his love, he cannot extend his embrace to a deeper level while still living in the flesh. The only way for a higher experience, a deeper and greater embrace of God, is after passing through death. There are many different views as to how man passes through death and how he arrives at the final embrace of Eternal Bliss. I have divided humanity's differing viewpoints into five general categories: a direct and instant arrival into "heaven" after death; a semi-direct arrival after passing judgment; a journey he must take for the sake of purification before acceptance can be made by the heavenly order of justice; another in which the resurrection of the body is actualized; and a long journey by means of a destruction and recreation of the entire cosmos. Often more than one of the above are mentioned by different groups within the same basic religion, for there is a constant struggle in the mind of men as to how to present God as both merciful and just as he accompanies man through his existential journey towards his final home.

A. A DIRECT AND INSTANT ARRIVAL IN HEAVEN

In the *Phaedo* it appears that <u>Socrates</u> is claiming a direct access to the company of heaven when he dies, for death is nothing other than the release of the soul from the body, and a return to its natural and eternal state. Even though Socrates refers to it as a journey, he does not speak of any impediments on the way to his direct entrance to the next world, a world that will be considerably happier and the company much better than the present world offers. He asked not to be grieved at his death, for he himself is not grieving over it: (Phaedo 63b).

> For I am quite ready to admit, Simmias and Cebes, that I ought to be grieved at death, if I were not persuaded in the first place that I am going to gods who are wise and good (of which I am as certain as I can be of any such matters), and secondly (though I am not so sure of this last) to men departed, better than those whom I leave behind; and therefore I do not grieve as I might have done, for I have good hope that there is yet something remaining for the dead.

Socrates goes on telling how the soul exists in itself, and in leaving the body it also leaves all the necessities and needs that the body has burdened the soul with. Therefore, a man prepares himself for the departure of the soul from the body with joy. In fact, after passing through death he will "attain the object to which all our efforts have been directed during my past life. So this journey which is now ordained for me carries a happy prospect for any other man also who believes that his mind has been prepared by purification."(Phaedo 67b). "I believe that I shall find good masters and friends in another world"(Phaedo 69e). For Socrates believed that the souls existed before in the eternal realm, before they were incarnated into human bodies, and therefore return to that same eternal realm when released from the body at death (Phaedo 76). That the soul has been made first as an eternal being and the body afterward as a special adventure for the soul is also well attested in <u>Plato</u>'s *Timaeus*, which is Plato's creation story. Finally Socrates clearly declares that the soul, "which is invisible, in passing to the place of the true heaven (Hades), which like her is invisible, and pure, and noble, and on her way to the good and wise God, whither, if God will, my soul is also soon to go." To those who believed that the soul dies with the body, Socrates replied "That can never be...The truth rather is, that the soul which is pure at departing and draws after her no bodily taint" will arrive in the eternal and pure world of God and men. For "the soul is in the very likeness of the Divine, and immortal, and intellectual, and uniform, and indissoluble, and unchangeable." (Phaedo 80). Socrates last words before he died were "Crito, I owe a cock to Asclepius, will you remember to pay the debt?" And the reply was "The debt shall be paid." (Phaedo 118). Asclepius was the god of healing, and Socrates' soul was about to be liberated from an aging body, and was to be soon restored to its eternal "health", and for that Socrates wanted to give a thank offering to Asclepius. Throughout Plato this is the theme of man's being and fate, made eternal and after the experience of the body, returned to its eternal purity and immortality.

Cicero, in his work, *The Commonwealth*, in *The Dream of Scipio*, praised Scipio in many ways, but particularly because of his defeat of Hannibal in Africa (thus called Scipio Africanus), which put an end to Carthage's threat to Roman rule in the Mediterranean. In so doing, he used Plato's theology to give comfort to those who loved Scipio, that is, Scipio's soul had returned to the eternal world whence it came. Nevertheless, he polluted Plato's doctrine by clothing it heavily in patriotism. He made the eternal land of bliss open, not to the good man as did Plato, but to the great patriotic warrior, a doctrine more suited to the Hinduism concept of the warrior caste of which Krishna (Bhagavad Gita) and Rama (Ramayana) belonged. Honoring warriors was indigenous to Roman history--one thinks of Horace's statement that it was sweet to die for one's country, and Cicero used it to reward Scipio with a speedy return to the eternal realm. Quotes from "Scipio's Dream" are: "All men who have saved or benefited their native land, or have enhanced its power, are assigned a special place in heaven where they may enjoy a life of eternal bliss." And again, "The soul...assuredly it is not created but is eternal... Now the noblest concerns of the soul have to do with the security of your country, and the soul which is employed and disciplined in such pursuits will fly more speedily to this abode, its natural home." The Christian Father Lactantius, himself a proud Roman, rejected such as a disgusting concept: "How great was the darkness in which you wandered, O Africanus, or rather, O poet, to imagine that men are allowed to mount to heaven through slaughter and bloodshed. To this vain opinion even Cicero gave his assent"(Lactantius, *Divine Institutes* 1.18.11). Unfortunately this idea of special eternal blessings heaped upon warriors continued to show itself in other religions also. Islam has a special place of glory for those who die in a holy war, a jihad. Christian popes during the corrupted crusades promised direct access to heaven, skipping purgatory, for those who died in the crusades. While both of these two latter cases it was not to die and kill for one's country, both were concerned about the expansion or at least protection of the influence of one's religion, yet the idea that by killing in mass slaughter one could be treated special by God in heaven was to turn religion over to a Viking and Valhalla euphoria of the joy of killing. As Plato said in his Laches there are many ways in which courage can be expressed, and to assign it only to war, even aggressive war for the purpose of destroying other people's freedom and to gain control over them and their natural resources is quite a pollution of the concept of courage. The crusades laid the foundation for the later idea that the white man of Europe was assigned by God a destiny and burden to conquer, civilize, and control all the peoples of the earth. For Christians often forget that Jesus said that it was the peacemakers and those who turned the other cheek that were the sons of God. When religions reward their believers with a direct access to heaven for deeds of violence, one wonders greatly about the motives of those high priests who control the teachings of those very religions.

Yet, there is the teaching in Christianity that one goes directly to heaven: from Jesus' words to the thief--"I say to you, this day you will be with me in heaven" to Paul's words that he desires to depart and to be with Christ and that in an instant one is changed from the corruptible to the incorruptible, and from Stephen's seeing the heavens opened to him as he was being stoned to death--all such words lead many Christians to believe that one goes directly to God at death. A general thought started by Paul himself is that one falls to sleep at death and is awaken either in heaven or at the time of his resurrection to heaven. Even the common prayer for children ends with "and if I die before I wake, I pray the Lord my soul to take". In Bede's Life of Cuthbert, it is said that at Boisil's death, "he entered into the joy of eternal bliss". Later of Cuthbert himself, it was said "with his mind rapt in the praise of the Lord, he sent forth his spirit to the bliss of Paradise."

B. SEMI-DIRECT PASSING INTO ETERNITY--THE NECESSITY OF JUDGMENT FIRST

It seems that most religions, including Christianity, also present a time of judgment after death to determine one's eternal fate. In the Osirian religion of Ancient Egypt judgment was an absolute necessity before one could enter the eternal realm of Osiris. For passage into the afterlife was not automatic, even though Osiris was a merciful god who cared for and loved his people, because he was morally demanding. When the day of reckoning came, Osiris would have the last word, if one even qualified to stand before him. As a preliminary test the deceased would have to appear in the "Hall of Double Right and Truth" and come before the 42 gods there, and each represented an ethical law. Before them, the deceased had to confess his purity in the form of negative statements: "I have not made any to suffer pain"; "I have not robbed another"; "I have done no murder"; "I have not committed adultery with the wife of any man": "I have not defrauded gods their offerings, nor have I committed any sacrilege". After the confession, the truth of his confession was tested by the scale of righteousness: a feather was on one scale and the weight of his sins upon the other, and if the weight of his evil deeds out-weighed the feather, he was condemned to an evil fate. However, if he was saved by the grace of the weight of the feather, Osiris granted him eternal life.

The Vedic Indians believed in a personal immortality but there seemed to be a difference in quality of being for those who were judged good and those who were not so virtuous. There were three different heavens: that of Yama, of Maruts, and of Vishnu. The lowest form of immortality was in the realm of Yama, which was a land of the fathers: "Unite with the fathers and with Yama, with good works, there is a reward in heaven. To home return, and leave all imperfection." The middle heaven was the realm of the Maruts, which seems rather vague, but the Maruts themselves were apparently immortals, and their fellowship was deemed a higher fellowship than that of the "fathers" of earth who were in the realm of Yama. The highest heaven was the realm of the God Vishnu, and it was the highest heaven, a place where men were exulting in the Gods with great joy, and also enjoyed the sweetness of Vishnu. It is to be noted here that the concept of reincarnation was not yet in the minds of the Indians, and first begins to appear in the Upanishads, but was not in the Rig Vedas.

In Zoroastrianism there is a judgment based on good works and the fate of the individual's soul is to be assigned to heaven, hell, or an itermediate domain. Man is born clean and with a free will, and therefore, he is responsible for all that he does, and all that he does will be judged and the goodness or the evil of his deeds will determine his eternal fate. There is no savitar, no advocate, no one to defend him or his actions, he is judged solely by his life and his deeds. For Zoroastrian doctrine of morality is based only upon: good thoughts (humata), good words (huxta), and good deeds (hvarshta). The person going to paradise is greeted by beauty in it feminine form, and the person sent to hell is greeted by ugliness in feminine form. The words of Yasna 33 state: "You (Mazda) give us our rewards in keeping with our actions", "Through Truth confer power: through the Good Mind, the good reward", and "Illumine the consciences of men through Truth." For the devotee wants a knowledge of good and evil and a good conscience to aid him in having good thoughts, good words, and good deeds. By praying to Ahura Mazda, one seeks his grace that he would be given a good mind and a knowledge of truth that he might follow the path of truth so that by his truthful deeds he would be spared at the judgment.

The Christian Gospels present Jesus as teaching that man will be judged by whether he does the will of God or not, whether he has done good or evil. The previous chapter showed this comprehensively and will not be repeated here, but, of course, it is proper also to this section in the progression of thought being presented. It is certainly clear that The Athanasian Creed, the third and last of the Ecumenical Creeds of the Christian Church proclaimed such and concludes with these words:

> From there he (Christ) shall come to judge the living and the dead.
> At whose coming all men shall rise again with their bodies; and shall
> give account of their own works. And they that have done good
> shall go into life everlasting: and they that have done evil, into
> everlasting fire.

Nicolas Berdyaev put this added concept to the importance of morality at the final judgment, that any system of ethics must be eschatological in nature, for it is not just a system by which man blesses his life here and now, but in every act and every choice he is determining his personality for eternity. A system of ethics simply cannot forget about the final judgment, and must concentrate of the inevitable death and victory over death, of resurrection and eternal life. Man must think of the Last Judgment, but also to "the creation of eternal, permanent, immortal goods and values which further the victory of eternity and prepare man for the end." 6.32   For then, and only then, has man understood the fulness of the Kingdom of God, and participated in his role in bringing about "positive results within the cosmic process."

In the Gnostic Hermetica an emphasis is put upon knowledge as a path to salvation, for the thinking is that without knowledge one is confused and does not know the proper path by which to live and is therefore condemned to make the wrong decisions. Somewhat like the prayer of Yasna 33 mentioned about, the worshipper seeks knowledge for it is the basis for all ethical decisions, and without that knowledge the passions of the body will overcome the good intentions of the soul. Libellus X of the Hermetica Corpus reads this way (7-9):

And human souls, when they have attained to a beginning of immortal life, change into daimons and thereafter pass on into the choral dance of the gods; that is the crowning glory of the soul. But if a soul, when it has entered a human body, persists in evil, it does not taste the sweets of immortal life, but is dragged back again; it reverses its course, and takes its way back to the creeping things; and that ill-fated soul, having failed to know itself, lives in servitude to uncouth and noxious bodies. And to this are evil souls condemned. And the evil of the soul is ignorance (AGNOSIA) For a soul of no knowledge of things that are, nor the nature of things, nor what is good...such a soul is controlled by passions of the body, and is burdened by the body, and even ruled by it, instead of ruling it. This is the soul's evil. But the virtue of the soul is knowledge, and he who has knowledge is good and pious.

And in the same Libellus, 15a, it states: "And only this, the knowledge of God, is man's salvation, for this is the ascent to Olympus, and a soul becomes good by this alone." Much of this is Platonic, as indeed, the entire Hermetica a form of Platonism, sometimes corrupted with the implication that the body and material universe are more than a hindrance but actually evil. Nevertheless, the final word is that the soul must be good and clothed in good works to receive paradise. For if he is not good, he is judged evil and falls back into a lower life or death that is variously described in Gnostic literature.

In the Norse religion, Snorri Sturluson in his work *The Deluding of Gylfi*, he wrote this in praise of Odin, the All-Father:

> His greatest achievement, however, is the making of man and
> giving him a soul which will live and never die, although his body
> decay to dust or burn to ashes. All righteous men shall live and be
> with him where it is called Gimle or Vingolf, but wicked men will
> go to Hel and thence to Niflhel, that is down in the ninth world.6.31

Here is again a judgment of man based upon his works. Those who have done good enjoy Odin in his heaven, whereas those who have done evil will stop off at Hel first and then descend lower to Niflhel.

C. A JOURNEY

A most explicit and long description of the journey after death before the final judgment is made is found in *The Tibetan Book of the Dead* in which a journey of fourteen days is explained in detail, before the judgment, based on karma, is finalized, at least for this particular incarnation. Such journeys after death were thought of by others also, including Socrates, but this teaching in *The Tibetan Book of the Dead* is the classical one of greatest detail. Actually it seems that the journey is a reflection of some of the mental fears and hopes that race through the mind of a person who is about to die, and therefore the work is one to comfort the dying. It is constantly telling the reader that the experiences or apparitions that appear are all mental and not be overly allured to those that are beautiful, that is, those that appear the first seven "days" and not to be frightened by the horrors of the "blood-sucking" deities of the last seven "days". For the "deities" are not in existence outside the person himself, for they are from within, his own "tutelary deities", and of those apparitions more fearful, they too are from within and one is not to be awed or terrified of them. One is to face them, acknowledge, and absorb them with a calm mind, and in this way one will be liberated from the cycle of reincarnations. In the section speaking of the final, the fourteenth day, one is told: "If all existing phenomena shining forth as divine shapes and radiances be recognized to be the emanations of one's own intellect, Buddhahood will be obtained at that very instant of recognition." And again, "The terrifying forms of the Lord of Death, exist not in reality, of this there is no doubt. Thus knowing this, all the fear and terror is self-dissipated; and, merging in the state of at-one-ment, Buddhahood is obtained." Thus one who is about to die is encouraged to read through the *Bardo Thodol* (The Tibetan Book of the Dead) three times, so that as he slips into unconsciousness and such things flash through his mind, he is prepared not to be fearful but accept with a calm faith that he is meeting his tutelary deities projected by his own mind, and in not being allured to them nor being terrified of them, he conquers them, is liberated, and is merged into Buddhahood. For its purely psychological comfort it is a work for all people of all cultures and religions. For the teachings of those journeys that are part of reality and actually take place there are two basic categories: that of reincarn- ation and of purgatorial cleansing.

1. Reincarnation

In the development of the Indian religion after the Vedas, the more advanced thinking that questioned the either-or, that is the salvation or the damnation, of a final judgment, seemed to be too decisive and too radical for both the mercy and justice of God. Exactly where the line to be drawn for mercy or whether or not a person had enough Karma to be given an ultimate and non-reversible sentence was in some ways too contrary to justify. Therefore, during the period of the Upanishads the ultimate mercy of the gods won the day, but not at the expense of justice itself, and the concept of reincarnation was born. If your *Karma* was not sufficient and you could not advance into eternity and enjoy the gods and all immortals, then you had to do life in the flesh over again in order to get it right. Most Indian thinking seems to imply that many reincarn- ations are needed for the average person to step into an eternal bliss, liberated forever from the need of qualifying for a joyous eternity. There is no hell, for that offends the mercy of the gods. Their goal is to provide bliss, eternal joy, for all, but they are not in a hurry and justice must be satisfied by the virtue of good living, *Karma*. What Westerners need to know and acknowledge is that the doctrine of reincarnation is not a primitive was of thinking, but a well advanced way of thinking in which both the mercy and the justice of the gods is given to men and also mankind is assured of eventually arriving at their eternal home. Likewise, it will be shown that the developing eschatological views of the West also have entertained reincarnation also, most notably Pythagoras and even Plato himself entertained it as a possible avenue to man's eternal bliss. However, let us look at the East first.

It must be clearly stated that the goal of the Indian gods is to bring men to themselves and bless them with eternal bliss, and that is to be emphasi- zed. The Khandogya Upanishad 4.15.6 states: "He leads them to Brahman (the Supreme God). This is the path of the Devas, the path that leads to Brahman. Those who proceed on that path, do not return to the life of man, yea, they do not return." They are beyond reincarnation. At the judgment there are two roads presented to those having been judged, the one that goes directly to Brahman and the other where the souls return to earth to be born again and again. The meeting place where the judgment was thought to have taken place, at least, by the author of the Kaushitake Upanishad, was the Moon. It states:

> And Kitra said: All who depart from this world (or this body) go
> to the moon. In the former, (bright) half, the moon delights in
> their spirits; in the other (dark) half, the moon sends them on
> to be born again. Verily, the moon is the door of the Svarga world
> (the heavenly world)....And according to his deeds and according
> to his knowledge he is born again here as a worm, or as an insect,
> or as a fish, or as a bird, or as a lion, or as a boar, or as a serpent,
> or as a tiger, or as a human, or as something else in different places.
> (1.2)

Here is must be stated that Hinduism is a very dogma free religion, and each may develop views that are not held by all, in fact there is much liberty of thought, and therefore, because of this very tolerant approach, they have no "heretics", no "anathemas" or religious persecutions, and also no one person can speak for all. The above quotation is a single teaching within a single Upanishad, and there are others who do not believe that a human will leave entirely the human race upon his return for rebirth, but will be lowered, if evil, in caste, or if his *Karma* was good, he will be upgraded in caste. One is totally in charge of one's destiny and must be a good person to be elevated and directed towards his ultimate release from the cycle of reincarnations. If he is a truly terrible human being bringing much suffering to the human race, then to be reincarnated as an insect or worm seems to many to be quite justifiable.

The Svetasvatara Upanishad states the goal this way:

When God is known, all fetters fall off, sufferings are destroyed,
and birth and death cease. From meditating on Him there arises,
on the dissolution of the body, the third state, that of universal
lordship...then passing even higher he is satisfied in the complete
bliss of Brahman (1.11)

It is obvious that such a doctrine demands the strictest morality. Control yourself and your actions because they will have an effect upon you for many future ages. Chapter 15 of the Srimad Bhagavadam strongly preaches self control and the doing of good even in the worst conditions.

Restrain yourself...If you desire the highest good, you must have
poise. Maintain your equanimity even if placed in dire extremities.
Do not let your peace be disturbed even if you are ridiculed or
slandered by others. Never return hatred for hatred, nor injury for
injury. If you desire the highest good, you must strive to free yourself from evil and ignorance.6.33

Most Hindus believe that in most all cases many rebirths are needed to accumulate the necessary virtue to liberate them from this cycle of rebirths.

Among the Greeks reincarnation appeared in earlier Orphism, in Pythagoras, Empedocles, and even Plato. Pythagoras thus forbad his disciples to eat meat, firmly believing that they had a soul that was in the process of reincarnation. Xenophanes joked about Pythagoras believing in reincarnation by repeating a story that Pythagoras once stopped the beating of a puppy and took pity upon it claiming to know in it a former friend, for he had "heard in the puppy's cries the voice of his former friend." Empedocles who likewise believed in reincarnation, said of himself, "For by now I have been born as a boy, a girl, a plant, a bird, and a dumb fish in the sea". Finally Plato referred to reincarnation, not only in the myth of Er at the end of his *Republic*, but also in the *Timaeus,* the *Laws*, and a long description in the *Phaedrus* (247-250). In the Timaeus (41e ff) he taught that the righteous person returns immediately after his death to "his native star, and there he would have a blessed and congenial existence." If, however, he never conquered the evil desires, he would be reincarnated to a more difficult life; both for a type of punishment and opportunity for rehabilitation. In the Laws (X 903d-905d), is a section which presents the order of justice established by the gods. Each person is rewarded according to his virtue: the virtuous go directly to "heaven" ("a special place of utter holiness" 904e), but those whose conduct was evil go through the refining process of reincarnation. Plato was not dogmatic about abstract concepts, but he certainly held reincarnation as a possibility in which the loving mercy and the justice of the gods could both be fulfilled. In closing this section on reincaration, I would like to quote <u>Paul</u> <u>Deussen</u> in his case for reincarnation.

> What comes after death? (then he considers the best of the only
> three options that he feels are available): inasmuch as we have only
> the choice between (1) annihilation, (2) eternal retribution in heaven
> or hell, and (3) transmigration. The first supposition is in conflict
> not only with a man's self-love, but with the innate certainty more
> deeply rooted than all knowledge of our metaphysical being as
> subject to no birth or dissolution. The second supposition, which
> opens up the prospect of eternal reward or punishment for an exist-
> ence so brief and liable to error, so exposed to all the accidents of
> upbringing and environment, is condemned at once by the unparal-
> led disproportion in which cause and effect here stand to one another.
> And for the empirical solution of the problem...only the third suppo-
> sition remains, that our existence is continued after death in other
> forms, other conditions of space and time, that it is in a certain sense
> a transmigration.6.34

2. Purgatory

The Christian Church in the West struggled with the preceding three options that Deussen presented, and added a fourth, a period of time for those caught between condemnation and salvation to suffer appropriately for the severity of their sins before being granted entrance into heaven. Such a place, called purgatory, never popular with the Greek Orthodox or Protestants, was not really as evil as most Protestants have made it out to be, at least in concept. It was trying to solve the problem of an eternal damnation for someone who was not totally evil, yet was not fit for the eternal kingdom of God. However, when greed took over the Western Church and profit was to be made by using the doctrine of purgatory, then it became a horrible doctrine that was supported by the Church for the sake of making money. The entire system of penance, relics, indulgences was corrupted. What was once an honest attempt to solve a philosophical question of the relationship of God's grace and God's justice came to be a tremendous burden upon the believers. In addition, the Church made hell so descriptive and fearful that people would have chosen complete annihilation to such eternal and brutal suffering.

The Protestants rejected the idea of the purgatory solution, and simply presented salvation by faith alone or by God's predestination. They followed Augustine, Anselm, Luther, and Calvin with Calvin doing the worst job in solving the problem of God's justice and God's loving grace. For Calvin taught that God, before the creation of the world predestined some of those who would be born in the future to heaven and others to hell. Such unfair partiality is, of course, a great affront to the grace and love of God, as well as to the dignity of His Person. Augustine himself was not guiltless in this teaching, also implying such a predestination of man. Anselm taught the "vicarious atonement" or "forensic" view of the atonement, in which one could die for another and the of transfer merits by penance or faith or devotion. Luther at least was inconsistent proclaiming "faith alone" and then saying that faith can no more be separated from good works than fire can be separated from light and heat. In short, the Protestants did not solve the problem of God's grace and justice. Gustaf Aulen, in 1930, tried to offer another way of atonement, rejecting both Anselm's forensic-vicarious view and that man was saved by following the Way of Jesus by offering a view that was often expressed by many of the early Church Fathers, which he described as *Christus Victor*, i.e. that God sent Christ to defeat the devil who had made a claim on man, because in sinning man became more like the devil than God and therefore fell into the realm and power of Satan. But in the 20th Century AD Satan no longer held any relevance to theologians and also it was felt that God never had to play games with Satan, and therefore never owed him any "victory" such as implied at the fall of man into sin. Again, the problem of man's comprehending both the justice and grace of God was not solved.

The time of purging appeared in other religions also. Zoroastrianism accepted a type of purgatory, but rejected hell.

> So understand, O mortal men, the Decrees
>   which Mazda has established regarding happiness and misery.
> There will be a long period of suffering for the wicked,
>   and salvation for the just, but thereafter,
> Eternal bliss shall prevail everywhere.(Yasna 30.11)

Plato in the *Phaedrus* 246-249 speaks at length of what seems a combination of reincarnation and a type of purgatorial punishing, but the punishing was not as bad as some of the Christian descriptions of hell. Plato, as did Zoroaster, believed that God made all souls to be immortal and to enjoy the heavenly realm, none would ever be left behind. Hell was not an option in Plato's understanding of God's nature, goodness, and love for his creatures. There are also some Christians who, not being satisfied with either purgatory or the concept of forensic and vicarious forgiveness in Christ simply by believing in his name, that have spoken of a type of Christian reincarnation, and these views can be read in the works of Rudolf Steiner's writings published by Anthroposophic Press. His views are based by in large on his interpretation of the Hebrew Scriptures and one verse in particular in the New Testament, John 9:1-3. "And passing along Jesus saw a man who was born blind. And the disciples asked Jesus, saying: "Rabbi, who sinned, this man or his parents, that he was born blind?" Jesus answered, "Neither this man sinned nor his parents, but he is blind that the works of God might be manifested in him." The disciples obviously had in mind the idea of "karma" of a previous life that was carried over to his birth into this one. For there is no other way that a man could cause his being born blind, except that it was merited by a previous life. Jesus neither confirmed their idea of the man's guilt that caused his blindness nor the guilt of his parents. He simply, in this case, said that he was born blind for the sake of manifesting God's glory which Jesus himself would establish by curing the man of his blindness and giving him sight. Since all the people in the neighborhood knew he had been blind from birth, they would know that Jesus did not "cure one pretending to be blind", and therefore God's glory would be made known. As I have shown in my book *Plato's Gift to Chrisitianity*, Greek thought pervaded the Jewish people of Jesus' age in Palestine as well as in the Diaspora, and, since, the Orphic cult, the Pythagoreans, Empedocles, and Plato all had entertained the idea of reincarnation, it is not surprising that the disciples also were aware of and, it seemed, influenced by it. Edward Reaugh Smith has written a book called *The Soul's Long Journey* in which he explains his Christian belief in reincarnation, and it would be helpful for those who are unfamiliar with the concept.

Thus the passing through death to arrive at heaven could also, in the minds of many, be a journey in which both the grace of God and the justice of God are executed for the benefit of man's salvation.

D. THE RESURRECTION OF THE BODY

Another view of passing through death and arriving whole on the other side is that one's physical body is resurrected. This was the teaching of the ancient Egyptians and is also found in some Jewish Intertestamental Literature. In *Second Book of Maccabees* the hope of the resurrection of the body is clearly expressed. In the story of the martyrdom of a woman's seven sons, when the third one was executed he, whose hands were chopped off first, stated that God would give them back to him. Then, when the fourth was about to die he verbally assaulted the king ordering his death that for the king, "there will be no resurrection to life"(2Mac 7:14), and in the death of Razis who after being surrounded by Nicanor's men, threw himself upon his sword and pulled out his entrails "calling upon the Lord of Life and Spirit to give them back again", that is, at the resurrection of the body (2Mac 14:41-16). The Christian Greek Scriptures speak of the resurrection of the body, but, at least according to Paul, it is a spiritual body, not a physical body that is raised. "It is sown a physical body, it is raised a spiritual body...I tell you this, brothers, flesh and blood cannot inherit the

Kingdom of God, nor does the perishable (physical body) inherit the imperishable"(I Cor 15:44, 50). Despite these words of Paul, the Apostles' Creed declares that one believes "in the resurrection of the flesh (Gk SARKOS and Latin CARNIS)". Therefore, Christianity is basically split in various ways as to whether or not there is going to be a fleshly body that is immortalized. I, being a Platonic Christian, personally believe in the immortality of the soul. For Jesus cautioned that the soul was man's real self, and not "to fear those who kill the body, but are unable to kill the soul (PSUCHE or PSYCHE)"(Mt 10:28). PSUCHE was, in Platonic theology, the eternal part of man that was created both before the body and lives on with God after the body dies.

E. DEATH AND RESURRECTION OF THE COSMOS

In <u>Norse</u> <u>mythology</u> there was the belief of the destruction and rebirth of the Cosmos takes place; and all, after total destructrion, will begin anew. In the story of Ragnarok it is stated:

So the end will begin.
...
The earth will start to shudder then.
...
Everything in heaven and earth and Hel will quiver.
...
Then Surt will fling fire in every direction.
Asgard and Midgard and Jotunheim and Niflheim will become
    furnaces--places of raging flame, swirling smoke, ashes, only ashes.
The nine worlds will burn and the gods will die.
The Einherjar will die, men and women and children in Midgard will
    die, elves and dwarfs will die, giants will die, monsters and
    creatures of the underworld will die, birds and animals will die.
The sun will be dark and there will be no stars in the sky.
The earth will sink into the sea.
...
...The earth will rise again out of the water, fair and green.
...
Vidar and Vali will still be alive.

> The sons of Vili and Ve will make up the new number, the gods in
> heaven, home of the winds.
> They will sit down in the sunlight and begin to talk
> ...
> There will be life and new life, life everywhere on earth.
> That was the end; and this is the beginning.

Snorri Sturluson adds in his version: "And you will think this strange, but the sun will have borne a daughter no less lovely than herself, and she will follow the paths of her mother." Thus the new beginning will be even more delightful.

Thus those of faith in God and human mortality are very optimistic about the future world, that is, if one casts aside the belief in hell, and I think most all western theologians have, and in the East there never was a real hell in concept. Passing through death, however done, will be a new beginning filled with the life more abundant, and in it the embrace of God will be fully enjoyed.

VII. THE ETERNAL EMBRACE OF GOD

A. THE EMBRACE OF GOD

In Hindu teachings Brahman is beyond description, yet it also implies that Brahman is *ananda*, i.e. bliss, and not as possessing bliss as an attribute but he is the very essence of bliss, much as the First Letter of John in the Christian Scriptures declares that God is love. Therefore, the embrace of Brahman would bring one into the very essence of bliss. Brahman is also declared to be light, and again, that means not a possessor of light or a bearer of light, but Light Itself. Light here, of course, is contrasted with darkness and in it one receives the greatest form of "enlightenment", vision, and warmth. The following passage can be found in the various Upanishads: Kath.5.15; S'vet.6.14; Mund.2.2.10 and also the Bhagavad Gita 15.6; and can therefore be considered a common teaching of all Hinduism.

> There no sun shines, nor glimmering star,

Nor yonder lightning, the fire of earth is quenched;
From him, who alone shines, all else borrows its brightness,
The whole world bursts into splendour at his shining.

This, again, sounds like the Christian Scriptures in speaking of God, for in John's vision of heaven described in the Book of Revelation, he proclaimed "And the city (the eternal new Jerusalem) has no need of sun or moon to shine upon it, for the glory of God enlightened it...there will not be night there (Rv 21:23-25). Night or darkness often implies fear and violence, but in God's presence the Eternal Jerusalem will never have to lock its gates, because "there will not be night there". The Laws of Manu (11.6) stated, after karma has been achieved, "one obtains after death heavenly bliss", i.e. the eternal embrace of Brahman. Shankara, speaking of Brahman, but using the word Atman, (in his *Crest-Jewel of Discrimination*) the "Self-existent Reality" tells us that "That Reality sees everything by its own light" and "...the Supreme Being...never ceases to experience infinite joy", for it is always the same.

Sarvepalli Radhakrishnan in describing the Hindu concept of salvation, wrote:

It is the *Moksa* of the Hindus, the *Nirvana* of the Buddhists, the
Kingdom of Heaven of the Christians. It is for Plato the life of
the untroubled perception of the Pure Idea. It is the realisation of
one's native form, the restoration of one's integrity of being...
Heaven is not a place where God lives but an order of being, a
world of spirit where the ideas of wisdom, love and beauty
exist eternally...The world process reaches its consummation
when every man knows himself to be the immortal spirit, the son
of God and is it 6.35

In brief, like the story of Jesus, it is the *Prodigal Son* coming home to the embrace of the Father, acknowledging that he is indeed, the son of the Father.

Seneca, a contemporary of Paul of Tarsus, described in a letter to Lucilius, man's death as the "birthday of eternity". He also used the figure of Light as the Eternal Presence.

The whole expanse of heaven will shine evenly; for day and night are interchanged only in the lowest atmosphere. Then you will say that you have lived in darkness, after you have seen, in your perfect state, the Perfect Light.6.36

For <u>Jesus</u> joy was certainly a central concept of heaven: "So you have sorrow now, but I will see you again and your hearts will rejoice, and no one will take your joy from you" (J 16:22). For in the Kingdom of Heaven those peacemakers of the earth will be called sons of God, and the pure in heart will see God, for He is the Father waiting in heaven. The spirit of man will rejoice to worship God in truth, and men will rejoice in having eternal life. Men will abide in the love of God and their joy will be full. Jesus will precede those who love him and prepare a place in the Great House of the Father. As the prodigal sons of the earth return to God, the Father will "run to embrace them and kiss them...clothe them with his best robes...put a ring on their fingers...have a feast of joy that all may make merry...the Father will rejoice and announce 'how fitting it is to make merry'".

The story of the "Prodigal Son" was called, by <u>Helmut</u> <u>Thielicke</u>, the "Waiting Father" for He in patience and in love awaited the return of his wayward son. <u>Kabir</u>, the Sufi, spoke of God as the Waiting Lover who never wavered in his love while he awaited the return of his beloved creature. Kabir's 86th Song manifested his feelings this way:

Serve your God, who has come into this temple of life!
...
He has awaited me for countless ages; because he loved me He has
  never lost his heart for me.
Yet I did not know the bliss that was so near to me,
  for my love was not yet awake.
But now, my Lover has made known to me the meaning
  of the note that struck my ear:
Now, my good fortune is come.
Kabir says: "Behold! How great is my good fortune!
  I have received the unending caress of my Beloved!"

The <u>Christian</u> <u>Mystics</u>, like the Sufis, often portray their deep love of God as a love relationship that is characterized by a deep romantic feeling, and even, sometimes, as a marriage as the consummation of that love. Bernard of Clairvaux in his essay "The Marriage of Love" considers his embrace of God to be a union as close as the intimacy of marriage itself.

> This is the marriage-contract of a truly spiritual and holy union: no, contract is too weak a description; it is an embrace...Nor need we fear that the inequality of the two partners will make the concurrence of their wills halting or lame, for love is no respecter of persons... But to a lover all these (other things) have lost their meaning.6.37

Thomas Traherne felt that one never sees life or the world correctly until one finds himself embracing God in heart and mind. "The image of God implanted in us, guided me to the manner wherein we were to enjoy. ...Your enjoyment of the world is never right, till every morning you awake in Heaven; see yourself in your Father's Palace; and look upon the skies, the earth, and the air as Celestial Joys: having such a reverend esteem of all, as if you were among the Angels."6.38 Francis of Sales explains in his Preface to his work *Introduction to the Devout Life* that he addressed his discourse to his soul, and named his soul Philothea (which is a Greek word meaning 'the love of God'). For Philothea signifies a soul that loves or is in love with God. He thus claims that the embrace of God is that act and feeling that comes when a man's soul is in a state of loving God, and in that rapture feels great joy. For in his section in which he meditates on Paradise (Chapter 16), he speaks this way of those who are in that eternal state: "O my God! How happy are they! Unceasingly they sing the sweet song of eternal love."

Leibniz, the philosophical mathematician, spoke of the happiness that is experienced by those who embrace God and will continue to embrace him in heaven. Leibniz believed that happiness will never be static but will continue in the realm of God and eternity to grow greater and more diversified throughout eternity, for that is the benefit of embracing God. In speaking of happiness he stated:

> I do not know whether the greatest pleasure is possible. I believe rather that it can grow ad infinitum; for we do not know how far our knowledge and our organs can be extended in all that eternity which awaits us. I believe then that happiness is a lasting pleasure;

which could not be so without there being a continual progress to new pleasures.6.39

And again he said it:

It may even be said that from the present time on, the love of God makes us enjoy a foretaste of future felicity...It is true that supreme felicity, by whatever beatific vision or knowledge of God it be accompanied, can never be full; because, since God is infinite, he cannot be wholly known. Therefore our happiness will never, and ought not, consist in full joy, where there would be nothing farther to desire, rendering our mind stupid; but in a perpetual progress to new pleasures and to new perfections.6.40

I would like to close this section with the simple and lovely words of Soren Kierkegaard who closed his discourse "The Expectation of Faith" with these words: "So we may understand that the same God who by his hand led us through the world, now withdraws it and opens His embrace to receive the longing soul."

B. VARIOUS IDEAS OF HEAVEN

Throughout this work there have been statements of belief that projected some general thoughts about the life after death and they involved the following: a nearness to the Ultimate Life Source and Its Eternal Being and Power, God, and the joy or bliss that comes from such a closeness to It; that such a Source of Life was Fatherly or Motherly and cared for them, not just for humanity's brief material existence, but for all of them and forever; that this "place" could be a type of Heaven in which all the human limitations known before are eliminated and, along with them, all negative elements of the physical life such as sorrows, pain, hunger, and death as well as all discomforts of societal living as rejection, status, fear of failure, and hopeless and loveless moments. The individuals themselves would be purged of all forms of weakness, ungodliness, and in place of them would be in full imitation of the virtues of the Creator. However, above these general concepts and hopes that man had for his eternal existence, there have been various other ways in which men and women have expressed their future existences.

E A Wallis Budge described the vision of heaven that can be deduced from the priest of Osiris and and Ra of ancient Egypt, claiming that the Osirian heaven was very much a replica of one's present material life, although by the influence of the teaching of Ra's priests there is some spirituality included. Budge stated:

> All these and similar statements point clearly to the fact that the reward which Osiris bestowed after death upon his follower was a life which he led in a region where corn, and wine, and oil, and water were abundant, and where circumstances permitted him to wear white linen robes and white sandals, and where he was not required to do work of any kind, and where he was able to perform his ablutions at will, and to repose whensoever it pleased him to do so. He possessed his own estate, or homestead, where he abode with his parents, and presumably with a wife, or wives, and family, and his heavenly life was to all intents and purposes nothing but a duplicate of his life upon earth. In several passages in the Pyramid Texts we also have allusions to a life in which his enjoyments and delights were of a more spiritual character, but it is evident that these represent the beliefs and doctrines of the priests of Ra, who declared that the blessed fed upon light, and were arrayed in light and became beings of light, and that the place wherein they lived was the boat of the Sun-god Ra.6.41

Elsewhere Budge said this of the abode of the blessed: "The gods of the Egyptians dwelt in a heaven with their Ka's and Khu's, and shadows, and there they received the blessed dead to dwell with them. This heaven was situated in the sky."6..42 Heaven, like earth, was a level square and was supported in the sky with four pillars at each corner. This was the image of earth for all mid-Eastern ancient thought: Egyptian, Babylonian, and Hebrew. But since the Babylonians and Hebrews did not believe man lived on after death, the "material" aspect of heaven and man's place in it was irrelevant and therefore not presented.

Plato believed in a pure home of the soul, whence it originally came, and that was the spiritual and ideal "heaven" in which the soul found itself to be joyously clothed in all the spiritual virtues that made it like unto God as much as possible. In sharp contrast to Egyptian thought, Plato thought of the eternal world as completely spiritual with a complete lack of any form of material existence. "Heaven" is described this way in the *Phaedrus* (247c-d):

> There abides the very being with which true knowledge is concern-ed; the colourless, formless, intangible essence, visible only to the mind, the pilot of the soul. The divine intelligence, being nurtured upon mind and pure knowledge, and the intelligence of every soul which is capable of receiving the "food" proper to it, rejoices at beholding reality, and once more gazing upon truth, is replenished and made glad until the revolution of the worlds brings her round again to the same place. In the revolution she beholds justice, and temperance, and knowledge absolute, not in the form of generation or of relation, which men call existence, but knowledge absolute in existence absolute.

One can see the obvious difference between the desires of the Egyptians who followed the faith of Osiris and those who were Platonists. Plato's world was totally spiritual and any talk of it had to be spiritualized to be understood, and therefore any reference to bodily comfort had to be understood in a strictly spiritual manner. Likewise the greatest good and blessing that gave joy to the ascended soul were not material in nature, but were spiritual and divine in nature, such as justice, temperance, and wisdom, those very attributes and characteristics of God that the man who best imitated then was capable of enjoying the absolute love and joy that was God Himself. Property, a "place" or farm, or wife, or cattle, or anything that seemed important to other religions of his day were considered totally irrelevant and, in fact, would have been hindrances to the development of perfection and happiness. For such "things" did not exist in material form in Plato's perfect world of the spirit. One will recall the story of the Sadducees who wanted to know which of her seven husbands would have her as wife in heaven (she kept remarrying after each one had died), and Jesus said that in heaven there is no marriage and being given into marriage for men will be like angels. In this conver-sation one can see the division of Egyptian thinking (the Sadducees) and the Platonic thinking in which Jesus expressed himself in rejecting their question and the basis of it. Paul of Tarsus, in First Corinthians, Chapter

15, speaks likewise of the spiritual aspect of man's existence and his step into immortality by being changed from a body that, being flesh and blood, is suspect to decay and mortality. While <u>Paul</u> does not speak much of what "heaven" is like, he does make it clear that the being who lives there is a spiritual being.

> And this I say to you, brothers, that flesh and blood is not able to
> inherit the kingdom of blood, nor corruption incorruption. Look!
> I am telling you a mystery. All of us are will fall asleep but all will
> be changed, in a moment, in a blink of the eye. For there will be a
> final trumpet, and by its sound, the dead will be raised incorrupt-
> ible, and we will have been changed.(I Cor. 15:50-52)

Paul is referring to flesh and blood as a unit, and is Paul's expression for the material body, and that is why the verb is in the singular, and that being, of flesh and blood, can not enter the kingdom of God: but, only the spiritual body. The <u>Hermetic</u> writings give us this joyous entrance into heaven: "And human souls, when they have attained to the begin- ning of immortal life, change into daimones (spiritual beings), and there- after pass on into the choral dance of the gods, that is the crowning glory of the soul."(Libellus 10.7). Actually this is just a rephrasing of Platonic thought, but it also shows, as did Plato, the division of body and soul, for the body must be released by the soul to enter into immortality.

<u>Kabir</u> stated that the one who lives in the life of Brahma experiences a foretaste of the world to come, as he is lifted high above his present earthy experience. "I have swept all tinsel away" he proclaimed in experiencing reality. For "There the sky is filled with music...no mention is made of rising and setting of the sun...In the ocean of manifestation, which is the light of love, day and night are felt to be one. Joy forever, no sorrow, no struggle! There I have seen joy filled to the brim, perfection of joy...There I have witnessed the sport of One Bliss." Bliss and happi- ness fill the heavens, and no bodily or earthly concerns are ever present.

<u>Hrabanus</u> <u>Maurus</u> wrote to Grimold, Abbot of St Gall, about their friendship in terms of the love that they shared for each other, and ended his short letter with the hopes that the future heaven will be one of their reunion:

> Christ keep thee well, where'er thou art, for me.

> Earth's self shall go and the swift wheel of heaven
> Perish and pass, before our love shall cease.
>   Do but remember me, as I do thee,
> And God, who brought us on this earth together,
>   Bring us together to his house of heaven.6.43

Peter Abelard wrote of the transcendental bliss in a devotion for Saturday Evening Vespers proclaiming peace beyond understanding, utter blessedness, the refreshing rest and joy being in the presence of the King, souls that celebrate an eternal holiday, and men and angels joining together in the eternal chorus and singing their rapture. Among most of the mystics God is such a focal point of joy and bliss that other things are often not even noticed, for all other things simply fade away in the Glory and Beauty of God.

While Martin Luther could talk loosely and mundanely about heaven in his "table talk" and speak, at least according to those who recorded his table talk, mundanely about the joys of heaven, even including his apparent love of dogs, with these words "There will be little dogs, with golden hair, shining like precious stones", yet in serious writing he was more hesitant in trying to describe the indescribable, at least in his Fourteen Consolations, the Seventh Chapter in which he stated:

> I do not now speak of the eternal and heavenly blessings which the
> blessed enjoy in the perfect wisdom of God. If I speak of them at all
> I do so only in faith and insofar as they come within the realm of my
> understanding.

This, of course, is for all of us to follow, for each of us will subjectively project his own feelings into such, yet, for the sake of human communication, we try to speak of such, at least to the limits of our understanding. We, naturally, think much of reunion with loved ones and perhaps some of the things that made our lives on earth so enjoyable like the music of Bach, Mozart, and Beethoven among others. Karl Barth when asked what music the angels sing in heaven answered that when they were before the throne they would sing Bach, but when they went home and sang with their families, they would sing Mozart. I would add that when they put on a performance for the entire heavenly realm, they would also sing Beethoven's Ninth "Choral--with Schiller's Ode to Joy" Symphony.

Perhaps it is not possible to say much more than what the Hindus say: "Brahman is Absolute Bliss". Or, maybe, Plato's words that "One sees Beauty Itself, face to face, and knows that he has become a beloved of God--God's eternal friend". Or, as most mystics would say, one is so overwhelmingly immersed in the Love of God that he really doesn't notice anything else. Whatever our limited and anthropomorphic minds may project, there is unlimited joy in the embrace of God and a feeling of absolute and eternal satisfaction in His presence.

CONCLUSION

This book has basically been an historical and philosophical study of man and religion and the unity between them from the very earliest appearance of man in the course of known history. It has included the cause and development of that unity of man and his religious being and the expressions and growth of that unity, as it speaks to the meaning of life and the human dilemma. It shows man's longing for continued life in any form and ultimately the desire for immortality in the very depth of eternity. Man's religious faith and love has given a joy and a power to that very life he experiences on earth in the material realm, and enhances both the idea of embracing a God of love, who is seen as his Father, and the universe as man's greater home, a house of immeasurable reality and beauty. The innate spirit of man, the daimon of love seeking eternal beauty, put into man's nature by God at creation, has driven man into the arms of that Kind Creator that he might embrace Absolute Beauty and Eternity Itself. The Hindus say, "Brahman is Bliss"; and Augustine declared that man has no rest until he rests in God. Again Jesus presented God as the Waiting Father with outstretched arms in patience waiting for the sons of earth to return home from their earthly journey. As the sons come home to this embrace of God, the festival of eternal joy commences, and those in the heavenly realm break out into song and dance, music and play, as man himself then joins in the Eternal Garden of Eden, the altar and presence of God.

GLOSSARY

Ahura Mazda: The name of God for Zarathushtra (Zoroaster) probably meaning "The Living One Who is Wise".

Allah: The Islamic name for God, and means "The God".

Ananda: The Hindu word for bliss: Brahman is often called "Bliss Itself." Also used for the name of Buddha's closest companion.

The Banquet: An earlier name given to Plato's Symposium.

Collegia Licita: A Latin word meaning the licit (legal/lawful) societies (colleges).

Corpus Hermeticum: Sacred books of the Gnostics attributed to Hermes Trismegistus, but in reality written at different times by different people.

Daimon (Daemon or Demon): A Platonic word meaning the Spirit of love of beauty that God put into man's inner parts that would drive him back to God Himself, The Absolute and Eternal Beauty, and would be restless until he met Beauty Itself (God) face to face.

Eros: A Greek word meaning love of the beautiful. In Plato it is an intensive form of Philia, friendship love. Planted within man as a daimon, it drives man fervently towards God, who is Absolute Beauty Itself, seeking his friendship in order to become a Theophilos (a loving friend of God).

Gathas: Written teachings of Zarathushtra.

Hindu Trinity: Brahman is beyond thought but expresses himself in three ways: Brahma (Creator), Vishnu (Preserver)--the one who has incarnations, the most famous is Krishna, and Shiva or Siva (Destroyer).

Hubris (Hybris): A Greek word meaning inordinate pride or arrogance especially of man's attitude before the gods.

Kabbala (Cabala): Jewish mystical texts.

Kabir: A Sufi.

Kami: The "vital force" that gives life to all nature in Shinto.

Karma: the virtue of man from his pious living.

Logos: A Greek word meaning logic or rational thought or word-order.

Metanoia: A Greek word, used by Plato to signify a changed mindset that formerly focused on the temporal world but now "sees" the spiritual world. In the Christian Scriptures it is usually translated as repentance or conversion.

Moira: A Greek word: the force of destiny or fate.

Numina: The Roman household gods.

Nous: A Greek word: mind or intellect often used by Heraclitus or Plato for God or the directing Mind of the universe.

Rig Veda (Rik Veda or Vedas): The oldest of Sacred Hindu writings.

Rumi: A Sufi.

Saga: Word used for the Icelandic wisdom writings.

Samadhi: An Indian (Hindu) term meaning the moment of illumination in which one experiences union with God.

Soli Invicto Comiti: To Mithra as the Friendly Unconquerable Sun.

Srimad Bhagavatam: "The Wisdom of God" is a holy writing of Hinduism.

Sufism: Islamic mysticism, the mystics themselves are called Sufis.

Theophilos: A Greek word meaning "A Friend of God" or "A Beloved of God."

Upanishads: Sacred Hindu writings of which there is a basic canon of twelve.

Yahweh (Jahweh): The God of the Hebrews meaning "It that is" or "He who is".

Yasna: Sacred Writings of Zoroastrianism and contains the Gathas.

NOTES

CHAPTER ONE

1.1   Adolf Harnack, <u>What is Christianity?</u>, trans. T B Sanders, p.41.
1.2   Siegfried Morenz, <u>Egyptian Religion</u>, trans A E Keep, pp.6-15.
1.3   Joseph M Kitagawa, <u>Religions of the East</u>, p.24.
1.4   E O James, <u>Seasonal Feasts and Festivals</u>, p.11.
1.5   Bronislaw Malinowski, <u>Magic, Science and Religion</u>, p.17.
1.6   Alfred North Whitehead, <u>The Aims of Education</u>, p.80.
1.7   <u>Leibniz Selections</u>, ed. P P Wiener, p.330.
1.8   Auguste Sabatier, <u>Outlines of a Philosophy of Religion</u>, p.1.
1.9   Immanuel Kant, <u>Lectures on Ethics</u>, p.81.
1.10   Nikolai Berdyaev, <u>Slavery and Freedom</u>, p.36.
1.11   Gabriel Marcel, <u>The Mystery of Being Vol. I</u>, p.239
1.12   John A O'Brien, <u>Eternal Answers for an Anxious Age</u>, p.152.
1.13   Alfred North Whitehead, <u>The Aims of Education</u>, p.13.
1.14   Ibid., p.75.
1.15   Ibid., p.80.
1.16   John Mansley Robinson, <u>An Introduction to Early Greek Philosophy</u>, p.8.

CHAPTER TWO

2.1   Abraham H Maslow, <u>Religious Values, and Peak-Experiences</u>, P.54.
2.2   Ibid., p.55.
2.3   Idries Shah, <u>The Way of the Sufi</u>, p.190.
2.4   <u>Indian Philosophy</u>, ed. Sarvepalli Radhakrishnan and Charles A Moore, p.613.
2.5   Cicero, <u>The Nature of the Gods</u>, p.87.
2.6   John Mansley Robinson, <u>An Introduction to Early Greek Philosophy</u>, p.52.
2.7   Abraham H Maslow, <u>Religious Values, and Peak-Experiences</u>, P.45.
2.8   Idris Shah, <u>The Way of Sufi</u>, p.103

2.9   Sri Chinmoy, Commentary on the Bhagavad Gita, p.115.

2.10   Swami Nikhilananda, The Upanishads, p.50.

2.11   Swami Prabhavananda, The Sermon on the Mount, According to Vedanta, p.90.

2.12   The Gathas of Zarathushtra, trans. Piloo Nanavutty, p.23.

2.13   Snorri Sturluson, The Prose Edda, trans. J I Young, p.31.

2.14   F C Happold, Mysticism, p.325.

2.15   John Burnet, Early Greek Philosophy, pp.135-136.

2.16   Srimad Bhagavatam, trans. Swami Prabhavananda, pp.68-69.

2.17   Cicero, Nature of the Gods, trans. H C P McGregor, pp.84-86.

2.18   Ibid., p.141.

2.19   Pierre Teilhard de Chardin, Hymns of the Universe, trans. Gerald Vann, p.31.

2.20   John Burnet, Early Greek Philosophy, p.119.

2.21   Ibid., p.140.

2.22   E A Budge, The Egyptian Book of the Dead, pp.LXXXII-LXXXIII.

2.23   Snorri Sturluson, The Prose Edda, P.48.

2.24   Aldous Huxley, The Perennial Philosophy, p.6.

2.25   F C Happold, Mysticism, p.222.

2.26   Ibid., p.222.

2.27   Ibid., p.222

2.28   Ibid., p.308

2.29   Siegfried Morenz, Egyptian Religion, p.65.

2.30   F C Happold, Mysticism, p.321.

2.31   Cicero, The Nature of the Gods, pp.124-125.

2.32   Mediaeval Latin Lyrics, Penguin Classics, p.64.

2.33   The Philokalia, Vol.2, trans. Palmer, Sherrard, Ware, p.96.

2.34   Leibniz, ed. P P Wiener, p.301.

2.35   The Ancient Near East, Vol.2, Ed. J B Pritchard, pp.108-112.

CHAPTER THREE

3.1   William Kelly Simpson, The Literature of Ancient Egypt, Pp.201-209.

3.2   Rudolf Bultmann, Primitive Christianity, p.46.

3.3   Cicero, The Nature of the Gods, p.185.
3.4   Karl Jaspers, Way to Wisdom, p.48.
3.5   Walter Lippmann, The Public Philosophy, p.131.
3.6   The Ancient Near East, Vol.1, ed. James B Pritchard, p.83.
3.7   Gilbert Murray, Five Stages of Greek Religion, pp.77-78.
3.8   Srimad Bhagavatam, trans. Swami Prabhavananda, p.245.
3.9   Beethoven: Letters, Journals and Conversations, trans. M
            Hamburger, p.61.
3.10   Ibid., pp.74,76.
3.11   Jaroslav Pelikan, Jesus Through the Centuries, p.83.
3.12   Alfred North Whitehead, The Aims of Education, pp.51-52.

CHAPTER FOUR

4.1   Srimad Bhagavatam, trans. Sweami Prabhavananda, pp.177-178.
4.2   Shankara, Crest-Jewel of Discrimination, p.67.
4.3   Joseph M. Kitagawa, Religions of the East, p.280.
4.4   Pierre Teilhard de Chardin, Hymn of the Universe, p.31.
4.5   Bronislaw Malinowski, Magic, Science, and Religion, p.23.
4.6   E A Wallis Budge, The Gods of the Egyptians, Vol.l, pp.115-116.
4.7   Apuleius, Metamorphosis XI.25, trans. Cumont.
4.8   Samuel Noah Kramer, History Begins at Sumer, pp.99,106,198.
4.9   Jason L Saunders, Greek and Roman Philosophers after Aristotle,
            Pp.149-150.
4.10   Snorri Sturluson, The Prose Edda, trans j I Young, p.31.
4.11   Jacob Grimm, Teutonic Mythology Vol.1., trans. J S Stallybrass,
            P.164.

CHAPTER FIVE

5.1   The Ancient Near East, ed. J B Pritchard, p.63.
5.2   Ibid., p.71.
5.3   Robert Frager, Heart, Self, and Soul, p.7.
5.4   Rrichard Maurice Bucke, Cosmic Consciousness, pp.121,123.
5.5   Sir Thomas Browne, Religio Medici, pp.15-16.

5.6   Meister Eckhart, trans. R B Blakney, pp.167-168.

5.7   Soren Kierkegaard, Edifying Discourses, Vol.2, p.129.

5.8   Ibid., p.150.

5.9   Auguste Sabatier, The Outlines of a Philosophy of Religion, p.15.

5.10   Ibid., p.146.

5.11   Nicolai Berdayaev, Slavery and Freedom, p.53.

5.12   Shankara, Crest-Jewel of Discrimination, p.43.

5.13   Idries Shah, The Way of Sufi, p.272.

5.14   Hegel: Lectures on the Philosophy of Religion, ed. P C Hodgson, P.95.

5.15   Ibid., pp.105-106.

5.16   Ibid., p. 460.

5.17   Sorfen Kierkegaard, Purity of Heart, p.154.

5.18   William James, The Varieties of Religious Experience, p.157.

5.19   Aldous Huxley, The Perennial Philosophy, p.134.

5.20   Karl Jaspers, Socrates, Buddha, Confuscius, Jesus, pp.78-79.

5.21   Rudolf Bultmann, Jesus Christ and Mythology, p.63.

5.22   Paul Tillich, The New Being, p.38.

5.23   Cicero, On the Good Life, pp. 89-90.

5.24   F C Happold, Mysticism, p.86.

5.25   Immanuel Kant, Lectures on Ethics, trans. L Infield, pp98-99.

5.26   Hegel, Lectures on the Philosophy of Religion, ed. P C Hodson, Pp.163-164.

5.27   Ralph Waldo Emerson, Self Reliance and Other Essays, p.33.

5.28   This I believe, ed. Raymond Swing, p.86.

5.29   Soren Kierkegaard, Purity of Heart, trans. D V Steere, p.51.

5.30   Ibid., p.107.

5.31   Thomas Merton, Spiritual Direction and Meditation, PP.46,48,58

5.32   Karl Jaspers, Way to Wisdom, P.47.

5.33   William James, The Varieties of Religious Experience, p.292.

5.34   Evelyn Underhill, The Mystics of the Church, pp.9-10.

5.35   Ibid., pp.10-11.

5.36   F C Happold, Mysticism, pp.45-47.

5.37   Back to the Sources: Reading the Classic Jewish Texts, ed. B W Holtz, pp.305-307.

5.38   Paul Deussen, The Philosophy of the Upanishads, pp.66-70.

5.39   Srimad Bhagavatam, trans. Swami Prabhavananda, p.76.

5.40   Shankara, op.cit.

5.41   The Philokalia, V.1, pp.31-32.

5.42   The Words of St Francis, J Meyer, p.4.

5.43   Thomas a Kempis, Imitation of Christ, p.28.

5.44   Immanuel Kant, Lectures on Ethics, p.173.

5.45   Ralph Waldo Emerson, Self-Reliance and Other Essays, pp.54-55

5.46   Srimad Bhagavatam, trans. Swami Prabhavananda, p.224.

5.47   The Preaching of Chrysostom, ed. J Pelikan, PP.151-152.

5.48   Gregory Palamas, The Triads, trans. N Gendle, pp.71-72.

5.49   Hegel's Phenomenology of Spirit, tans. A V Miller, pp.264-265.

5.50   This I believe, ed. R Swing, PP.210-211.

5.51   Leo Tolstoy, The Kingdom of God is Within You, p.101.

5.52   Emmanuel Swedenborg, Divine Love and Wisdom, p.20.

5.53   Jacque Maritain, Education at the Crossroads, p.11.

5.54   Ibid., pp.23-24.

5.55   Srimad Bhagavatam, trans. Swami Prabhavananda, p.4.

5.56   Idries Shah, The Way of Sufi, p.80.

5.57   The Philokalia, Vol.1, p.198.

5.58   Ibid., Vol.2, p.107.

5.59   John A T Robinson, Honest to God, p.116.

5.60   Daniel Day Williams, The Spirit and the Forms of Love, p.67.

5.61.   Soren Kierkegaard, Purity of Heart, p.60.

CHAPTER SIX

6.1   Gregory Palamas, The Triads, p.33.

6.2   The Philokalia, Vol.1, p.24.

6.3   St John of the Cross, Dark Night of the Soul, p.72.

6.4   Aldous Huxley, The Perennial Philosophy, p.212.

6.5   Richard Maurice Buck, Cosmic Consciousness, p.3.

6.6   Jack Dean Kingsbury, The Parables of Jesus in Matthew 13, p.62.

6.7   Peter Brown, Augustine of Hippo, p.95.

6.8   Abraham H Maslow, Religions, Values and Peak-Experiences,
            P.29.

6.9   Meister Eckhart, trans R B Blakney, p.79.

6.10   Indian Philosophy, ed. S Radhakrisnan and C A Moore, p.618.

6.11   Abraham H Maslow, op.cit., p.XIV.

6.12   F C Happold, <u>Mysticism</u>, p.256.

6.13   John Mansley Robinson, <u>An Introduction to Early Greek Philosophy</u>, p.159.

6.14   <u>The Philokalia</u>, Vol.1, p.290.

6.15   <u>The Philokalia</u>, Vol.2, p.32.

6.16   Ibid., pp.281-282.

6.17   F C Happold, <u>Mysticism</u>, p.251.

6.18   <u>Songs of Kabir</u>, trans. Tabindranath Tagore, pp.54-55.

6.19   <u>Rumi</u>, tans. C Barks, p.108.

6.20   <u>Meister Eckhart</u>, trans. R B Blakney, p.132.

6.21   Swami Prabhavananda, <u>The Sermon on the Mount According to Vedanta</u>, p.80.

6.22   <u>Meister Eckhart</u>, op.cit., p.50.

6.23   <u>Songs of Kabir</u>, Trans. R Tagore, p.81.

6.24   Ibid., pp.39-40.

6.25   Idries Shah, op.cit., p.95.

6.26   Robert Frager, op.cit., p.65.

6.27   Gabriel Marcel, <u>The Mystery of Being, Vol.2, Faith and Reality</u>, P.73.

6.28   Pierre Teilhard de Chardin, op.cit., p.19.

6.29   Eva Mary Drew and Sidney Drew, <u>Bach,</u> p.35.

6.30   Ralph Waldo Emerson, op.cit., p.62.

6.31   Snorri Sturluson, <u>The Prose Edda</u>, p.31.

6.32   Nicolas Berdyaev, <u>The Destiny of Man</u>, p.263.

6.33   <u>Srimad Bhavagatam</u>, op.cit., p.288.

6.34   Paul Deussen, <u>The Philosophy of the Upanishads</u>, pp.314-315.

6.35   <u>Indian Philosophy</u>, ed. S Radhakrisnan and C A More, pp.635-6.

6.36   Rudolf Bultmann, <u>Primitive Christianity</u>, p.151.

6.37   F C Happold, <u>Mysticism</u>, p.238.

6.38   Ibid., pp.370-371.

6.39   Leibniz, op.cit., pp.436-437.

6.40   Ibid., pp.532-533.

6.41   E A Wallis Budge, <u>The Gods of Ancient Egypt,</u>Vol.2,pp.118-119.

6.42   E A Wallis Budge, <u>The Egyptian Book of the Dead</u>, p.CI.

6.43   <u>Mediaeval Latin Lyrics</u>, trans. H. Waddell, p.121.

A SHORT BIBLIOGRAPHY

The Ancient Near East, Vols 1-2. Edited by J.B. Pritchard. Princeton, NJ: Princeton U. Press, 1958 and 1975.

Arberry, A.J. Aspects of Islamic Civilization. Ann Arbor: University of Michigan Press, 1967.

St Anselm. Proslogium; Monologium; etc. Translated by S.N. Deane. La Salle, Illinois: Open Court Publishing Co., 1951.

St Augustine. The Confessions of Saint Augustine. Translated by E.B. Pusey. New York: The Modern Library, 1949.

St. Augustine. The Confessions of St. Augustine. Translated by J.K. Ryan. Garden City, N.Y. Image Books, 1962.

Aulen, Gustaf. Christus Victor. Translated by A.G. Hebert. New York: The Macmillan Co., 1961.

Basham, A.L. The Wonder That Was India. New York: Grove Press, Inc. 1959.

Beethoven. Translated by M. Hamburger. Garden City, N.Y. Doubleday, 1960.

Berdyaev, Nicolas. The Destiny of Man. New York: Harper Brothers, 1960.

          Slavery and Freedom. Translated by R.M. French. New York: Charles Scribner's Sons, 1944.

Bergson, Henri. The Two Sources of Morality and Religion. Translated by R.A. Audra and C. Brereton. Garden City, N.Y: Doubleday, 1935.

          Time and Free Will. New York: Harper Brothers, 1960.

Bernard, Abbot of Clairvaux. The Steps Of Humility. Translated by G.B. Burch. Notre Dame, Indiana: University of Notre Dame, 1963.

Boethius. The Consolation of Philosophy. Edited by J.J. Buchanan. New York: Frederick Ungar, 1957.

Boisen, Anton T. The Exploration Of The Inner World. New York: Harper Brothers, 1936.

Brown, Peter. Augustine Of Hippo. Berkeley: University of California, 1975.

Browne, Thomas. Religio Medici. New York: Dutton, 1965.

Bucke, Richard Maurice. Cosmic Consciousness. New York: Penguin Putnam Inc., 1923.

Budge, E. A. Wallis. The Gods of the Egyptians Vols 1-2. New York: Dover, 1969.

The Egyptian Book Of The Dead. New York: Dover, 1967.

Bultmann, Rudolf. Primitive Christianity. Translated by R.H. Fuller. New York: Meridian Books, 1959.

Jesus And The Word. Translated by L.P. Smith and E. H. Lantero. New York: Charles Scribner's Sons, 1958.

Jesus Christ And Mythology. New York: Charles Scribner's Sons, 1958.

Burnet, John. Early Greek Philosophy. Cleveland: The World Publishing Co., 1930.

Cassirer, Ernst. Language And Myth. Translated by S.K. Langer. Dover, 1946.

A Celtic Miscellany. Translated by K.H. Jackson. Baltimore, Maryland: Penguin Books, 1971.

Sri Chinmoy. Commentary of the Bhagavad Gita. New York: Rudolf Steiner, 1973.

Cicero. On The Good Life. Translated by M. Grant. Baltimore, Maryland: Penguin Books, 1971.

. On the Commonwealth. Translated by G.H. Sabine and S.B. Smith. New York: Liberal Arts Press, 1929.

The Nature Of The Gods. Translated by H.C.P. McGregor, New York: Penguin Books, 1984.

Confucius. Translated by J. Legge. New York: Dover, 1971.

Conze, Edward. Buddhism: Its Essence and Development. New York: Dover, 1951.

Copleston, Frederick. A History of Philosophy, Vol. I. Westminster, Maryland. The Newman Press, 1966.

Cornford, F.M. From Religion to Philosophy. New York: Mineola, Dover, 2004.

Crossley-Holland, Kevin. The Norse Myths. New York: Pantheon, 1980.

Cumont, Franz. The Mysteries of Mithra. New York: Dover, 1956.

Dante (Alighieri). The Divine Comedy. Translated by H.R. Huse, New York: Reinhart & Co., 1958.

Deussen, Paul. The Philosophy of the Upanishads. New York: Dover, 1966.

Duchesne-Guillemin, Zoroastrianism. New York: Harper & Row, 1966.

Meister Eckhart. Translated by R.B. Blakney. New York: Harper
    Brothers, 1941.

The Edicts of Asoka. Translated by N.A. Nikam and R. Mckeon.
    Chicago: University of Chicago Press, 1966.

Ehrlich, Jerry Dell. Plato's Gift To Christianity. San Diego: Academic
    Christian Press, 2001.

            Building A Life By Carpenter Jesus. San Diego:
    Academic Christian Press, 2003.

Einstein, Albert. The World As I See It. New York: The Wisdom
    Library, 1949.

Emerson, Ralph Waldo. Self-Reliance and Other Essays. New York:
    Dover, 1993.

Erickson, Carolly. The Medieval Vision. New York: Oxford University
    Press, 1976.

Epictetus. Translated by George Long. Chicago: Encyclopaedia
            Britannica, 1952.

Ferguson, John. The Religions Of The Roman Empire. Ithaca, N.Y:
    Cornell University Press, 1985.

Frager, Robert. Heart, Self, & Soul. Wheaton, Illinois: Quest Books,
    1999.

The Words of Saint Francis (Assisi). Edited J. Meyer. Chicago, Illinois:
    Franciscan Herald Press, 1952.

St. Francis of Sales. Introduction to the Devout Life. Translated by J.K.
    Ryan. Garden City, N.Y: Image Books, 1949.

Frazer, James George. The Golden Bough. New York, N.Y: MacMillan
    Co., 1950.

The Portable Greek Reader. Edited by W.H. Auden. New York: Viking
    Press, 1955.

Graves, Robert. The Greek Myths: 1. Baltimore, MD: Penguin Books,
    1969.

Grew, Eva and Sydney. Bach. New York, N.Y: Collier Books, 1962.

Grimm, Jacob. Teutonic Mythology Vol. I. New York: Dover, 1966.

Guillaume, Alfred. Islam. Baltimore, MD: Penguin Books, 1964.

Hammarskjold, Dag. Markings. Translated by L. Sjobergf & W.H.
    Auden. New York: Alfred A Knopf, 1964.

King Harald's Saga: From Snorri Sturlsuson's Heimskringla. Translated
        by M. Magnusson and H Palsson. Baltimore, Maryland: Penguin
        Books, 1970.

Happold, F. C. Mysticism. Baltimore, Maryland: Penguin Books, 1963.

Harnack, Adolf. What is Christianity? Translation by T. B. Saunders.
        New York: Harper Torchbooks, 1957.

Hegel, G.W.F. Phenomenology Of Spirit. Translated by A.V. Miller.
        New York: Oxford University Press, 1977.

                Lectures On The Philosophy Of Religion. Edited by Peter
        C. Hodgson. Berkeley: University of California Press, 1987.

Hermetica Vol. I. Translated by Walter Scott. Boston: Shambhala, 1985.

Hesiod and Theognis. Translated by Dorothea Wender. Baltimore, Md:
        1973.

Holtz, Barry W. Back To The Sources: Reading The Classic Jewish
        Texts. New York: Summit Books, 1984.

Huizinga, Johan. Homo Ludens. Boston: The Beacon Press, 1950.

Huxley, Aldous. The Perennial Philosophy. New York: Harper & Row,
        1970.

Indian Philosophy. Edited by S. Radhakrishnan and C. A. Moore.
        Princeton, NJ: Princeton University Press, 1957.

James, E.O. Seasonal Feasts and Festivals. U.S.A: Barnes & Noble,1963.

James, William. The Varieties of Religious Experience. New York,
        Mentor Books, 1958.

                Essays on Faith and Morals. Cleveland: Meridian Books,
        1962.

Jaspers, Karl. Way To Wisdom. Translated by R. Manheim. New Haven:
        Yale University Press, 1954.

                Man in the Modern Age. Garden City, N.Y: Doubleday
        Anchor Books, 1957.

                Socrates, Buddha, Confucius, Jesus. New York: Harcourt,
        Brace & World, 1957.

St. John of the Cross. Dark Night of the Soul. Mineola, N.Y: Dover,
        2003.

Songs of Kabir. Translated by R. Tagore. York Beach, Maine: Samuel
        Weiser, Inc., 1998.

Kaltenmark, Max. Lao Tzu and Taoism. Stanford, CA: Stanford
        University Press, 1965.

Kant, Immaneul. Lectures On Ethics. Translated by L. Infield. New
        York: Harper & Row, 1930.

Kitagawa, Joseph M. Religions of the East. Philadelphia: Westminster
        Press, 1960.

Kierkegaard, Soren. Edifying Discourses, Vols 1-2. Minneapolis, MN:
        Augsburg Publishing House, 1962.
                Purity of Heart. New York: Harper & Brothers, 1938.

Kingsbury, J.D. The Parables of Jesus in Matthew 13. London: SPCK,
        1969.

The Koran Interpreted. Translation by A.J. Arberry. Toronto: The
        Macmillan Canada, 1969.

Kramer, Samuel Noah. History Begins At Sumer. Garden City, N.Y:
        Doubleday Anchor, 1959.

Diogenes Laertius. Lives of Eminent Philosophers, Vol.1-2. Translated
        By R.D. Hicks. Cambridge, MA: Harvard University Press, 1995.

Laxdaela Saga. Translated by M. Magnusson and H. Palsson. Baltimore,
        MD: Penguin Books, 1969.

Leff, Gordon. Medieval Thought. Baltimore, MD: Penguin Books, 1958.

Leibniz: Selections. Edited by P.P. Wiener. New York: C. Scribner's
        Sons, 1951.

Lewis, C. S. The Discarded Image. Cambridge: Cambridge Univeristy
        Press: 1964.

The Literature of Ancient Egypt. Edited by W. Simpson. New Haven:
        Yale U. Press, 1973.

Lives of the Saints. Translated by J.F. Webb. Edited by R. Baldick and
        B. Radice. Baltimore, MD: Penguin Books, 1973.

Lippmann, Walter. The Public Philosophy. New York: Mentor Book,
        1955.

The Table Talk of Martin Luther. Edited by Thomas S. Kepler. New
        York: The World Publishing Co., 1952.

Luther's Works Vols. 42-43. Philadelphia: Fortress Press, 1968,1969.

Malinowski, Bronislaw. Magic, Science and Religion. Garden City, N.Y:
        Doubleday Anchor, 1954.

The Laws of Manu. Tanslated by G. Buehler. New York: Dover, 1969.

Marcel, Gabirel. Homo Viator. Translated by E. Craufurd. New York:
        Harper & Brothers, 1962.
                The Mystery of Being, Vols 1-2. Chicago, IL: Henry
        Regnery Co., 1949.

Maritain, Jacques. A Preface To Metaphysics. New York: Mentor Omega
    Book, 1962.
         Education at the Crossroads. New Haven: Yale U. Press,
    1943.

Maslow, Abraham H. Religious Values, And Peak-Experiences. New
    York: Penguin Books, 1970.

Mediaeval Latin Lyrics. Translated by Helen Waddell. Middlesex,
    England: Penguin Books, 1962.

Merton, Thomas. Seeds of Destruction. New York: Farrar, Straus, and
    Giroux, 1964.
         Spiritual Direction. Collegeville, MN: 1960.

Mo Tzu. Translated by B. Watson. New York: Columbia U. Press, 1966.

Morenz, Siegfried. Egyptian Religion. Translated by A.E. Keep. Ithaca,
    N.Y: Cornell U. Press. 1992.

Myth And Mythmaking. Edited by Henry A.Murray. Boston: Beacon
    Press, 1968.

Nida, Eugene A. And Smalley, William A. Introducing Animism. New
    York: Friendship Press, 1959.

Niebuhr, Reinhold. Beyond Tragedy. New York: Charles Scribner's
    Sons, 1937.

Nikhilananda, Swami. Hinduism. New York: Harper & Brothers, 1958.

Niles, D.T. Buddhism and the Claims of Christ. Richmond, VA: John
    Knox Press, 1967.

Nilsson, Martin P. A History Of Greek Religion. New York: W.W.
    Norton & Co. L964.

Njal's Saga. Translated by M. Magnusson and H. Palsson. Baltimore,
    MD: Penguin Books, 1970.

Nurbakhsh, Javad. Jesus In The Eyes Of The Sufis. London: Khaniqahi-
    Nimatullahi Publications, 1983.

O'Brien, John A. Eternal Answers for an Anxious Age. Englewood
    Cliffs, NJ: Prentice-Hall, Inc. 1962.

Ovid. Metamorphoses. Translated by Rolfe Humphries. Bloomington:
    Indiana U. Press, 1961.

Palamas, Gregory. The Triads. Translation by N. Gendle. Mahwah, NJ:
    Paulist Press, 1983.

Pelikan, Jaroslav. Jesus Through The Centuries. New York: Harper &
    Row, 1985.

The Philokalia Vols 1-2. Translated by Palmer, Sherrard, and Ware.
    London: Faber & Faber, 1979.

Odes of Pindar. Translated by C.M. Bowra. Baltimore, MD: Penguin
    Books, 1969.

The Dialogues of Plato Vols 1-2. Translated by B. Jowett. New York:
    Random House, 1937.

Plotinus. The Enneads. Translated by S. MacKenna. New York: Penguin
    Books, 1991.

The Essential Plotinus. Translated by Elmer O'Brien. New York: Mentor
    Books, 1964.

Prabhavananda, Swami. The Sermon on the Mount according to
    Vedanta. New York: New American Library, 1972.

Pseudo-Dionysius. Translation by C. Luibheid. Mahwah, NY: Paulist
    Press, 1987.

The Rig Veda. Translated by R.T.H. Griffith. USA: Motilal Banarsidass
    Publishers, 1992.

Robinson, John A.T. Honest To God. Philadelphia: Westminster Press,
    1963.

Robinson, John Mansley. An Introduction To Early Greek Philosophers.
    Boston: Houghton Mifflin Co., 1968.

Rose, H.J. Religion In Greece And Rome. New York: Harper & Row,
    1959.

Ross, Floyd H. & Hills, Tynette. The Great Religions. New York:
    Premier Books, 1965.

Rougemont, Denis de. Love In The Western World. Greenwich, CT:
    Fawcett Publications, 1966.

The Essential Rumi. Translations by C. Barks with J. Moyne. Edison,
    NJ: Castle Books, 1977.

Sabatier, Auguste. Outline Of A Philosophy Of Religion. Translated by
    T.A. Seed. New York: Harper & Brothers, 1957.

Schiller, Friedrich. On The Aesthetic Education Of Man. Translated by
    R. Snell. New York: Frederick Ungar, 1965.
        An Anthology For Our Time. New York: Frederick
    Ungar, 1959.

Schleiermacher, Friedrich. Christmas Eve: Dialogue on the Incarnation.
    Translated by T.N. Tice. Richmond, VA: John Knox Press, 1967.
        On Religion. Translation by J. Oman. New York: Harper
    & Brothers, 1958.

Shah, Idries. The Way of Sufi. New York: E.P. Dutton, 1970.

Shankara. Crest-Jewel of Discrimination. Translated by S Prabhavananda
 And C. Isherwood. New York: New American Library, 1947.

The Situation Ethics Debate. Edited by Harvey Cox. Philadelphia:
 Westminster Press, 1968.

Srimad Bhagavatam. Translated by Swami Prabhavananda. New York:
 Capricorn Books, 1968.

Smith, Edward Reaugh. The Soul's Long Journey. Great Barrington,
 MA: Steiner Books, 2003.

Snorri Sturluson. The Prose Edda. Translation by J.I. Young. Berkeley:
 U. Of California Press, 1973.

Swedenborg, Emanuel. Divine Love and Wisdom. Translated by J. C.
 Ager. New York: Citadel Press, 1965.

The Texts of Taoism, Vols 1-2. Translated by James Legge. New York:
 Dover, 1962,

Teilhard de Chardin, Pierre. Hymn Of The Universe. New York: Harper
 & Row, 1972.

Thomas A Kempis. The Imitation Of Christ. New York: Books, Inc. ND.

The Tibetan Book of the Dead. Edited by W.Y. Evans-Wentz. Oxford:
 Oxford U. Press, 1972.

Tillich, Paul. The New Being. New York: Charles Scribner's Sons, 1955.
 Christianity and the Encounter of the World Religions.
 New York: Columbia U. Press, 1963.
 The Shaking Of The Foundations. New York: Charles
 Scribner's Sons, 1948.
 The Courage To Be. New Haven: Yale U. Press, 1963.
 Theology of Culture. New York: Oxford U. Press, 1964.

Tolstoy, Leo. The Kingdom of God is Within You. Translation by Leo
 Wiener. USA: Farrar, Straus & Dudahy, 1961.

Tomlin, E.W.F. The Oriental Philosophers. New York: Harper & Row,
 1963.

Underhill, Evelyn. The Mystics of the Church. New York: Schocken
 Books, 1964.

The Upanisads, Vols 1-2. Translated by F. Max Mueller. New York:
 Dover, 1962.

The Upanishads. Translated by Swami Nikhilananda. New York. Harper
 & Row, 1963.

White, J.E. Manchip. Ancient Egypt. New York: Dover, 1970.

Whitehead, Alfred North. The Aims of Education. New York: Mentor Books, 1955.

Williams, Daniel Day. The Spirit and the Forms of Love. New York: Harper & Row, 1968.

Wilson, John A. The Culture of Ancient Egypt. Chicago: U. Of Chicago Press, 1975.

The Wisdom of China and India. Edited by Lin Yutang. New York: The Modern Library, 1955.

The Gathas of Zarathushtra. Translation by Piloo Nanavutty. Ahmedabad: Mapin Publishing, 1999.

INDEX

Abelard, Peter 231
Aeschylus 34
Angels 69-70
Animism 17ff
Anselm of Canterbury 138, 150, 164
Aristotle 80, 86
Asoka, Edicts of 136, 196-197
Athanasian Creed 212
Augustine of Hippo 190, 194, 199
Aulen, Gustaf 219-220
Baba Kuhi 200
Bach, Johann Sebastian 98-99, 206-207
Barth, Karl 231
Basil 60
Bede 210
Beethoven 99-100
Berdeyaev, Nikolai 16, 140, 212-213
Bernard of Clairvaux 151, 226-227
Bhagavad Gita 165-166
Boethius 75
von Braun, Wernher 25
Brown, Peter 190
Browne, Thomas 139
Bucke, Richard Maurice 155, 189
Buddhism 82, 90
Budge, E.A.Wallis 51, 228
Bultmann, Rudolf 146
Chandra X-ray telescope 9
Chinese 80ff, 97
Sri Chinmoy 44
Christian Scriptures 178-179, 193-194, 198-199, 221-222, 225
Christianity 126-128, 178-179
Chrysostom 168-169
Cicero 41, 49, 66, 74, 83, 150, 209

Cleanthes 118-120
Clutton-Brock, Arthur 176
Collegia Licita 68, 121
Confucius 39, 90, 104
Corpus Hermeticum 44, 74, 175,
Cornford, F.M. 38, 86
Crosby, Fanny J. 205
Dante 158, 188
Deussen, Paul 159, 218
Diadochos of Photiki 199
Diogenes Laertius 116-118
Egyptians 46, 54, 56, 78, 111, 222
Egyptian Book of the Dead 90
Einstein, Albert 9, 21
Emerson, Ralph Waldo 152, 163-164, 207
Empedocles (Empedokles) 178, 196, 204, 217
Epictetus 117
Evagrios The Solitary 161, 175
Fine, Lawrence 157
Frager, Robert 135
Francis of Assisi 162
Frazer, Sir James (The Golden Bough) 29
Gilgamesh Epic 131
Gnosticism 124-126, 213
Gospel of John 63, 187
Greeks 79-80, 95ff
Gregory Palamas 60, 169, 187
Grew, Eva Mary & Sidney 206
Grimm, Jacob 129
Hahn, Otto 22,
Hakim Jami 206
Hammarskjoeld, Dag 23
Hammurabi, Code of 89
Happold, F.C. 158
Harnack, Adolf 11
Hebrew Scriptures 52, 79, 90, 202
Hegel, G.W.F. 40, 91, 143, 151, 170, 188
Hellenism 55

Heraclitus 48
Herschel, William 9
Hesiod 50, 178, 196
Hesychios the Priest 180
Hilton, Walter 63
Hindus 56, 91, 104, 112ff, 160, 165, 175, 178, 203-204, 215ff, 223
Hittites *Telepinus Myth* 88
Holtz, Barry H. 156
Huxley, Aldous 144
Ibn el-Arabi 179
Imitation of Christ 139, 187
Incarnations of Vishnu 64
Isaiah the Solitary 187
Islam 55, 128
James, E.O. 12, 32
James, William 144, 155, 158-159
Jaspers, Karl 86, 145, 153-154
Jesus Christ 149-150, 166-168, 225
John of the Cross 24, 138, 150, 187, 191, 201, 205
Judaism (see Hebrews also) 115-116, 221
Julian of Norwich 47
Jupiter 64
Kabir 60, 91, 105-6, 139, 161, 179, 195, 200, 225, 230
Kant, Immanuel 15, 151, 162-163, 169-170
A Kempis, Thomas 162
Kierkegaard, Soren 139, 144, 152-153, 181, 192, 227
Kingsbury, Jack Dean 189
Kitagawa, Joseph M. 12
Koran 195
Kramer, Samuel Noah 111
Lactantius 209
Lao Tzu 59, 80-81
Leibniz, G.W.F. 14, 76, 175, 189, 226-227
Lippmann, Walter 87
Lucifer 74-75
Luther, Martin 97-98, 192, 231
Malinowski, Bronislaw 12, 110

Marcel, Gabriel 16, 206
Maritain, Jacques 176
Maslow, Abraham H. 10, 39, 42, 190-191, 193
Maurus, Hrabanus 230-231
Maximus the Confessor 60, 75, 180-181, 200
Mayo, Charles 152
Meister Eckhart 139, 169, 191, 201, 204
Merton, Thomas 153
Mo Tzu 166, 177, 197
Moira 38ff
Morenz, Siegried 11
Morgan, John Pierpont 20
Moses 62
Myths 84ff
Nabonidus 76-77
Names of God 43ff
Norsemen 30, 35, 53, 129, 200, 215, 222-223
Numina 123-124
Osiris 111-112, 133, 211, 228
Otto, Rudolf 39
Ovid 52
Pantheism 107ff
Paul of Tarsus 75, 229-230
Pelikan, Jaroslav 101, 205
Plato and Platonism, 13, 56, 59, 73, 93-95, 114ff, 133-135, 172-175,
       178, 197-198, 204, 208, 217-218, 228-229
Plotinus 136-137, 204
Swami Prabhavananda 44
Pseudo-Dionysius 47, 72, 137
Pythagoras 80, 204, 217
Radhakrishnan, Sarvepalli 193, 224
Rgi Veda 35-36, 46, 132, 146, 159, 211
Robinson, John A.T. 181
Romans 104, 120-124
Rumi, Jalaludin 43, 97, 194-195, 201
Sabatier, August 15, 140
Sanai (Hadiqa) 40
Sarapis 122

Sartre, Jean-Paul 25
Schiller, F. 99-100, 202
Schleiermacher, F. 41, 91, 195
Schweitzer, Albert 22
Seneca 162, 224
Shah, Idries 142
Shankara 58. 108, 136, 142, 160
Siddhartha Gotema 185
Smith, Edward Reaugh 221
Smith, John 188
Snorri Sturluson (see Norsemen)
Socrates 208
Srimad Bhagavatam 14, 48, 58, 62, 96, 107, 113, 142, 148, 160, 165
       196, 217
Steiner, Rudolf 220
Sufis 142-143, 160, 200, 205-206
Sumerians 111
Swedenborg, Emanuel 175-176
Symeon Metaphrastes 169
Tagore, Rabindranath 161
Teilhard de Chardin, Pierre 9, 49, 106, 109, 140, 206
Theodorus the Ascetic 200
Tibetan Book of the Dead 214-215
Tillich, Paul 146
Tolstoy, Leo 170-171, 207
Torah 186
Underhill, Evelyn 156, 158
Upanishad Aitarey 132
Upanishad Brihadaranyaka 148
Upanishad Katha 147
Upanishad Kaushitake 216
Upanishad Khandogya 132, 216
Upanishad Mundaka 202
Upanishad Svetasvatara 192, 217
Upanishad Taittiriyaka 187
Upanishad Talavakara 56
Vedas (see Rig Veda)
Vyasa 113-114

Wagner, Richard 17ff, 102
Wesley, John 191
Whitehead, Alfred North 12, 23, 101, 135
Williams, Daniel Day 181
Xenophanes 217
Zarathushtra 14, 45, 58, 67, 104, 131, 148, 166, 185
Zoroastrianism 212, 220